M000006905

Soul Chaser

Devotions to Anchor the Soul

Loren Paul Decker

Published by
IngramSpark

Soul Chaser

www.ingramspark.com

Cover design by Amanda Decker.

ISBN 978-0-692-15835-7

Printed in the United States of America

In Memory of Tom Howard

Soul Chaser - The Introduction

Devotions to Anchor the Soul

Within the pages of my first book, "I Love You, Church; Modern Parables" I described a parable as a story which explains the 'unknown,' by placing it beside the 'known.' The term parable finds its origin in the Greek language. Para-bollo simply means to "throw alongside." One can explain deep and mysterious spiritual truths by connecting them to ordinary events or items. A parable, in other words, takes the things we see every day and ties them to eternity. Jesus often used parables to give the crowds a glimpse of forever. "The kingdom of God is like...," He would say, and then go on to tell a story about Himself and His Kingdom using farming or shepherding; things well known to his listeners.

I am convinced that spiritual truths abound, unseen, in our everyday world. So, in this book, Soul Chaser, I will attempt to connect heaven and earth with stories of life from our earthbound condition, in hope that they will transport you far beyond. What we ultimately believe rests not in our minds, but in our souls. Truth settles deep there, grounded in the understanding that God chases us down, each one, in order to arrest our attention and show us the way home. As you read the chapters, look for the deeper truths that your mind may have noticed, but that only your soul can recognize. These truths will shape you, at your soul core, into a believer.

The telling of my personal experiences are mostly factual and, to the best of my recollection, "as-they-happened". For some of the non-personal stories I have attempted to "flesh out" the characters and themes using a little "Sanctified Imagination." Those stories are meant to show us how some events could have occurred. So, you may notice an extra character or conversation [not found in the Bible, let's say,] or a historical Biblical event with circumstances described a little broader than what we know for certain. Hopefully you will see that my desire is to enrich your reading experience but never to mislead you. Events described as they could have been do not change what we know did occur. Jesus came to save us. He is the only One who can. I can add nothing to that truth. My hope is that these imaginative pages (some inspired by ancient legends—some from me) will be obvious to you as you read. Your Bible is the true account of what happened to real people. In these pages you will read what happened in my life as a result.

Loren Paul Decker / Freetown, Massachusetts

Acknowledgements

Thank you Amanda for always loving me and for living happily ever after. I love you so much. Thanks to my children, Ash, Brett, Evangeline, Lane, Mercedes, Prudence, True and Rory Jude. Thank you "Mary Sketties," Jack and Heather for the proofreading. Thank you Lydia for editing. To Ed and Kathy K, my friends that encourage me so, thank you both. Dan and Ali - I love you... Cousin Jane Heald - thank you for your support. Jim Deering, you are such a friend... 'thank you' is not enough. Milton - I remember. Jesus - I believe.

A special 'thank you' to my friend, whose name means "The Beautiful Face of Jesus." God bless you, my brother.

Endorsements

I have known Loren Decker for most of my life. His writing has always captured my imagination. His ability to paint a picture with words makes me want to read one more page, one more chapter or just one more story. Soul Chaser is just such a book. Pick it up and you will find yourself wanting to read, "just one more story."

Jeff Barksdale
Lead Pastor / Lifecoast Church
Palm Coast, Florida

I have rarely read anything that has gripped me and moved me as much as Loren Decker's "Soul Chaser." If Norman Rockwell wrote books instead of painting pictures, I strongly suspect that they would read like this one! This book is absolutely critical for a believer desiring to share the living hope of God's love with a broken world. Loren's spiritual perspective as a lover of Christ is woven into these stories with such beauty and honesty that even the coldest cynic will find them captivating! Thank you, Loren, you are a treasure.

Randy Stonehill
Recording Artist

Time can change many things. When I first met Loren Paul Decker he was just finishing up his college years. I had been requested to visit his dad's church to show a movie and present a brief spiritual message. My wife and I pulled our car into the church parking lot and this gangly, unbelievably tall, long-haired, blond young man dashed down from his home next door to greet us—dressed only in a pair of white overalls. Our hearts were won over immediately. Since then time has passed close to 40 years, still good friends, Loren has become an experienced man of God, a beloved pastor, a wonderful husband and father, and an author. His books are filled with the wisdom of God and personal experience that comes only from walking hand in hand with his Lord Jesus Christ. You will find a refreshing look at how much Jesus loves you and me, as you move from story to story.

Jim Deering – Retired from many things,
except for the Lord's service.

Some books haunt you. Soul Chaser, is that kind of book on steroids. As I read this book I sometimes found myself laughing, at other times weeping and on every page I heard "the soft sound of sandaled feet." I encountered Jesus in different, surprising and refreshing ways. "Soul shaping" is a delicate and important art and this book will show you how God does it. You won't look at the "normal" the same way again… and you'll encounter Jesus in places where you didn't expect he would show. Read this book and give it to everyone you know. They will "rise up and call you blessed."

Steve Brown
Author, Seminary Professor
Broadcaster—Key Life Network

Today, with all of the demands and distractions on our time, it's no easy task to impact readers, let alone captivate them. My longtime friend Pastor Loren Decker manages to accomplish both things with "Soul Chaser." You're sure to be touched by his stories, you'll smile a lot and most likely laugh and weep some. I certainly did. And as a non-Christian, I found the lessons and allegories to be both universal and meaningful.

Jordan Rich
WBZ Radio and podcast host

Loren Decker has been my pastor since our church "Lifehouse' began. What has always drawn me to Loren's teachings is his gift for storytelling. Having been a school teacher for close to 30 years, I know the power of a good story. It can inspire us and motivate us to change the way we think and understand our world, our Creator, ourselves, and how we respond to others. Each Sunday, Loren never fails to inspire me with his ability to weave scriptural truths with day-to-day stories much the same as Jesus did with parables. "Soul Chaser" does the same thing. As I read these stories, I felt like Mary, the sister of Lazarus (New Testament characters), as she chose to sit at the feet of Jesus and listen intently to every word He spoke. They are real stories that teach divine truths. They are humorous and heartbreaking. Most importantly, these stories reveal the true character of Jesus Christ and his overwhelming love, mercy, and compassion for each of us. When you open this book, it's as if Jesus opens his welcoming arms wide to invite you in for a soul hug. It's a book and a hug you don't want to miss!

Karen Kelly
Member, Lifehouse Church

LOREN PAUL DECKER
Senior Pastor of LifeHouse Church

Contents

Soul Chaser

"...That the trial of your faith,
being much more precious than of gold that perisheth,
though it be tried with fire,
might be found unto praise and honour and glory
at the appearing of Jesus Christ:"
1 Peter 1:7

There is a barn in Brattleboro, Vermont that is dear to my heart. On the loft door is an Amish style rendering of a man mounted on a horse. The bold script reads "Enter His Gates With Thanksgiving." My mother was the artist who created the beautiful design. I will share that story in a few page turns. But, for now, it is sufficient to say that like the barn door, this book is crafted to help create in us a desire to live well and in doing so, find ourselves at the end of our life's journey, fully prepared to enter His gates with great gladness of heart. Some parts of this book will cause you to smile. Other sections may make you feel sad. It is all a part of living in what one ancient writer called, the Valley of the Shadow of Death. Yet, the shadow need not be feared. In fact, the brevity of life can be welcomed shade when we consider how rough our journey.

As the years roll on, I have come to the realization that most of my life experience is behind, not before me. This knowledge has a way of sharpening my focus. I should have things largely sorted out by this time. There are mysteries still to ponder, but the wonder of life is now focused on eternity (directly ahead) and not planet earth. In my youth, some considered me to be wonderful. I guess you could say I was indeed, that... full of wonder. I wondered about my future spouse. Who could she be? I wondered about schooling. Which colleges should I apply to, and my career. What was I good at? There were so many questions to be asked and I did wonder if they would be answered well.

Then, one day I understood, most of the questions have already been asked. I live with my choices – some good, some bad.

My testing is just about done. Only a final exam lies ahead. And I am filled with wonder once again as I consider our forever life just beyond view.

So, for my family, and the generations yet to come, I will begin this book by listing some of the wonderful questions I wrestled with, which caused me to be a fortunate and blessed older man.

First, I considered the significance of faith. I questioned if the things of this earth really paled in comparison to spiritual matters in their ability to afford pleasure and meaning. Well, not really. I found that real pleasure is available in this world if you wish to pursue it. However, pleasure cannot sustain you in this life, nor prepare you for the next. It just isn't a worthwhile pursuit. You pay a lot for pleasure, but it doesn't last long. Just ask someone who owns a boat.

Remember the story Jesus told, about a man who had lots of cash? He told himself it was pleasure time. "Eat, drink and be merry," was how he put it. But, he made the mistake of thinking more wealth meant more time. Like a carnival ride, the pleasure thrill is short lived, very costly and leaves you feeling a bit sick. The more you chase pleasure, the further it goes from you, leaving nothing but tired, retold stories in its wake. There is no spirit in that stale bread. Yet, many aging people spend their later years chewing on the stuff of yesterday. Worldly pleasure grows old faster than we do.

On the other hand, genuine faith makes you pleasing to God and to know His pleasure is life changing. It arrives without an ounce of mirth, on waves of trouble and heartache that can and will prepare you for a noble and eternal life. You will miss God's favor if you are chasing after pleasure on your own. God's purpose trumps pleasure every time.

I also wondered about greatness and fame, and the prospect of my achieving it. In my youth, I was surrounded by many whom the world considered great. Personalities from radio and television, the sports world, musicians… I met so many. I learned that greatness is fleeting in the eyes of the world. Celebrity status is fickle and temporary. There is nothing more pitiful than needing attention from others to sustain one's happiness. Many seniors learn that they miss the status their career afforded them, and discover, too late, that, in reality, status was what they were working for all along. Not for the company or the team, not even for the end product… but for themselves. Serve self for a lifetime and you'll wind up alone at the table. Many have devoted their lives to that pre-occupation and pursuit of self-satisfaction only to have it turn out like ashes in their mouth. Attention and greatness are never one in the same. Don't mistake one for the other. True greatness comes from lifting up others, not propelling yourself alone to the top.

I also wondered about relationships. Why does it seem that family is perched on such a flimsy framework? More families than ever are going through divorce. Abuse and neglect are commonplace in homes across the world. As a pastor, I have learned that saying "I do," on your wedding day, is a ceremonial, surface nod in the right direction. However, when the bones are aching and the eyelids heavy, saying "I will" is another animal altogether. For that matter, "I won't" may come as the hardest phrase of all.

Temptation is not sin, unless you engage it. When faced with temptation to err against one's family, it is vital to remember that the whole is greater than the sum of the individual parts. Belonging is a blessing worth keeping, and there is no substitute lifestyle that is better than family.

These are but three of the questions that filled my younger days with wonder. Together, with a host of other questions that life brings over the years, we all find the resultant wonder begins to shape our soul. We know less, but believe more. We answer less, but ask more.

You may find yourself asking soul questions as you go through this book. You may also find some answers along the way. There is journaling space at the end of each chapter; a place for you to personalize the pages and chart the truths you discover. You will also find a summary sentence to help remember the point of each story. I have called these "Dropping Anchor," for they offer a place to be still and reflect… to anchor deep in the harbor of God's truth. There you will meet the Soul Chaser. There He will speak to you in language that you recognize as your very own.

Shaping a soul is an arduous affair. The deep truths hide in deep places. They are not obvious to us upon first glance. One must not expect the eternal to ride in like a victor. No, rather it is through loss and distress that we discover the reason for life. Fruit does not grow on mountaintops; fruit grows in the valleys. So come and walk in wonder with me as we discover some choice fruit that grows along this valley path. We will travel together on the journey that leads us home. Our soul stretches toward heaven, where our wonder will fall away, to be replaced by one Answer. In Him, the Soul Chaser, all wonder resides.

Father God, you are wonderful in all your ways. Help me to focus on truth this day. I desire to build my life's foundation on eternal things that heaven offers rather than the fleeting pleasures of earth. Fill my heart with wonder and lead me to answers that you promise to reveal to those who seek your face. Amen

Dropping Anchor: *If you seek only pleasure you will miss God's favor.*

___

___

___

___

PHIBBY

"And David said, Is there yet any
that is left of the house of Saul,
that I may shew him kindness for Jonathan's sake?"
2nd Samuel 9:1

Ziba was annoyed. A royal messenger had just come to his door holding official credentials of the King's palace. It was certainly out of the norm for Ziba to have contact with Zion. But, as he unfolded the package containing a scroll with the royal seal it became obvious. He had been summoned by the King to the royal palace in Jerusalem. "For what purpose?" he muttered to himself. Still, one doesn't resist a King's request, and so, despite his misgivings and questions, Ziba began the two day journey from his farm to the capital city. He carried the official royal orders with him. Ziba had an appointment with King David at the palace in Jerusalem.

Ziba had once lived in a palace. As a servant to King Saul, David's predecessor and Israel's first king, he carried much responsibility. He was a popular figure with the merchants as he made his way around the shops and vendors of the capital city. He loved the early morning markets. There he would load up with produce and meats for the staff and family back at the King's residence. Ziba had been a happy man. That is, until that fateful day when word came that King Saul and his son, Prince Jonathan had both been killed in a battle with the Philistines. Father and son, king and prince, snuffed out in a moment's time. David, the shepherd had taken control of the government and now reigned as Israel's king. Ziba kept a low profile, but remained the sole tenant of Saul's western stockade and villa. He farmed the fertile fields and made himself to be, in his estimation, a wealthy landowner. After all, there was no one else to claim the property and the locals never questioned Ziba nor his expert care of the lands. All seemed in order. There was, however, one son of Jonathan whom Ziba could not account for. A missing strand in the once royal story. A lost son. "Mephibosheth," said Ziba aloud, trying to focus his thoughts. "A noble prince doesn't just disappear," thought Ziba. He had to admit, he was not actively searching for the whereabouts of this lost once and future king. He had a good thing going at the villa and he wanted to keep it that way. Any one of Saul's true family members could easily make a claim on the fertile farmlands and Ziba would lose everything.

Yet, for now his only thoughts were questions as to why King David had requested his presence. "This can't be anything good," he mused as he entered the iron gate that stretched around the palace compound.

Far away from David's palace in a ghetto town on the south side of the kingdom the day had dawned for Mephibosheth as had so many before. He languished in poverty and self-pity, a lame man who could not walk, begging on the filthy streets of Lo-debar. He lived there in a colony of poor men, a street pack as it were… tough men who roamed the city like jackals looking for sustenance. They were always helpful to the crippled Mephibosheth, for he was one of their own. Rumor had it that he was once a rich child—a prince in a palace. "Phibby" as he was known, had no recollection of his early years. "Do I seem as a prince?" he would ask anyone who questioned the story. Still, some nights, while alone on his mat he would dream of a regal room with a banquet table filled with the finest of foods. The dream was so real that he often awoke with a start only to have the vision drift from his mind like so much smoke. On these nights, he would drift back to sleep with a lump in his throat, longing to return to the royal feast in his dream. But, daylight proved Lo-debar to be no shining city, and the scraps he begged for were not on the menu in the palace of his dreams.

Back in Jerusalem, Ziba was escorted by guards to the inner chambers of the King's palace. Considering his own experience in Saul's household, Ziba was surprised to find himself so nervous. He sat down in an anteroom next to a huge oaken door, a guard standing at attention on his left and his right. As he waited, he noticed the beautiful artwork on the palace walls. On the closest wall there hung a magnificent painting of David slaying the giant Goliath. It captured the moment that the rock from David's sling caught the huge Philistine in the forehead. The fierce warrior's knees had started to buckle in the painting and it was obvious the battle was over. On the opposite side of the chamber, there was another piece of art. "David and Jonathan," Ziba considered as he recognized the two men in the portrait. They were pictured in an embrace both dressed in full military gear. Theirs had been a legendary friendship until Jonathan's life was cut short in battle.

"I miss him every day." The voice behind him startled Ziba back to reality. He turned and saw King David himself standing in the open doorway. "I couldn't help but notice you were studying that picture of Jonathan and myself. Come in, Ziba. Come in now and sit. I have a question to ask of you." Feeling quite welcomed, Ziba followed the King into the private room that awaited them. Once seated, a servant appeared and poured two cups of wine from a pitcher. The drink was cool on his throat and the wine went down quickly. "I guess I am a little nervous," he fumbled to say.

"Tell me, Ziba... what of Saul's household. Are there any survivors?" The King drew near to his guest. Ziba noted the intensity in David's eyes. "I want to bless any living descendant of the household of Saul as a tribute to my love for Jonathan." Ziba listened intently as the King described how devastated he had been when Jonathan had perished in battle. Many years had passed since then, and David now wanted to honor the memory of his friend. "I recall he had a young son who would be a grown man by now," stated David. "His name was Mephibosheth." "I well recall the little prince," replied Ziba, "but I lost track of him over time. The last news I heard came to my ears years ago. The report had stated that Mephibosheth was living on the streets of Lo-debar, begging and crippled in both feet. It was an unfortunate accident that crippled him." Ziba failed to mention that he had never investigated the sighting nor, truth be told, had he ever looked anywhere for the lost lad. He did tell the king about that day when Saul and Jonathan lost their lives. Fearing the invading Philistine army, a nanny had attempted to flee the palace with young prince Mephibosheth. However she fell from her horse and the child fell hard as well, breaking his back on the cobblestone pathway. He was hidden away from sight by the horrified nursemaid and eventually time forgot them both. "How he ended up in Lo-debar I know not," said Ziba, finishing his tale. "Nor do I know if he remains there to this day."

King David clapped his hands together, summoning the guards outside the door. "Get a caravan together at once!" he barked. "You are headed for Lo-debar to search for the son of Jonathan. Mephibosheth will be known immediately for he is a lame man who begs on the streets of that God forsaken ghetto." The guard turned on his heel and left the room. Turning to Ziba, David remarked, "If he is there, those soldiers will find him and bring him here to me."

Later, back in Lo-debar, the village was buzzing with news of a column of soldiers from the royal palace who were searching for someone all through the streets and back alleys of the hamlet. "It's Phibby!" said a young child running down the main thoroughfare. "The soldiers are looking for Phibby!" A panic washed over and through the lame beggar. "Me?" he worried, "what is their business to be with me?" Before he could guess at an answer, a group of armed soldiers came rushing around the corner just one block away. Mephibosheth tried desperately to crawl for cover but they had already seen him. It was of no use. In a moment, they stood over him and one, the leader, snapped to attention. The others followed as one. No one said a word for a moment, and then, the leader spoke, "Mephibosheth?" "I am he," stammered the beggar from the dust. "Come with us then, you have business with the king."

As he spoke, the soldier bent down and gathered the waif of a man in his arms. He handed him over to a second soldier who placed the astonished lame man on a cart which was pulled by two other men in uniform. They were quite a sight as they made their way down the dirty streets out onto the highway—heading due north to the capital city. People lined the street for nearly a mile, hoping to learn what favor or tragedy had come to their Phibby. There was plenty of speculation as to both in his own mind as they bumped along the main road. The soldiers were not saying much, to him or each other. But as they neared the palace, you could sense their pace quicken as they burst into song. It was a strange song that Phibby had never heard before. It spoke of Jehovah the Shepherd and the words and melody cut right through the anxiety that the poor man felt. When the song finished with "I will dwell in the house of Jehovah, forever," Phibby could not hold back. "What song is this that you sing?" he asked the soldier nearest him. "It was written by King David himself," came the reply. "It's beautiful," Mephibosheth remarked. "Did you hear that, men?" shouted the one in command. "Our guest likes the sound of your singing." So they sang it again. That is how they entered the gates of the royal city… singing. The song did not stop until they reached the palace of King David himself.

Mephibosheth sat in wonder as all attention turned to him. He was given a bath by the same team of servants who took him from the cart. Then he was carried to a large bedroom with a stunning set of windows and a porch where one could see snow covered Mt. Hermon in the distance, He was given a robe to put on and a silver bracelet for his wrist. "What kindness is this?" he asked one of the servants. "Is this a joke at a poor man's expense?" "Nay," replied the steward. "It is the kindness of King David. We all share in its glory. We are bringing you to him now." With those words, echoing in his heart, Mephibosheth was carried through the corridors and into a large banquet hall. As they entered, Mephibosheth gasped. It was the very room of his dreams. The table was spread before him, just as he had seen it during the long, lonely nights in Lo-debar. Around the room were beautiful people dressed in elegance. And there, at the head of the table sat the king. All conversation ceased as he raised his hand and everyone's attention was turned to their guest.

"Mephibosheth, the son of Jonathan the Prince, the son of Saul, the king; you are welcome to my table," stated David as he motioned for Mephibosheth to be placed in the seat of honor next to him. "You are to dine here every day with my household." "But I am nothing but a dirt dog," countered the astonished guest of honor. "What could you want with me?"

"I want you to be part of the royal family." The King was crying, "The love I had for your father, I will pour out on you. As long as you live you shall live and dine as a king… You shall not want for any good thing, I have arranged for the profits of your grandfather's farm be put in your account. Ziba will see to it. You are now a wealthy man" Reaching for a nearby instrument, David plucked the strings in a melody Mephibosheth now recognized. Everyone around the table joined and sang "Jehovah is my shepherd, I shall not want. He brings me to green pastures and restores my soul." One new voice rose clearly above the rest. Phibby sang with a joy he had never known.

> *Father God, You have brought me into your family and have treated me with great kindness. I am undeserving - but grateful beyond words. Amen*

Dropping Anchor: *Our beneficent king brings joy to His Kingdom. He makes room at the table for the lowly of heart.*

____

____

____

____

The Least Of These

"... Verily I say unto you, Inasmuch as
ye have done it
unto one of the least of these My brethren,
ye have done it unto Me."
Matthew 25:40

I once heard the story of some homeless people who gave away thousands of dollars. As far as I know, it is a true story. It took place in a major US city. Which city it was I have forgotten, but that is beside the point. Here's how the story goes;

Nearby to the homeless shelter, which served many displaced adults, there was a small church. The congregants of the house of worship often brought meals to their homeless neighbors. Clothing drives were organized during the winter months. During the warmer weather, large pitchers of lemonade often found their way to the shelter to be served with the evening meal. Over time, the relationship grew to a regular mission outreach for the church friends, and a deep sense of appreciation was returned by those in the shelter.

One day, the pastor of the church had the idea of starting a Bible study at the shelter. He presented the concept to the director of the facility and received prompt permission to get underway. So, the following Monday evening, the reverend and a few congregation members showed up and began teaching the Word of God. The class grew quickly and before long, some of the street people were asking for their own Bibles. These were readily provided. It soon became commonplace to see a homeless man or woman reading the Holy Scriptures in an alley, the subway, or any other downtown location.

After several months of ministry, the pastor began a study series in the Gospel of Matthew. In the pages of that New Testament book, many of the homeless found Jesus to be irresistible and they gave their hearts to follow after the Savior. The weekly study group became a vital lifeline for pastor and homeless alike. It was during that study of Matthew that a wonderful thing occurred.

Reaching the twenty-fifth chapter of Matthew's account, they came upon the story of the sheep and the goats. Hearing how loving service to the 'least of these' was credited in the kingdom as service to the King, one of the homeless men raised his hand and said, "I guess that must be about us. We must be the least on the list." That prompted a rousing discussion amongst the shelter dwellers as to whether or not they were indeed, the poorest of the poor. Reaching into his Bible, the minister pulled out a flyer he had received in the mail, telling of a missionary organization and their efforts to supply drinking water for some African villages. Looking at the photos of the malnourished children of one village, the study group came to an agreement that they were, despite being homeless, indeed better off than the families of these villages in Africa. They at least had access to drinking water at the shelter. "So, what can we do for them?" one homeless woman queried. "We have nothing to give."

Their penniless plight notwithstanding, the homeless men and women were determined to find a way to help. How they accomplished this was inspirational. Instead of asking for money on the streets each day—they took canisters and flyers, and began raising funds for an African village in desperate need of a well to provide drinking water. It was slow going at first, but as the story began to get out, people were more responsive. It became the norm for a street person to return home at nightfall with twenty dollars in change, which was added to the growing total in the big jug on the dining room table.

After several months of collecting spare change, the day came to count the money they had raised. The jug was emptied and the counting revealed the amazing sum of over three thousand dollars. That was enough for a new well in three villages! The particular project they chose to fund was known for building a small playground for the children of the stricken village, complete with a merry go round serving as a cap for the new well. As the children spun around and around, water was pumped to the village.

The result of their efforts brought joy and dignity to the homeless in the shelter and revival to the little church. Water for the far away village provided for more than anyone had ever imagined. And it was all so simple. Jesus said a cup of cold water given in His name would not be overlooked in the Kingdom. Imagine how He feels about three wells, three playgrounds and three thousand dollar's worth of change, collected by those determined to find someone needier than themselves. The Kingdom grows. The children of the King carry out His business, dancing through the dark. The King is pleased. Amen.

Father God, may I look to ease the suffering of someone less fortunate than myself. May I be generous with the little that I possess. There is always an opportunity to give. Amen

Dropping Anchor: *There is always someone in your sphere of influence that needs your help. You can make a difference no matter what your circumstances.*

____

____

____

____

LeClaire, Iowa

"And when he cometh home,
he calleth together his friends and neighbours,
saying unto them, Rejoice with me;
for I have found my sheep which was lost.'"
Luke 15:6

Everyone said they were too young to get married, but they were in love and nothing, it seemed, could keep them apart. So, he was just eighteen and she was a little bit younger when they said their vows before a local Justice of the Peace. They got themselves a little second floor apartment over a thrift store and began their dream of living happily ever after.

When their first baby arrived, she quit her job at the market and he took on a second job to make ends meet. With the arrival of baby number two, he added a weekend shift as a security guard at the local factory. Their dream of being happy, together, seemed but a memory now, buried under a pile of diapers and overdue bills.

One day, after a third child was born, she stood in front of a sink full of dishes with the crying baby on the floor beside her and two toddlers pulling at her apron strings. She said aloud, "I'm out of here," and she closed the door behind her and was gone.

When he got home from work that evening, the house was a mess. The toddlers were in the playpen and the baby in his crib—but she was nowhere to be found. He washed the dishes that were in the sink and managed to whip up some pancakes for supper. He got the children into their beds and read them a story. All the while, his heart was beating fast and his head felt numb. Where was she? Was she hurt? He finally sat down to collect his thoughts. Just then, the telephone rang. He answered it and asked. "Where are you??" There was no answer, not a sound on the other end. Finally, her voice broke the silence. "Are the kids ok?" she asked. "I managed to feed them and get them in bed," he replied. With that, the receiver clicked and the line went dead. "Where are you?" he asked again, this time to no one.

Over the next week, she would call to inquire about the children. He begged to know where she was, but she wouldn't say. He would plead with her to come home. "I love you," he would always exclaim. But, the telephone connection would go dead each time without any conversation. "Where are you?" he would ask the empty space in their bed when sleep wouldn't come. Days turned into weeks and weeks became months.

The calls became less frequent and eventually they ceased altogether. The questions from the children became fewer as well. Desperate, he hired a private detective to investigate her whereabouts. The report came back that she was in Le Claire, Iowa. He scraped together what little savings they had and bought a plane ticket. He landed in Sioux City and bought a bus ticket to Le Claire. He located the third rate hotel where she was staying and climbed the stairs to the fourth floor. He knocked on the filthy door and she answered. "I love you. Can I take you home?" was all he could manage to say. She burst into tears and fell into his arms. They began the long trip home in a rented car, silent in their seats.

When he could hold it no longer, he asked the question, "I told you I loved you. Why wouldn't you come home until now?" "Those were just your words," she replied. "But, then you came for me."

God is like that. His word could have been all He offered us. "Where are you?" he called to the first fallen ones who hid themselves from Love in a Garden long ago. And, the Word became flesh, and He came looking for us. He will surely find us and take us home.

Father God, You did not leave us lost and hiding. You loved us enough to leave heaven on a rescue mission to earth. Thank you for never giving up on me. You are my Soul Chaser. Amen

Dropping Anchor: *Our God is a soul chaser. He always comes looking for lost ones.*

A Stranger That I Know

"...this sickness is not unto death, but for the glory of God, that the Son of God might be glorified thereby."
John 11:4

About nine years ago, I was introduced to a stranger. Ever since that initial meeting, he has followed me wherever I go. Some days he follows at a distance, while at other times he climbs up my back and makes me carry him through the day. He becomes such a difficult burden to shoulder, and I am hesitant to tell you about him. I want to spare anyone and everyone from knowing this cruel, invasive stranger. If you have encountered Mr. Parkinson, you know well what I mean.

He arrives quietly... even benignly. You are told that it is a progressive disease - but that you can live with it. So, the stranger arrives carrying hope and you grab that from him first. But hope gives way to harsh reality fairly quickly. Hope doesn't help you when your body won't move. Hope can't calm the anxiety that this Parkinson's fellow brings along with him. You struggle to get into bed at night, knowing full well, that when you wake up the next morning, Mr. Parkinson will be there to greet you. All your life, sickness has come and gone… the flu, a cold, the chicken pox… you always feel better after a short time. Not so with this illness. It worsens with passing time. You begin to feel like a burden to those you love. They are forced to accommodate the disease on your behalf. They must slow their own pace to a maddening rate in order to walk beside you. The things you long to do for them, they must do for you. You tell yourself to rise above it, but this hole is deep. The walls are high. It is bigger than you. You cannot overcome it. It's as if you are going to have the flu for the rest of your life and each day it will get a little worse. You don't have "feeling better" to look forward to. And so hope gets swept away. Fortunately, the Stranger is carrying something else in his pack.

There is something stronger that breaks the icy grip of the stranger who has now, moved in. It is a rare and valuable gift the stranger brought with him. He offers grace. I did not know that the stranger in my life who causes suffering was also going to be the one to introduce me to grace. My life is now filled with grace. But while Mr. Parkinson clamors for attention, grace rides in beneath the radar. You have to know what you are looking for. It is much like the people you see at airports, holding signs with a name written on it. You must wait for grace. But after a time, his personality and demeanor push Parkinson's aside

Grace, grace and more grace. You need grace to forgive your own rebellious body. You need grace from others that are annoyed by the presence of this stranger who tags along everywhere you go. You need grace from God who allowed you this cross to bear. The cross, you discover, does come with grace attached. That grace carries renewed hope to replace the meager hope you once had, but lost along the way. God's grace looks over Mr. Parkinson's shoulder when he brings you his cold morning greeting. It takes great effort to look past the stranger's presence and into the Face of God, but you learn that grace is stronger and thus, you reach for his hand.

God, help me to hold on.

> *Father God, on those days when your face is hidden from sight, let my faith keep me strong. I pray that I won't doubt in the dark what I believed in the light. Amen*

Dropping Anchor: *Grace is found in the strangest of places. It is a severe gift indeed.*

____

____

____

____

Sons Of The Father

"For it became Him, for whom are all things,
and by whom are all things,
in bringing many sons unto glory,
to make the captain of their salvation
perfect through sufferings."
Hebrews 2:10

As I write this, my son True is three years old. His little brother, Rory just turned two. They are remarkable boys, and I love them dearly. They are growing up in our home environment that is constructed on a foundation of love. They are not exposed to harsh talk or angry attitudes. We are fortunate that our family gets along very well. We like each other. And, because we are so fond of our family, we are always doing things for one another... little things that add up to a great amount of love and affection.

Every morning, as soon as the sky changes from black to predawn grey, True bounds into our room and announces "Its morning! Mr. Sun is waking up!" We are always glad to see him. At the first sound of his footsteps on the stairs, we smile and wait for his appearance at our door. His morning greeting and cheery personality are not unlike Mr. Sun himself, brightening every corner of our room. Rory, on the other hand, stays in his bed and waits for me to come and get him. He is simple and sweet, crawling out from under a pile of blankets. "Up!" he says. I gather him up as he wraps his chubby arms around my neck and down the stairway we go. "Mama!" he says as I plop him in bed next to Amanda. Together they cuddle and chirp morning rhymes and melodies.

My job is to break out the cereal and fill their awaiting bowls with breakfast. True likes his blue, plastic bowl with the matching blue, plastic spoon. Rory doesn't care which bowl he secures, as long as there is cereal in it. They play happily throughout the day, expressing themselves with mud puddle splashing and rock throwing. Rory likes to play "Throw Ball Stairs," a game that involves bouncing a ball up and down the stairs, as the name implies. Often they just run in a big circle around the living room, chasing each other and giggling hysterically. True leads the way and Rory stumps along close behind.

Each night at bedtime, we read a book and sing familiar lullabies. They technically are not lullabies in the traditional sense. A little U2 followed by a bit of Neil Young puts them in quiet mode. Sleep is not far behind.

It is life. It is love. But if it all ended suddenly and I was to die today, the harsh reality is that my boys would remember none of my life with them...Years from now they would have to explain, "I never really knew my dad..." Since birth, they have lived in the security of my great love for them, but none of it would be remembered in the coming decades. If I were to go now, I would be the forgotten father. They would be my orphaned children.

We are all orphaned in this same sense. God gave us life. But, God is not visible. As a result, we don't remember Him. Just as my son would long for stories of his dad, we grow up listening to stories in Sunday school or catechism, trying to piece together a picture of a Father we have never seen. Just as my son would be pleased to hear someone remark in future years, "You remind me of your father." so should we endeavor to hear those same words spoken of us. I will leave behind writings that express my love for my children, just as our heavenly Father left us a Book, but it will be up to them to read and believe. I will be waiting to embrace them but they will also have to believe that dream will come true - afterward.

We too, have a brother; a loved one so close he even tasted death on our behalf. The Father was so pleased with Him; He raised him up in eternal life. It is ours as well, this life that lasts. We will someday see our distant Father who loved us before we knew what love was. This is the heritage we have always felt as we have journeyed through our days on earth, believing we are not home yet. Our Father, we believe, is waiting to meet us. How do we know He is real having never glimpsed? Look around you... Love is everywhere.

Today, I am still here on planet earth with my family. I am still putting my picture of the Father together. But, the biggest piece is securely in place. I know that He is good and that He loves me. He put his song in my heart and I sing it each evening to my children, for they are His children, too. Orphaned? Not today. What a gift - this life of ours. We are sons of a loving father.

Father God, help me to be grateful for every day I have with my family. My children are a gift from your loving hand and my prayer is that they will grow securely and strong in that love. Amen

Dropping Anchor: *Sweet words for heaven's child to hear, are these, "You remind me of your Father."*

Nain

"And it came to pass the day after, that He went into a city called Nain;
and many of His disciples went with Him, and much people."
Luke 7:11

She awoke with a start. Her eyes seemed swollen shut and she was slow to adjust to the sunlight that beamed through her curtains. "What time is it?" she wondered aloud. Had she been crying in her sleep? Her eyelids seemed like sandpaper. "Why didn't Jesse wake me?" she wondered. Had her son gone out to the barn already? "I'll put on some breakfast and then go help him bring in the eggs," she said to no one. She lay still on her bed, her feet unwilling to make the short trip to the kitchen. With a jolt, her yesterday came rushing in like a flood. The broken fence, the horses loose, her son Jesse insisting that all would be okay… then that terrible kick to his chest by the bay horse. The force had sent him falling backward. He hit his head with a mighty blow on the feeding trough, and when she got to him his heart had stopped beating. Despite her valiant and desperate attempts to revive him, the brute force had done too much damage. "Jesse's dead." The sound of her own voice shocked her. It was no dream then, the day before had brought a misery she could not hold back. She gasped and then rose to her feet, still hesitating at the thought of going into the kitchen. Instead, she stood all alone in the middle of the bedroom floor and gave way to a torrent of tears.

She did not answer the knock on the door. "Unless you are bringing my son back to me you can go away!" she cried. "Miriam, let us in," came a voice she recognized as that of her sister. "We have traveled all night to be with you." Miriam got up from her knees and lifted the latch on the door. "Who knew one could reach Nain in a night's journey," said the weary traveler. "We left as soon as the news reached us. Show me the boy." "In there… in the kitchen." Miriam pointed and nodded her head in the direction of the tiny kitchen. A low moan escaped from the sister. Miriam's only son lay on the table, shirtless. A wound of deep purple, black and yellow spread on his torso… Miriam peeked in the doorway. "My beautiful boy," she managed to whisper. "Take courage, Miriam. We have work to do," her sister answered matter-of-factly.

Several hours later the two women lifted the body into a roughly hewn pine box. They placed the lid over the top and just before sliding it into place, Miriam bent low to kiss the forehead of her son. "One last kiss," she said through her tears. She couldn't help but think that it had only been six years before when she had buried her husband. Jesse had been the strong one ever since – the man of the family. Now he was gone. "What am I going to do?" she wailed as she buried her face in her sister's shoulder.

Toward evening, as the sun sank low in the sky, friends and neighbors gathered for the burial procession. The tombs of Nain were located on the far slope of the hill upon which the little village was perched. The sad widow walked at the front of the slow procession, her heart aching with every step. Slowly they began to descend the roadway that would take them to the graves. After a while of somber, silent walking, a cackle of laughter broke in on the funeral march. It was distant but it could not be mistaken. Someone was laughing. She lifted her head to see the source of the annoyance. There, coming toward them was a band of men and women making their way up the hills toward her town. They were surely oblivious to her plight. "This is no day for laughter..." she muttered.

As the two groups closed the distance between them, she noticed that the leader of the group below had seen them and was waving his hands to quiet his followers. They all took notice as he pointed toward the procession and lifted a finger to his lips. "Hush," he was close enough for her to hear. The man and his now quiet followers stood off to the side of the trail so the funeral procession could pass by. Reverently, they lowered their heads. Some of the women knelt in the dirt. But, the one in the lead… each time Miriam raised her eyes he was looking directly at her. He would not shift his gaze. Then, as the two groups came side by side—he stepped out and took her by the arm. "Stop," was all he said.

"Who is this man who would interrupt a widow in her sorrow," she fussed. "This is the height of rudeness." "What is your business with me?" she asked aloud.

Without a word he led her to the side of the pine box that held her dead son. To her astonishment and disgust he reached up and lifted the lid from the top. Then! What was this? The man reached his hand into the coffin. Everyone gasped as he drew out the dead man's hand, held in his own. That was enough for Miriam. She pulled away and stomped in the dust—raising her small fist at the intruder who was, yes! He was smiling. She was just about to let her words fly when she heard a familiar voice. "Mother!" said Jesse, sitting upright in the box. "Help me with these wrappings, will you? Why have we slept so late? The sun is low in the sky and I still have a fence to mend."

Suddenly the laughter she had noticed from afar was coming from within her as joy spilled from her lips in glad shrieks and loud peals of the most inexpressible happiness she had ever known. Rushing to her son, she began to pull and tear at the burial garb. There was no more yellow bruising on his chest! She gathered her son into her frail arms and cradled him like she did when he was a small child. "Mother, why are we near the tombs?" asked Jesse. "Never mind son… never mind." Dizzy with excitement she turned to the Man who had stopped the funeral. She began to thank Him, but He raised a finger to His lips and simply said, "Be on your way home with your son, for this is a day for laughter!"

Thus it was that the two groups merged into one and made the way back up the hill to the village of Nain, the name of which means "beautiful green pastures." They were all led now by one Man… laughter their language, springing up from the peace in their souls. Amen.

Father God, someday you will turn every funeral into a dance - even mine. Amen

Dropping Anchor: *Life ascends... death descends. The two will always meet, but life happily interrupts death's cold greeting.*

____

____

____

____

The Pieta

"For we are His workmanship, created in Christ Jesus unto good works, which God hath before ordained that we should walk in them."
Ephesians 2:10

It is a phenomenal sculpture. Known as the Pieta, it was created more than half a millennium ago by a young artist in his early twenties. That artist, Michelangelo formed the incredible masterpiece from one block of marble stone, which he himself chose from a quarry. He labored with chisel and rasp for nearly two years before presenting his gift to the world.

The sculpture is heart wrenching to view. Mary, the mother of Jesus is holding her lifeless son after his death upon a wooden cross. Her face, downcast, is somehow serene though her heart is broken within. The Christ is laid across her knees, as if he were again a child listening to his mother's sweet lullaby. Perhaps she is singing to him in the image of cold stone.

Michelangelo's incredible work of art has been on display since the year 1500. It sits now in St. Peter's Basilica in Vatican City. It was there, in 1972 that the unthinkable occurred. On Pentecost Sunday of that year, a crazed man wielding a hammer broke from a crowd of onlookers and attacked the statue. Before he could be restrained he had swung his hammer fifteen times, damaging the sculpture in horrific fashion. The pieces of the ruined art were scattered in every direction. Some, no bigger than a child's fingernail, were blown by the breezes, never to be found again.

What to do? That was the question that had to be addressed. There was only one answer: restoration. A team of brilliant scientists and artists began the painstaking work of repairing the broken artwork. Any thought of throwing the sculpture away in its damaged condition was dismissed immediately. You don't toss a masterpiece on the trash heap. No… its value is so great, it must be restored. Nearly two years later, the sculpture was re-gifted to the world, resurrected and whole.

You know, an evil prince once attacked God's creation long ago, attempting to forever mar the image of the Divine in us. He hacked away, until we were unrecognizable and ruined. But the Master did not throw us to the junk pile. He painstakingly restored us. He did this for one reason and one reason only. We are of great value. Heaven considers you and me to be a masterpiece. The Bible does not lie when it tells us; "For we are His masterpiece, created in Christ Jesus for good works…"

It is said that a tourist who witnessed the attack on the Pieta, picked up a small chip of the broken marble stone that landed at his feet. He planned to keep the small piece of the masterpiece as a souvenir. Months later, at home in America, he learned of the restoration process that was ongoing in Rome. He packaged the stone chip in a box and mailed it anonymously to Italy along with a note of explanation. The marble chip was returned to the restoration team where they found it to be the perfect fit for which they had been searching.

Perhaps someone has a piece of you that you are missing and need returned. Keep an eye on your spiritual mailbox. Your restoration is taking place. The One in charge of the restoring has been known to work a little miracle or two in the process. He is the Perfect Artist. One day, His restoration of us will be on display for the universe to see. What was once considered to be ruined, ready to be discarded, will forever reign—completely restored.

Father God, in your grace you are restoring me from the ravages of sin and separation from you. I surrender to your sculpting hands that shape my soul for eternity in your heaven. Amen

Dropping Anchor: *You are a masterpiece, restored.*

Author's note:
There is some evidence and much folklore that suggests Jesus walked on the shores and hills of England before He began His public ministry in Palestine at thirty years of age. Similar stories place Him in India and the Orient. The Bible does not tell us of these ventures, so we cannot know for certain. We do know that Joseph of Arimathea, the man who gave his tomb for the burial of the crucified Jesus, was, in all likelihood, a blood relative of the Christ. Tradition tells us that Joseph was the Virgin Mary's uncle, and therefore played an active role in the Holy Family after the death of Joseph of Nazareth, the husband of Mary and earthly parent to Jesus.

The tin trade was a lucrative enterprise for many years prior to the birth of Christ. Reliable tradition states that Joseph of Arimathea was very successful as a tin merchant, running his fleet of ships along the trade route from the mines of Britannia (Great Britain) to the Mid-East. Tin ore was necessary for the making of bronze and bronze was in high demand in the Mediterranean region. Did the boy Jesus sail to Europe with his daring great-uncle? It surely is not beyond the realm of possibility. He certainly was comfortable on the water. He walked upon it. He slept on board a storm tossed vessel. And, He called fishermen first. An ancient hymn that most in England have known since childhood references the folklore…

And did those feet in ancient time.
Walk upon England's mountains green:
And was the holy Lamb of God,
On England's pleasant pastures seen?*

Our next story finds its roots in the tradition and legend that surround the early years of Jesus.

---

*Jerusalem, William Blake 1810

Saving The Tin Man

"And Joseph had taken the body..."
Matthew 27:59

The salt spray was blinding as the wind battered the groaning ship. Joseph shielded his eyes and scanned the main deck. They were riding very low in the water, their hold below, full of a rich haul of ore from the tin mines of Britannia. The wind was driving them ahead in the full onslaught of the storm, and the boat was in present danger of going under, there could be no doubt. Joseph of Arimathea had often made this run, but this time he was especially concerned. He was carrying more than just his cargo of raw tin. This time he had his niece, Mary and her thirteen year old son, Jesus Bar-Joseph on board the freighter. Mary, recently widowed, had agreed to go on the journey to assist her wealthy uncle, and young Jesus had come aboard for his first real job as a cabin boy.

Joseph, a successful tin merchant had thought the change of scenery and the adventure of the boundless sea would do Mary and Jesus some good. Mary's husband had passed away just four months before. The family had been settled in Nazareth where Joseph labored as a less than successful woodworker, always struggling to overcome public ridicule. Years before, prior to his marriage to Mary, the carpenter had claimed to have been visited by angels in a dream. He asserted that Jesus was not his actual son, but was Jehovah God in the flesh. "Rome has little time left to oppress us," he was known to say. "Our Jesus will become a mighty king and lead the nation to freedom." The local townsfolk considered him crazy, and though his work was first-rate, his customers were few. He passed away quite suddenly, leaving Mary alone to find work to support the family. Joseph, her uncle, had thought the merchant trip to Britannia would be a good distraction for his niece and he promised to pay her to serve as cook aboard ship. Jesus had signed on to assist his mother.

"We may have to jettison some of the load!" The cry of the first mate came over the howling wind. "I don't like this one bit," Joseph called back, pointing to the waves breaking over the hull. "We are riding too low in the waves," the crew member warned. "Any one of these breakers could swamp us and take us to the bottom!" "If that occurs," said Joseph with a worried expression that he was unable to hide, "we will likely all perish. We are miles and miles from any land and the sea is very cold." The weather was now growing even fiercer as the two men hollered above the horrible whining of wind and wood. Joseph was about to call out "All hands on deck!" in an effort to assemble the crew and begin the dangerous task of lightening the ship's cargo when suddenly, everything stopped. The wind instantly changed to a fair and gentle breeze. The sun appeared high in the sky and the angry waves ceased their battering of the vessel, instead, becoming calm and quiet as they gently lapped the sides of the ship.

Joseph of Arimathea let out a low whistle. "What just happened?" His voice quivered as he asked the question. The first mate responded with a nod towards the bow of the boat. There stood the young Jesus, arms extended, his head turned toward heaven. Just as Joseph was about to call out to Jesus—the young lad turned and looked directly into his eyes. His face, framed by his long wet hair, broke into a broad grin. He hopped down off the rolled canvas sail he was perched upon and walked past the stymied crew.

Coming alongside his great uncle, his face grew solemn. "Before too long, it will be my turn to face a storm angrier than this one today," Jesus stated matter-of-factly. He looked deep into Joseph's eyes. "It will require your own bravery and courage. On that day, remember this one. I will be with you always, I promise."

"Did you just... was it you who... the wind and waves... gone!?! We were about to die!" Joseph struggled for words.

"Shhhh..." Jesus put his finger to his lips. "Just remember what has occurred," the young man said earnestly. "There is something more powerful than death."

Some two decades later, Joseph buttressed himself against another howling gale as he walked the narrow path from Golgotha, just outside of Jerusalem. His nephew, Jesus was hanging dead on a Roman cross behind him, atop the rugged hill. Joseph was on his way to the temple to bargain with the chief priests for the body of Jesus. "I will place it in my own tomb," he told them. Moments later a crack of thunder split the sky as the wind moaned through the columns of the portico. But, Joseph's thoughts were back some twenty years earlier, on board a sinking ship in the middle of the Great Sea. He recalled the immediate calm that silenced that storm. He recalled the words that the young Jesus had told him to remember... "I will be with you always, I promise." The peace that conquered an ocean gale now conquered Joseph's own troubled heart. It was inside of him. "I remember," the tin merchant said aloud. "In fact, I shall never forget. I am but a battered, sinking vessel in the boundless ocean of heaven's peace. And, you, Jesus, are forever my captain, the only One who is stronger than death itself."

Father God, Jesus came on a mission to earth - to bring peace to my storm tossed soul. Jesus, be my captain always. Forgive me and guide me to your safe harbor. Amen

Dropping Anchor: *Storms make great sailors.*

____

____

____

____

Bridle Party

"Now if we put the bits into the horses' mouths so that they will obey us we direct their entire body as well."
James 3:3

We pulled into our driveway, glad to be home after a long day. We took the familiar left turn off Braley Road and came down the small hill which brings us to the parking area connected to our spacious backyard.

"Horses!" Prudence was the first to see them. "Horses dad," she said again. This time she pointed to our yard. There they were, three big horses, pleasantly munching on my green grass. Our arrival on the scene did not seem to faze them as they plucked at clumps of clover and weeds. They barely looked up from their eating. "Dining out, tonight ?" I tried to sound clever and humorous as I approached them. It's not every day I talk to large animals at such close range. "I wonder where they came from?" I asked Amanda, who was still in the safety of the car. No sooner had I asked the question when a young lady in cowboy boots came dashing into our yard. "They broke down a stockade fence and got away from the corral about a half a mile from here," the out of breath neighbor announced. "I just called the owner and let them know their horses were out."

I did not want the horses to venture into the street where they could cause an accident or hurt someone. So, I called for backup. The young lady in the boots grabbed the rope lead around the grey horse and began stroking the mane of the black one right beside her. I focused on a magnificent brown horse that seemed just a bit jumpy. Remembering that we had plenty of apples in the car, fresh from the grocery store where we had just been, I called for the kids to toss me the bags of fruit. "Horses like apples," I said rather hopefully. The brown horse looked curiously at the bag of green apples which I now held before him. I fished one out of the plastic and held it out for the beast. He gladly chomped it, devouring it in just seconds. I reached for the rope that was around the neck of my hungry visitor, and produced another apple from the bag. I figured the owner would show up soon and I was pretty sure I could keep the apples coming until then.

The girl in cowboy boots got some carrots that my wife tossed to her from the passenger's seat and that's when I made a discovery. Actually, I made two discoveries. Number one, the brown horse in my care preferred carrots to apples. He definitely wanted "in" on the carrot action his buddies were enjoying. Number two, if brown horse decided to go get a carrot, I was going with him. My strength was no match for his power. I could not restrain him.

Just then, the owner of the horses came running into our impromptu rodeo and proceeded to throw a bridle over each horse's head. Once on, a bit was fitted into the mouth of each animal and suddenly they were no longer independent nor free roaming. No, they were tame and obedient. One could even say "orderly." It was obvious that the bit and bridle had been utilized many times on my hoofed friends. The owner had trained each horse by introducing the metal bit and increasing it's usage over many weeks.

At the moment when the brown horse had decided to move, despite my hold on him, I recognized that I was no match for his amazing strength. If you have ever arm wrestled someone whose strength is superior to yours, you know there is that instant when you realize you are not going to triumph. The other guy is going to win. Some things in our lives are bigger than we are. Parkinson's fits that bill in my life. I can hold it at bay for a time - but I cannot stop it. Maybe for you, it's an addiction. You have used all your power to keep it at bay, but it is relentless. It is stronger than you are. You can feel the collapse of hope as your arm is pushed closer and closer to the table and eventual defeat. You will never match the power that opposes you - but look! The Owner comes running and has just the proper tool to subdue the dark horse. Like a bit in the mouth, it's just a small thing, but used repeatedly over time, the beast gives way to submission and you are declared a victor. It is strategy, not simply strength that you require. A solid strategy can control unbridled strength every time.

> *Father God, please help me to respond to your leadership and direction so that I won't be inclined to go wherever I feel I may want to go. May small actions of mine be a blessing to others. Amen*

Dropping Anchor: *Small actions, repeated over time, yield big results...*

____

____

____

____

O.G.

"For though I am free, I am a slave to all men..."
1st Corinthians 9:19 [paraphrased]

His name is Richard, but I will always call him "O.G." In fact, more often than not, he will refer to himself as the Old Gangster. But, you have to say it like he does, "Ol' Gangstah" in order to get it just right. The Ol' Gangstah... "O.G." for short. He picked up the name in prison, yet he was one of the most unlikely inmates you would ever want to meet.

You see, Richard, err... O.G. was a sedate real estate salesman. A member of my congregation, we suspected he had a wild story or two from his youth, but as an older, mature gentleman, he seemed far removed from any sort of trouble. He was dependable and caring, a true man of God.

One night, while driving home from church, he was pulled over by a local policeman. "You have a tail light out," said the officer. "Better get that fixed in the morning." Richard agreed and waited patiently while the officer sat behind him in the cruiser. "He is taking a long time..." thought my friend. "I wonder what's up." When the officer returned he wore a stern face and ordered Richard to get out of his car. "I'm afraid I am going to have to arrest you," he said. "For my tail light?" asked Richard in shock. "There's a warrant out for you—has been for a long time, apparently," reported the officer. "You can see a judge in the morning."

He spent the rest of that night in the local jail, waiting for the morning to bring answers. He racked his brain, trying to make sense of the circumstance, but he just could not recall any reason for which he should be imprisoned. The next day, in court, the judge showed little sympathy. A bad check some two decades before had been on his record as an offense that he had somehow dismissed from memory. "Sixty days in prison," he heard the court officer say. In disbelief, O.G. was handcuffed and led to a holding cell where he awaited transport to the county jail. There he was processed in and taken to the block that was to be his home for the next two months. His orange jumpsuit hung off his skinny frame like it was made for someone twice his size. He carried the sheet and a pillow that were handed to him sometime during the check-in. As the door swung open on its heavy hinges he stared at a cell block full of inmates who were all looking back at him. Adopting his toughest pose, he said "Hi fellas," and casually tossed his gear up on an empty bunk, like he had done this one hundred times before.

"Look at the Ol' Gangstah," breathed one inmate, glancing up from his poker game... Everyone chuckled and then returned their attention to the cards. O.G. climbed up to his bunk and pretended to nap while hiding his tears in the pillow. "How could you allow this to happen?" he asked God. "It isn't fair at all." O.G. was caught off guard by the answer. "I am here with you," he felt the Lord say. "You are needed here." O.G. argued a bit, wondering why it was he that God needed in such a place. A few weeks later he got the answer.

One particular inmate had been incarcerated for many months. He had served his time, but he was genuinely nervous about being released the next day. His greatest fear was that his children would be like strangers now. Would he fit into their lives? "O.G.?" His whisper came through the gathering morning light. "I seen you pray, man. Will you pray for me?" The inmate's voice carried across the block from where his bed lay. "I'm scared to go home." O.G. climbed down from his bunk and sat on the edge of his cell mate's bed. When he finished his prayer, the Old Gangstah was shocked to hear a chorus of 'Amens' carry back to his ears. "O.G. I need some of that," said one particularly tough inmate. "I do too," said another. "Me too!" said a third. O.G. spent the morning praying bunk to bunk, man to man. When he finally collapsed back in his own bed, he wore a smile a mile wide.

Sixty days. O.G. went to the mission field for two months. There, he picked up a nickname and a new confidence in God. Why? He was dependable and caring… A true man of God.

Father God, I will go anywhere you lead me - even beyond my comfort zone. I want to be your ambassador despite difficult circumstances. Amen

Dropping Anchor: *God needs us in places where He wants to be known.*

____

____

____

____

Lola's Story

"For ye are bought with a price..."
1st Corinthians 6:20

Lola is an incredible woman, one that you just know has done a lot of living in her fifty some years. She has a merry laugh that comes readily, but it had to be fought for. You can tell. There are hints of sadness around the edges of her face that never disappear, even when she smiles.

Originally from the Deep South, she was orphaned and placed with distant relatives in a major New England city. She quickly grew accustomed to the realities of inner-city life. Drugs and gangs were nothing if not normal in her childhood, and by the time she turned thirteen, she had entered the world of the streets. She lost herself there. Tossed from boyfriend to boyfriend, bouncing from party to party, she discovered life to be hard, even as a young teen. She was considered beautiful by all; the dark skin of her face framed by glorious black braids. Beauty can be a burden, she quickly learned.

Once a week or so, she would find a seat in the back row of pews at Saint Patrick's cathedral, a giant stone edifice filled with dark hallways and wood paneled rooms that glowed in the diffused light of their stained glass windows. No one ever bothered her here, not even the kindly priest who always nodded his head in welcome. Here she could think. She remembered her mama's stories of the generations of family that preceded her, especially the true tales of her great-grandmother. Back in the 1800's, Lola's great-granny was an evangelist who travelled the southern states as a free woman, preaching the Gospel under tents or open sky. There, in Saint Patrick's, in the glow of the colorful, windowed patriarchs who looked down from on high, Lola would pray to the God her ancestor knew and loved. He seemed distant and beyond reach, but she prayed just the same. One day, when she was sixteen, He answered.

She had been hanging out in a recently abandoned house that friends had labeled a 'good place to party.' For several days they stayed there, shooting drugs and stealing bread from a local bakery. By mid-week however, they were out of food, drugs and money. Not wanting the party to end, the young man Lola currently considered her boy-friend, announced that he was going out to get provisions. Everyone knew what this meant. He took a small handgun with him. An hour or so later he returned, out of breath, with a load of cash and drugs. "I hit a dealer," he said in a frightened voice. "I didn't know he was dealing, but I sure scared him good and I took all his junk off him. He was just a kid, man… I don't think he saw where I went. There's no way anyone will find us here." He sat down next to Lola and proceeded to get high. Something was wrong, she could tell. She could feel it in the atmosphere. She got up from her seat on the floor and went toward the filthy bathroom, instructing another girl not to take her spot while she was gone. As she closed the door behind her, she saw the girl had ignored her admonition and had already taken her place, next to the young man.

A strong and foul odor filled the bathroom, and Lola quickly traced the source of the stench to the closet that was filled with old clothes. Running some water over her hands and onto her face, she tried to clear her head. Just then, a loud bang and a commotion of voices came from outside the tiny bathroom. She knew in an instant that they had been followed and found by the pillaged dealer. Frantically, she looked for somewhere to hide. Her only option was the closet, so she dove in and covered herself with the filthy laundry. Gagging from the smell, she sat motionless praying for her life. She heard a voice she knew to be her boyfriend, begging for his life. Then she heard a scream, followed by the unmistakable sound of a shotgun blast. Silence. Then another shot. Then the bathroom door creaked open on its hinges. "Look in the closet," someone said. Carlotta froze as the closet opened. From where she hid she could see the blue steel of the gun barrel. She closed her eyes tightly and prayed. Just as she expected to be discovered, a fit of coughing came to her ears. The man holding the shotgun squawked, “Man! That stuff smells terrible. Let’s get out of here.”

Lola stayed until she heard nothing, and then came out of hiding. The house was empty except for two dead bodies… her boyfriend was one, and next to him laid the girl who had taken her seat. “That could’ve been me,” she cried as she fled from the house. She remembered praying in the closet, and as she ran home she thought about the dead girl who had been in her place. Before she reached her house, she had decided that the rest of her life, she would make a difference in young lives. If God had spared her, it must be for a reason.

That was more than thirty years ago. Today, Lola is a prevention and intervention specialist, having helped hundreds of women to get off drugs and then to stay clean. She carries that ready smile wherever she goes. But, yes, you can see the sadness there too. I imagine her great grandmother looked much the same.

Father God, I am amazed that you sent Jesus to die in my place. Your plan of salvation shows just how wonderful you are and how great your love is. I accept your gift of eternal life and I promise to start living it, this very day. Amen

Dropping Anchor: *Does your life reflect true gratitude for the opportunity grace offers?*

____

____

____

____

Reflecting Light

"Ye are the light of the world..."
Matthew 5:14

The two great lights that rule the sky were fashioned by the Creator to impart a lesson. The sun rules the day with its golden glow illuminating all. The moon stands guard over the night hours, reflecting the sun and bringing light to the black sky. We are to understand that God is light; there is no darkness in Him at all. We however are surrounded by present darkness as this tired old earth swallows up the light. While He was with us here, Jesus told us that He is the Light of the World. He is the Source. Later He added a little nugget telling us that WE are the Light of the World; like the moon in the dark sky, reflectors of the Source.

It stands to reason, that the more light we reflect, the brighter the night around us. You can often see the reflection of the light of Jesus in a believer's face. You can recognize a family resemblance. In contrast, you can notice darkness in a person's countenance too. But, remember—there is no darkness in Father God at all, not one bit. We are part of a different family altogether; a family of light.

There is a choice we all must make: God who is light... or self (for without Him we are in darkness) which means we're in for a long walk on a dark road. If self is your choice, then the original Selfish One moves in and teases you into believing that Love is a myth. He'll try to convince you that right and wrong are the same... and that in the end, you are worthless. He is a dark entity, with a good pitch—having been cast out of heaven to the earth, where he now roams looking for an easy mark. His homeless condition is a consequence of his own choice of loyalty to self. He speaks the native language of a fallen planet. Satan brings darkness to the world. He is the opposite of the Light. He is the Prince of Darkness.

His language is lies, the dialect of darkness. He is fully aware that there is a Home to be found... he understands that there is a solid rock to rest upon. But, he is a wanderer, a homeless vagabond who pretends to be royalty. Those who believe his claim of inheritance wander themselves—away from Love.

I once was a wanderer too, looking and hoping that there was Light somewhere in the dark night. It came to me in the encouraging words of a brother.

He was a well-known musician, having had both secular and sacred career success and I was his host for the day. He was in town to perform a concert later that night, but the afternoon hours were mine to fill. I took him to a bar that I frequented where the steak tips were out of this world. We talked for hours—and I peppered him with questions. He finally looked across the table and said, "Loren, I don't have all the answers, but I do know this... I see Jesus in you." No sweeter words could have come to my ears. I was reflecting the Light after all. From that day to this—it is all I have ever tried to do—reflect the glorious Light of Jesus to a dark world.

If Jesus is the life choice you make, your spirit will be sweet and overflowing no matter your situation. You will know the reality of True Love and it will carry you Home to a place where you are worth everything to your Father who dwells there in perfect Light.

Father God, shine brightly on me and I will reflect your light to a darkened world. Amen

Dropping Anchor: *That which fills you - spills from you.*

____

____

____

____

Two Funerals And A Wedding

"A merry heart doeth good like a medicine: but a broken spirit drieth the bones."
Proverbs 17:22

A friend of mine, who pastored for many years, often recounted the story of the first funeral he ever officiated. It was during the Vietnam era, a sad time for our nation as many of our brave soldiers came home to their families in a flag-draped wooden casket. Thus, it was that his first funeral was a military affair, complete with honor guard and twenty one gun salute. As he began to pray at the graveside, the military honor guard assembled behind the mourners. With guns aimed high, they prepared to fire upon his scripted "amen." The nervous pastor finished his prayer and indeed, as he said "amen," the first volley went up from the military rifles, sending a loud boom and a cloud of smoke into the air. It caught more than one of those in attendance by surprise. At the sound of the gunfire, one elderly lady standing near the casket fainted and fell to the ground. A small boy's horrified voice was heard to call out, "They shot Grandma!" Despite the genuine somberness of the situation, more than one in attendance had to stifle a chuckle.

Sometimes, we find ourselves having to laugh just a bit at our own set of unexpected circumstances. That same pastor friend of mine was a bit nearsighted. Preparing for another funeral he conducted years later, he found he had misplaced his glasses. Not wanting to be late for the interment, he decided to go on without them. To make matters worse, the weather was stormy. As the mourners approached the open grave with the casket secured above the deep hole, heads were down as the wind and rain battered their slow procession. No one saw the missed step my short-sighted friend made just as the mourners drew near. Down he slipped into the freshly dug grave—leaving the amazed family to wonder, "Where did the reverend go?" When he finally summoned for help from his lowly position, several family members truly thought the "Help me out!" they heard came from... well, you get the picture. "Aren't you glad the Lord never has an off day?" he would always say, whenever I begged to hear his stories again.

The set of "bad day stories" recited by my reverend friend always included one of his first weddings. The church where he pastored was the setting for this bumble. As the story goes, the old sound system had recently been upgraded, complete with the addition of a new, wireless, lapel microphone. A bit of a tech-junkie, my friend couldn't wait to try out the new equipment. He arrived early and secured the new microphone to his suit jacket and giving a test or two, he listened to the sound quality as it filled the sanctuary. Pleased, he shut the sound board off and since he was early, he went to his office to brush up on his homily. As the noon hour approached, the church began to fill up with guests. A rather sudden and uncomfortable queasy feeling sent my friend on a quick run from his office to the men's room, just before the ceremony was to begin. Meanwhile, an unsuspecting volunteer from the Audio Committee turned the soundboard on, and piping over the speakers came the sounds of true gastric distress, picked up ever so keenly by the new wireless microphone on the suit jacket lapel. No one, including the amazed member of the audio team, knew where the sound came from or who was finding such relief until the finish came with a great flush and an audible, "That's better!" Everyone immediately recognized the voice as that of their pastor. No one had the heart to tell him why so many red faces greeted him as he entered the nearly full and very quiet sanctuary. "Not my best day," he would always offer as a reflection.

Not having an easy time of it today? Remember, our God promises that joy comes in the morning. Sometimes you have to hunt through some hardship to find it, but you will.

Each new day is a gift from heaven, where joy resides and there is never a bad day.

Father God, there are many people near me who have not laughed or even smiled for some time. We must share our joy and perhaps a big belly laugh whenever we can. Our laughter brings happiness to heaven's throne. Amen

Dropping Anchor: *Don't take yourself too seriously… that is if you expect others to.*

____

____

____

____

Nostalgia

"forgetting those things which are behind..."
Philippians 3:13

Nostalgia... If you live in that cerebral district, you are likely unhappy with the circumstances of the here and now. Some spend their time living on memories, forced backward by today's pain or just a simple dissatisfaction with the present day's unfolding. Or, perhaps it is the future they fear. For example, classic rock was just, well, rock until an aging generation began missing screaming guitar solos. Lost in a modern sea of computerized techno-beats, they longed for arena filling anthems, and so made a safe place on the radio dial where they could always return. And, there they dwell. No thank you. The future does come spilling into the present like a mad rush of water—sweeping away all in its path. But, it is neither to be feared, nor avoided. Consider the source! It is poured out of heaven itself from the wells and springs where love abides and time does not. There is no going back. We know this full well. Since retreat is not an option, should we not cease listening to the drum cadences of yesteryear and turn our eyes to the front?

It's a longstanding issue. Nostalgia did not ride in on hair mousse and mullets. The ancient wanderers of Israel longed to return back home from the desert, even though they were looking back to the slave chains of Pharaoh. What it boils down to is trust. The Jewish population was carrying a promise from on high that spoke of a future land, flowing with milk and honey. These delicacies were not available in the wilderness, but rather than looking ahead in faith, they found it simpler to look backward toward the spice and bite of Egyptian garlic and onions. These ingredients make good pizza toppings, but are poor substitutes for sweet milk and honey.

Years ago, I was conducting a Teen 12-Step meeting in the church where I pastor. Noting the sudden passing of a friend, the youths were talking seriously about life and its brevity. "If I ever die..." one young man began to muse. I stopped him mid-sentence and replaced his spoken "if" with a "when". It will happen. The life to death ratio stands at one to one. You cannot tune this reality out. You can't survive on the memory of yesterday's lunch. We must push on in faith. If we listen, we will hear Love calling us forward over the crashing drums and whispered complaints of our past.

Love never fails. It never changes. It is the one thing that will carry you from decade to decade and into eternity, for it is the very stuff that matters. When God chose to reveal Himself to us—He chose love as the method. The coming future is a love story. But, you must accept love on its own terms. Negotiations are meaningless. Love has made a way but it is narrow. And only a few find it. The rest of earth's populace is left to spin the dial in hopes they will find something familiar to lean on. They will sing along in classic fashion until the final song is played, and that last hymn will begin with a resounding "Hallelujah!" It will pour forth in a welcome wave of newness, sweeping away all past and present. The future is coming, but fear not. It is a love song that the angels sing... Alpha to Omega... beginning to end.

Father God, You have authored a love story like no other and we are the main characters in your book. The adventure of being loved by you is breathtaking. When I consider the ending you have prepared for your loved ones it makes each new day exciting. Help me to live in love toward all of your creation. Amen

Dropping Anchor: *The future pours forth from heaven's boundless river and flows through our hearts as Love.*

____

____

____

____

The Bishop

"Pride goeth before destruction..."
Proverbs 16:18

Sometimes pride creeps into our lives and we become quite pleased with ourselves. Pride was the first sin in the universe, a sin committed by the first sinner, Lucifer himself. He was subtle, mind you. He was able to roam free in God's universe, anywhere he pleased, which caused him no end of delight. Wherever he travelled, he was known and admired. This attention became like a tonic to his growing sense of self-importance, but he continued to play his role of underling well. Day by day he would present himself before the Lord, and each time he did, he would eye the power seat with mischievous jealousy, and a sense that he was destined to sit upon the glorious throne. Lucifer did not love his Creator.

Well, he gave it a shot... a power play, if you will. For the first time in eternal non-time, a will contrary to God's perfect will was proclaimed as the devil stated, "I will ascend to the throne. I will make myself like the most high." And so, error was born. Satan was cast out of heaven—for in that place, only humble hearts can reside.

The story is told of a bishop who became very prideful. He told one and all, both small and great that he alone heard from God. He carried himself in pompous fashion—his stern countenance a reflection of his grand ego. He was revered by his congregants, and esteemed in the marketplace. One day, however, word came to him that a local peasant woman had a daily conversation with God. "Impossible," fumed the bishop. "God speaks to bishops, not peasants." Nevertheless, the reports continued to reach his ears and so he sent for her. Dutifully, at the set time, the old woman appeared at the bishop's opulent office and was ushered in. From behind his massive desk he thundered, "So you hold conversations with the Almighty?" The humble peasant replied in the affirmative. "I don't believe you," growled the cleric. Quietly but firmly, the woman held her ground until the bishop finally remarked, "Alright then, let us put this to a test. The next time you hold conversation with God, why not ask him to tell you the last sin I committed." With that, he sent the woman from his office. The next morning, he was surprised to find her waiting for him outside his door.

"Well, did God talk to you?" he asked. "Yessir," came her reply. "And did you ask the question I gave you?" She nodded. A bit nervous now, the bishop continued, "So then, what did he tell you? What was the last sin I committed?" After a lengthy pause came the peasant woman's answer. "He said he couldn't remember."

On the issue of forgiveness, the Bible tells us that even the angels look in wonder at the redemption we have been offered. Pride rejects grace, and heaven knows nothing of that potentiality. There, in glory, they are amazed that most of mankind will not consider the lowly path of the Savior. It's always been the same story—pride chases away love for anyone but self. It can even chase you out of heaven.

Father God, what a blessing to know that in Christ my sins are forgiven, and may I always remember to be forgiving of all those whose lives surround me. Amen

Dropping Anchor: *God does not remember our sin. He does remember the cross.*

____

____

____

____

Rory And The Bowling Pin

"...Trouble not yourselves; for his life is in Him."
Acts 20:10

In my office, there on the window sill, sits a bowling pin. Yes, a bowling pin. A ten pin to be exact. It's very old. When I went off to college, just after the earth's core cooled, (around 1976) a dear friend of mine gave me the bowling pin as a gift. It doesn't seem like much, but it was meaningful. It sat on my dorm bookshelf for four years. It decorated my office at Songtime radio for the next nearly twenty years, and now it has a place in my office window at LifeHouse. It has been there as long as I have, over fifteen years.

Well, yesterday I nearly threw it away. It fell on baby Rory's head. It could have killed him. It is rather weighty, and it fell from the window sill—a pretty fair height. It had been a beautiful morning up until the accidental "beaning" of Baby Rory. The weather was getting cooler, carrying hints of autumn with every light breeze that floated into my open office window. We shut off the air conditioning system and let the perfect weather fill my office. My wife and small children were with me. The kids enjoy time in my study. Knick knacks and collectibles gathered over the years are sources of entertainment for them. A snow globe featuring the Nativity and a cast iron dog that works as a nutcracker are the most sought after playthings. Too young to play with the makeshift toys, Rory was taking a nap in his little bouncy seat right beneath the open window. An unexpected gust of wind happened to blow the blinds in, knocking the pin from its perch and sending it like a missile down, down, to where it bounced off of Rory's four month old head.

He screamed. I jumped from my desk and ran to try and assess what happened. I had heard the sound of the pin hitting Rory and then the floor, but I had not seen it occur. While I tried to put the scene before me together, Amanda scooped up the distraught baby and held him close. He was hurt, there could be no doubt. A large and growing lump on his head displayed both the damage and the point of impact.

Parental experience caused us to determine immediately that we were headed for the ER. This was not your average knock. We climbed into our Ford and tore out of the church parking lot, headed for the trauma care center in the next town. Flashers on, I drove at speeds of nearly one hundred miles per hour along the highway. We pulled into the entrance marked "Emergency" and Amanda ran in with Rory in her arms. I parked the car in a lot near the ambulances. Rory was taken to a treatment area and then sent for X-Rays. While we waited for X-Rays to tell us if his skull was fractured, we prayed. As word got around, many of our friends arrived and called to check-in. Finally, the word came to us that the X-Rays proved negative. After four hours of observation, the hospital sent us home, none the worse for wear.

Relief was everywhere. We celebrated God's goodness with a lobster dinner. An impromptu gathering of friends and boiled sea creatures brought a relaxing end to a long day. I couldn't help but think however, of the homes where the news of the day was not as good as what we had received on Rory. Maybe your diagnoses came with bad reports. Perhaps your X-Rays revealed breaks, or tumors. Please know that you were not forgotten in our reverie. We stand with you. We will celebrate life, but we will remember with you just how fragile it is.

Father God, I pray for your strong hand of protection to cover my loved ones and family this day. And, I pray for the children of this world who are so small and vulnerable - that your angels would guard them night and day. Help me to be a protector of the innocent. Amen.

Dropping Anchor: *Know that you are not forgotten.*

Celestial Story

"...I will be like the most High."
Isaiah 14:14

It was long ago in a land that time would never touch. The Merciful One ruled over a vast and beautiful kingdom with lovingkindness and grace. He had created this special kingdom to be his home and He called it Eden. It was to be the first of two Edens.

The celestial kingdom knew no borders, had no guards. It had a capital city where the Merciful One sat on His throne. Surrounded by panoramic beauty and light, the King kept order according to His beneficent will. He was adored by all of His creation. Cherubim and Seraphim kept a loving vigil around the throne of their King. Their service to Him was born from hearts of love and gratitude. Laughter and merriment flowed as freely as the golden wine that was poured readily for one and all. Thirst was never known. A crystal river bubbled up from the majestic mountain called Zion and it flowed lazily throughout the villages and hamlets of Eden. Along its banks grew forests green and fertile plains where wheat and barley grew tall and strong. The Tree of Life was found on the outskirts of the city, rooted deep in the rich soil of eternity. To taste of its fruit meant life eternal. Gemstones of breathtaking beauty paved the pathways and highways of the city and those who traveled in this fair land were often slowed to a near stop just by looking at the beauty beneath their feet.

All was loveliness and light and would be for all eternity if not for the Light-Bearer, Lucifer. Such was the name of the closest created being to the throne room of Eden. He orchestrated the music sung by the king's angel choirs. He was music itself, for as he moved about, his aura created anthems that burst forth from his very being. He directed his disciples to praise only their King for the beauty found within him, for Merciful One had indeed, authored the life that Lucifer enjoyed. Until...

Just how it happened, no one knows. It is a secret lost forever. Lucifer began to love himself more than his king. We tell our tales of myths and legends here on our earth, the second Eden, that surely echo back to the prideful fall of Lucifer. The ancient Greeks told of Narcissus who saw his own reflection and fell in love. They told of the boastful heart of Niobe whose end was to be made into stone. Pride is forever linked to a fall in the Holy Scriptures—but it all began in one heart... the heart of the Light-Bearer. He was lifted up in pride. Until that fateful moment, the Merciful One's will was the only will there was. It held full sway in the glorious land of the first Eden. Yet, the moment that Lucifer stated "I will ascend to the holy throne—I will be as the Most High," a contrary will found existence and a heart to call home. Sin was born.

News traveled quickly throughout the Kingdom. A dark cloud had risen over the once perfect light. Everyone waited to see what the Merciful One would do to restore order. Chaos was breaking out in the villages of Eden as the land-dwellers heard the news of the rebellion. Some rushed to defend the capital city. Others found the dark stain of pride had taken root in their own hearts and they secretly admired Lucifer's bold claim. Yes, they even pledged their allegiance to the Opposition and they criticized openly, those who did not join their cause.

In secret, they rallied their numbers and planned a march to Zion. There, they would brandish weapons and in a military-style coup, install Lucifer upon the throne. All they deemed necessary was to force the Merciful One to show unrighteous anger, and thus de-throne Himself by committing a wrong.

So, the appointed day came and they marched with taunts and curses, jeers and lies upon their sneering lips. "We will hear these words again," said the Merciful One to His loyal Son as the angry band approached. "They will someday fall upon your own back like a whip. But that will be the story for another time for we will defeat this sin then, at that future moment. It is yet to come." "Of course," said the obedient Son. "Today, we will send these rebels away to be victims of themselves and of their own pride. I have prepared a second Eden on an orb called Earth. There, pride will rule and sin abound until we conquer the rebellious hearts of the race of men that will live there under their hard rule of sin. Their greedy hearts will attempt to establish a rival kingdom and will launch crusade after crusade against our own rightful rule. But we will have the final win on a mountain like this one. It is to be called Calvary." The Son nodded. "And, what weapon will we choose to win such victory?" He asked the Father of Mercy. "Love," came the answer, "Always love."

Father God, we all must choose your will or our own. Today I declare my allegiance to you and to all that is good... I will serve you all of my days and then for eternity. I love you. Amen

Dropping Anchor: *Love is a force to be used as a weapon. No enemy is stronger.*

___

___

___

___

Timmy Two

"And when he heard that it was Jesus of Nazareth,
he began to cry out, and say,
'Jesus, thou Son of David, have mercy on me.'"
Mark 10:47

Timaeus, or Tim as he was known in the village, was very fond of his young son. He had a deep affection for the awkward, sometimes invasive behavior that the boy had exhibited since, "the dreadful mistake," as Tim called it. The mistake was his own fault. Timaeus always considered that he was the one responsible. Years ago, he had noticed some discoloration in his son's eyes, and that they were irritated much of the time. Timaeus, following the advice of a relative, took his young son to a medical man in another village. The self-appointed physician decided to cure the problem with a mixture of mercury, herbs and acid. The mixture was prepared and applied, covering the boy's eyes in a slimy paste. When the would-be doctor rinsed away the potion, Tim's little son was left sightless. He was six years old.

Timaeus spent all of his free time with his blind son. "Timmy Two" was how he was known to the villagers. He was a loud youth. It seemed that the loss of his sense of sight caused him to overcompensate with sheer vocal volume. You could hear Timmy Two from across the marketplace, carrying clearly over the noise of the pushcart fish hawkers and the droning hum of the shoppers. The only place he was ever known to be quiet was down at the shore. There he would sit for hours, listening for the sound of his father's voice. Timaeus was the captain of a fishing vessel that ventured out on the great lake early each morning before dawn. The blind child would awaken to an empty house and begin to fix himself breakfast. His father had taught him how to fetch an egg from the chicken coop. He knew just where the wood for the stove was kept and he dutifully stoked the fire in the hearth while he waited for his egg to boil. He was alone at these times. He never knew his mother. She had no place in his memory nor his heart. Timaeus never spoke of her.

Timmy Two spent his days in the village marketplace. He was well known as a "nudge" to the vendors. Always underfoot, he would pass the hours waiting for the afternoon sun to feel cooler on his brow, a sure sign that evening was coming. That could mean but one thing. His father would be coming in with the day's catch. Timmy Two would head for the docks and await the familiar sound of his Abba, calling orders to his crew. As soon as the ship was near enough, the silent boy would exchange listening for calling. "Abba, do you see me?" he would cry, waving his arms above his head. The senior Tim would wave back and call, "Coming, child! Let us go home together!" As soon as the ship docked, Timmy Two would follow the sound of his Abba's calling voice and run to his open arms. His father would then take his boy's hand in his strong grip and gently lead Timmy Two through the narrow streets. An unlikely pair, they were ship captain and blind boy together on their way home.

This is how it was until the day his father's ship did not return to port. No one was sure what had happened to the captain and his crew. The blind child would not be moved from the dock where he waited silently for days on end. He sat, listening for the familiar sound of his Abba, calling to him. But the sound did not come. The days became weeks and the weeks became months. In time, the months turned to years. Timmy Two began the descent downward to the only life available to him… life on the street. He became a beggar... a blind beggar, who was still known as the son of Timaeus, or "Bartimaeus."

His condition was dreadful. He was pitied by many but ignored by most. The mystery of his long lost father disappeared into yesterday's news. The past was indeed a sad mystery, but the future was certainly bleaker still. His home was the street, both night and day. The alms that folks occasionally tossed his way, he kept in a leather pouch until he had collected enough to buy bread from the baker. "Alms, alms for a blind man," Bartimaeus would call. His loud voice carried throughout the market, causing some to give way to the annoyance. "Hush, loudmouth!" Their words had no effect. The beggar called for aid despite their rude protests. Thus the years rolled on, and on.

One morning in the marketplace, Bartimaeus heard a commotion. There were excited voices discussing a recent visit by two disciples of a rabbi named Jesus, who was said to be a miracle worker. The duo that had come to the village had spoken in glowing terms of this rabbi, claiming he was the promised Messiah. Bartimaeus did not hear of it personally as they had set up in the temple—a place he was not welcomed. However, in the wake of their visit, he caught some reference to Jesus giving sight to the blind. Could this be? His heart ached with curiosity.

That night, he slept fitfully. He dreamed of his father. In his dream, he was a boy again, walking home from the docks, his hand tucked snugly in his Abba's strong grip. When he awoke it was midmorning. He could tell the hour by turning his face to the warm sun. For some reason, on this morning, the market was strangely quiet. It seemed nearly empty.

"Where is everyone?" he asked no one in particular. Just then, a loud cheer could be heard out by the road that led around the village. "What could it be?" Bartimaeus asked himself. As quickly as he could, he scurried toward the sound of excited voices. "It's Jesus!" said a woman in the crowd. The blind beggar was close enough to hear her. "He's coming right this way!"

Something burst inside of Bartimaeus. He began to cry out, his loud voice carrying over the crowd. "Jesus! Can you see me?" Bartimaeus was wildly waving his arms above his head. "Be still, beggar," said one nearby. Another fumed, "Hush, loudmouth," and pushed him down in the dust. But Bartimaeus could not be silenced. His booming voice rose higher still. "Son of David, have mercy on me! Son of David, have mercy on this blind man..." Suddenly the crowd drew quiet. Bartimaeus strained his ears trying to discern what was happening. Everything was still. And then, a voice next to him, "He's calling for you." Then another voice spoke, "Yes, Timmy Two. The rabbi is calling for you." The crowd began to push him forward, parting like a wave to let him through. "Hurry!" they urged, but Bartimaeus needed no urging. He began to run toward a voice that he could now hear clearly. "That's right! Come to me, son." The sound of it reminded him of his Abba's voice. He fell to the ground, embracing the rabbi's feet.

"What do you want me to do for you?" asked Jesus. "I want to see!" sobbed the beggar. "Do you believe I can do this for you?" asked the Rabbi. "Yes, yes" came the reply. "Then you shall have what you ask for," said Jesus. At that moment, Bartimaeus looked up into the gentle face of his Healer... It was a smile that he could see! Looking around at the astonished crowd, he bellowed, "I CAN SEE!" Cheers ascended from the people, praising this great gift. Men thumped Bartimaeus on the back. Women hugged him for joy. But Bartimaeus would not turn from the face of Jesus.

"Come with me," said the Rabbi. "My Father is very fond of you..." As he slipped his hand into the strong grip of Jesus, the crowd began to move again, following an unlikely pair. They were Jesus, the son of David, and Bartimaeus, a child of God... together, on their way home.

Father God, Your love is the strongest tug in the universe. It pulls my heart toward you. It conquers kings and kingdoms. It always has and always will. I love you because you loved me - unconditionally and undeservedly. Thank you. Amen

Dropping Anchor: *You will not be overlooked by Jesus, even if the world turns away.*

___

___

___

___

Fires And Foundations

"...Behold, I lay in Zion for a foundation a stone, a tried stone, a precious cornerstone, a sure foundation: he that believeth shall not make haste."
Isaiah 28:16

Acushnet, a little town which borders the famous seaport of New Bedford, Massachusetts, is foundational to my life experience. It's the town where I grew up. My father, the Reverend Stanley Decker, left his childhood home in upstate New York to settle in Acushnet. He answered a posting for a pastoral position and came to be the cleric of the local Baptist church. Oddly enough, he had heard of Acushnet some ten years before becoming the pastor. An article on the newswire was picked up by the weekly paper in his hometown. By chance, a slow news week meant that the article actually made it to press. My father had a paper route in rural New York and happened upon the story. Apparently, he never forgot it. It was a less than complimentary story about the all-volunteer Acushnet fire brigade and how their plodding responses to alarms gave them a reputation for saving foundations.

Acushnet was named for the tribe of Native Americans who lived there centuries before my family came along. The Cushena Indians were mostly friendly folk. They had a few off years of being disagreeable when they rallied behind one chieftain called Philip who led an insurrection against the advancing white man (King Philip's War.) Plymouth Plantation and other neighboring settlements became locked in battle with the displaced tribes of Native Americans. The Cushenas burned the white men's homes to the ground within their own territory, leaving only smoldering foundations, no doubt a foreshadowing of things to come. The sturdy settlers rebuilt their homes however and the local Indians eventually settled back in next to them. Apparently they would rather fish than fight.

By the time my father came to town, Acushnet was emerging as a bedroom community, a suburb of New Bedford and Fall River, close enough to the Boston beltway to be a favorable spot for the new "commuters." No doubt Dad appreciated the location of the church parsonage, his new home. It was a quarter mile from the local firehouse. Volunteer firefighters arrived at breakneck speeds whenever the old alarm on top of the barn sounded. The "barn," or firehouse, was just big enough to house the two old fire trucks that were owned by the town. Whenever a blaze broke out, the siren atop the building would wind its way toward full volume, a sound that could be heard for many miles. The volunteers would respond, the first ones there would take truck number One and the rest would come after in old number Two. A slate blackboard inside the barn would cite the address of the fire, hastily scrawled in white chalk as a guide for latecomers to follow. This was key for my dad.

At the first sound of the wailing alarm, my father would spring into action. He would run the short distance to the firehouse, check the address written on the blackboard and more often than not, he would race back home, hop in his Oldsmobile and rush to the scene. Once there, he would console victims, or help run a hose; he did whatever was needed. It was a fine day for me when he finally considered me old enough to ride along with him on one of these missions. Thereafter, at the first sound of the siren, we would look at each other with that sense of excitement that comes only from a dramatic interruption in the routine. I would match him stride for stride down Main Street, past Bud Harding's gas station and into the open door of the barn. Dad would check the chalkboard and depending on the information there, he would grab my arm and sprint back to the Decker driveway, where the Olds awaited. "Let's go!" he would say. The V8 would roar into action and off we would race, to lend aid as best we could.

Lending aid was an expected part of the fabric and history of Acushnet. We have Laura Keene to thank for that. There is a road named in her honor on the southeast side of town. She is a foundational character in the story of Acushnet, indeed in the story of the United States. Laura Keene was a British born actress who had a fairly good run as a leading lady in the live theater of the Civil War period. Her chief claim to fame came in April of 1865 when she took the stage at Ford's Theater in the nation's capital. The President of the United States was in attendance on Saturday the 15th of the month to catch Laura's performance in "Our American Cousin." Also in attendance was John Wilkes Booth, who entered the theater and climbed up the backstairs to the presidential viewing box, where he put a single bullet into the head of the unsuspecting President. Booth then jumped to the stage below and screamed "Thus it is with tyrants." Many in attendance pegged Mr. Booth as part of the evening's performance. Some in the audience applauded. Ms. Keene however ran to the edge of the stage, calling for a doctor in the house. She then dashed to the stricken leader, cradling his bleeding head in her lap until medical help arrived.

So shaken by the assassination was Ms. Keene that she retired from the theater and moved to, of all places, Acushnet. There she lived out her days on a farm in relative seclusion. No doubt she was asked to tell the story of that fateful night in Washington over and again. She became enough of a local celebrity to have an avenue named in her honor. If you go there today, you will see her old farmhouse is still standing. The foundation is secure.

I have long since moved from Acushnet, although I did not settle far from my roots. I now live just one town over. But I don't go back much; things are too different now. The Baptist parsonage, my boyhood home, was sold and moved by truck to a different location. It was pulled right up and off its foundation. The old firehouse stands empty, replaced by a modern, downtown facility featuring state of the art rescue trucks. There are no more volunteer firemen either; a full time firefighting staff mans the new station. If ever one was interested, the old chalkboard is still visible on the back wall of the now vacant barn that once housed old Number One and Number Two. You can see it if you put your face close to the window and block the light by cupping your hands against the glass. It hangs there like a museum piece. If I ever do go looking, I sense my dad isn't far behind. I then imagine the old alarm beginning its winding into a full wail, and my dad, sprinting home from the station, saying "Let's go!" I guess in the end, Dad did better than just saving a foundation, for he, the pastor from Acushnet, gave me mine.

> *Father God, I thank you for my heritage - for those who taught me how to live and how to love. They built a roadway for me to walk upon and it led me to you. Amen*

Dropping Anchor: *A good father allows his son to stand upon his shoulders. From there he can get a pretty good glimpse of the future.*

____

____

____

____

Do Re Me

"Woe unto them that join house to house,
that lay field to field, till there be no place,
that they may be placed alone in the midst of the earth!"
Isaiah 5:8

It is a mistake we often make. People see themselves as individuals, standing alone. "It's my life, after all," we are known to say. We shrink back and retreat into our privacy at every opportunity. Headphones attached to personal listening devices are commonplace, providing instant isolation—wherever you may be. Modern radio can be formatted to fit our own private playlists. Computers have become so personal that we can wear them on a wrist as watches. The internet allows us to forgo a trip to the library, instead, bringing the library to us. We are crowded as a populace, yet we have never been more alone.

This was never God's intent with his race of humans. Eve was formed from Adam's rib—and every human being since that initial creation has been fashioned within the life of another. We are a single strain manifested in multiple persons. The older you get, the more you realize that life is an amazing gift—but life is not about me. We are but a single note played in a grand symphony, forever connected within the melody of generations that form as a song in the mouth of the Singer.

It is likely that past generations understood this connection more fully. They set out for new worlds and even fought world wars to ensure that pioneers would prevail, not tyrants. These ancestors of ours sensed a genuine responsibility to the generations yet unborn. They wanted future descendants to have a better life than they did. Today we forge ahead on cyberspace with ME leading the way. We post endless texted tributes to our own lives and snap countless photos of self and not scenery. We have been swallowed by a cause, but the cause is personal. It is us. It is me.

Jesus opposed this very concept while he walked the planet. He had twelve followers, yet He treated them as one. Even the betrayer received equal treatment. When the Lord announced that one of his disciples was to turn on him, the group did not all stare knowingly at Judas Iscariot. No, they looked at themselves and asked, "Is it me?" Jesus had walked with the disciples for three years without giving away a clue that there was a rogue in their midst. He had established unity—at least in principle. There were times when Jesus was not close by and his followers turned to infighting. "What have you boys been talking about?" he would ask. "Nothing, really." they would answer; embarrassed by the greed in their own souls. It is much the same to this day. When his followers are fighting, he's usually not around.

Humanity was meant, designed, to be connected. We are connected, even when we pray. When the occasion rose to teach the Twelve how to pray, Jesus instructed them to use the word "Our" not "My". "Our Father in heaven," presents much differently than "My father...." The prayer continues "Give us this day our daily bread." Unity continues, established. We are eating together. We are sharing a meal (pass the potatoes). He goes on... "Lead us (not me) not into temptation, but deliver us from evil." This means that I may have to encourage someone to stay on the straight and narrow path. There really is strength in numbers. There is not a single "me" in the entire instructional prayer. I am left to ponder the nature of our prayer lives. Are not most of them constructed on things concerning me? Jesus could pose the question of us, "What are you talking about?" "Nothing much… just me," we would answer. Just think of the result if we prayed less for ourselves and more for the needs of our family, friends, neighbors, and leaders.

Yes, life is a grand gift, but not if we consume it on ourselves; it is, instead, to be given away. A single note symphony would never please the ear of the Listener. He longs to hear us harmonize. We are notes played together in a chorus that spans the generations. Warm up your voice. Join the song. Do Re Me—I mean "we."

Father God, I pray that I won't be a soloist. Make me a humble harmonizer. Amen

Dropping Anchor: *Harmony cannot be achieved in a song sung solo.*

____
____
____
____

The Barn In Brattleboro

"Enter into His gates with thanksgiving, and into His courts with praise: be thankful unto Him, and bless His name."
Psalm 100:4

If you ever happen to travel through Brattleboro, Vermont, be sure to ride along on old Route 9 away from the center of town, and head northwest toward Bennington. Just up from town about a mile or two you'll see the West Brattleboro Baptist Church on your right. If you stop in, Pastor Steve will greet you warmly. If you don't have time for a visit, at least drive slowly past the church and neighboring parsonage. At the end of the driveway between the two buildings is a white barn. On the loft doorway is a decorative, Amish-style painting featuring an intricate design with a man on horseback. It reads "Enter His Gates With Thanksgiving." My mother painted that many years ago during the time when my dad pastored the little church there on Western Avenue.

The senior Deckers truly enjoyed their years in Vermont. "It's like going to heaven, early!" they were known to say. They came to their northern home later in life; my father was pushing sixty when they arrived. The local "pulpit search and supply committee" was looking for someone with experience to serve as the next pastor. They got their man. The work he accomplished while ministering there has now been felt through several generations of grateful Brattleboro families. He served faithfully for more than a decade. Heart and soul invested, he forged a legacy of integrity and love. But, I want to return our focus back to that barn door which my mother painted.

She was not young either when she and dad relocated to Brattleboro. A fine artist, she quickly earned a respect and reputation for her watercolors and oils. Many homes in Vermont still have a Ruth Decker original hanging on a wall... but, the door high upon the barn in her backyard? It represents an amazing artistic achievement. She had to have conceived the idea first and foremost.

Where you and I would've seen only a barn door, she saw a canvas. She must have spent many hours perched on a ladder in order to accomplish her art. Twenty feet in the air with brush in hand, she surely labored for many days on the project. In the end, she had rendered a beautiful image which remains to this day.

Some people leave a mess wherever they have been; others leave beauty in their wake. That old barn door is a testament, really, to the lives of Stan and Ruth Decker. They both labored to make things better around them. And when it came time for them to find a place more wonderful than Vermont to call home, they entered His gates with thanksgiving. When my turn comes to enter those same gates, I pray they will be standing at the end of the driveway, waving me home. I carry that dream with me. I miss them, but, not for too much longer. I'll go to see them soon. They both live due north of here, just up from town a little way.

> *Father God, may I leave beauty behind me as I journey to your home. I will gladly enter your gates - safe for all eternity. Amen*

Dropping Anchor: *Is there beauty in your life's wake - or just troubled waters?*

____

____

____

____

Yusef And The Bible

"For which I am an ambassador in bonds:
that therein I may speak boldly, as I ought to speak."
Ephesians 6:20

Yusef was a warrior. He was a hunter. He was a leader of his tribe. He and his family lived deep in the Congo region of the continent of Africa. He had never seen a white person, except for one time when he visited the city of Bakool as a youth. There he had learned that the ways of the white man differed from anything he had ever seen. In that seaport city, money and power were the driving forces that propelled men in their pursuits of wealth and fame. "People look out for only themselves," he said to his parents upon his return to his village. The people of Yusef's tribe were not that way. Everyone had a part to play in the life of the community. From the youngest to the oldest, each person carried responsibility. No job was unimportant.

Yusef was one who hunted game to feed his village. He became expert at tracking and trapping wild animals and the women of the tribe often marveled at the amount of fresh meat he provided for their tables. However, drought came to the region, a seemingly endless dry season that turned the rivers into baked clay. Game became scarce as the animals moved on to higher country. Each hunting trip took Yusef farther and farther from his village home.

One day he found himself in a region he had not travelled before. He was tracking an animal when he noticed a strange new set of tracks nearby. Following them, he happened upon a jeep parked under a shade tree, with a lone white woman dozing in the driver's seat. Yusef was more than curious about the stranger and he shyly cleared his throat. She awoke with a start and seeing Yusef she scrambled to her feet. "Greetings," said the woman in Yusef's own language. She smiled as she spoke. Yusef returned her greeting but his attention was on the jeep. Seeing his curiosity, the driver, who was a missionary to the region, offered to give Yusef a ride. He accepted and off they bounced and spun—with Yusef barely hanging on. They returned a half hour later, laughing loudly at their escapade. Together they shared a humble meal while the missionary also shared some readings from a little black book she called the "Bible."

Yusef was enthralled. He had never heard such an amazing truth as that which came from the pages of the little book. Such a good God it described... compassionate and forgiving. His heart beat fast within as he prayed for the first time to this Jesus that the woman spoke of. He felt brand new, and he knew he would never be the same again. Bidding a hasty goodbye he ran all the way home to his village, preparing to share the good news of Jesus with them. Arriving with much commotion, he summoned the tribe to the center of the village announcing he had news to share. As his friends and neighbors came together, he began to tell them of his new found faith. Instead of receiving the words with gladness however, dark clouds gathered on the faces of the villagers. They began to shout at Yusef, and then their anger boiled over into violence. They beat Yusef with rods and whips until he was unable to stand. Dragging him out into the swamp behind the compound, they left him lying in his own blood. Barely conscious, Yusef wondered why his tribesmen had behaved in such a manner. "Maybe I didn't tell it right," he surmised. Rehearsing the details as best he could recall from the lady missionary and her Bible, he summoned up his strength and stumbled back into the village. Expecting to hear an apology, the village people gathered around once again. And, once again, Yusef began to tell them of God's love.

If the first beating wasn't bad enough, the second one was worse. Thinking him to be dead, they heaved his body back into the swamp. Yusef laid there for two days. In great pain, he crawled back to the village center and tried again to speak. He told the amazed villagers about God's love and forgiveness. He felt too weak to continue although he tried hard to give the message as he had first heard it. He, instead, passed out from exhaustion and pain. However, when he awoke, he was not back in the swamp—he was in his own bed. As his eyes fluttered open, he saw his village friends gathered around his bedside. "You have caused us to believe," said one. "Tell us again of this good news."

Today there stands a church in the center of the village, right where Yusef had first spoken to his friends on that day when he first heard the Gospel. Yusef is an old man now, but he still serves as pastor to the little village. He preaches the eternal truth from the pulpit of that little church. He carries no ill will for the beatings he took. Instead he carries his own copy of the little black book that changed his life—the Bible.

Father God, Your written word is etched upon my heart. It is good news, indeed and I believe it is true. Help me to follow your truth no matter the cost. Amen

Dropping Anchor: *Your life, not your words tell the story.*

___

___

___

___

The Bat Bus

"...Follow Me, and I will make you fishers of men."
Matthew 4:19

Some stories stick with you. Here's one that has stayed in my heart. It was told at a conference I attended many years ago. It went something like this.

As I recall, a minister (We will call him Pastor Mike) served a church in the Deep South. It was a large church, and getting larger. They eventually needed to hire a youth minister to keep up with the growing number of young people in the congregation. Well, this was in the early 1970's during the Jesus People era. Youth pastors didn't come in three piece suits in those days. The young man who was hired came on staff, complete with long hair, which he wore in a ponytail, his face framed with a flowing beard and sandals on his feet. Pastor Mike had his doubts but the young cleric had a love for God and boundless enthusiasm, and before long, he had proven to be an effective addition to the ministry team.

As part of his responsibilities, the new youth pastor also oversaw the bus ministry which transported many children from the neighborhoods to the church on Sunday morning. The Sunday school program relied on these yellow busses. It was a vital ministry but it needed a "shot in the arm" as the numbers of riders had begun to fall off in recent months. Some of the busses had seen better days and were now showing their age.

"I'd like to paint bus number four," said the youth pastor from the door of Pastor Mike's office. He had poked his head in for one of those "got a second?" conversations. "Is it in the budget?" asked the senior pastor in return. Mike pictured the vehicle with a fresh coat of yellow paint. "It won't cost much," came the answer. Pastor Mike ran some numbers in his head, and considered the size of the bus. "It'll probably be more than you think," he said. "But go ahead and get it done." "Thanks Pastor Mike," said the youth pastor as he went whistling down the hall. A couple of hours later he was back at Mike's office door.

"All set," he said excitedly. "You wanna see it?" Pastor Mike looked at his watch. It was still an hour before lunchtime. "How could you get it painted so quickly?" he asked as the pair headed for the parking lot. As they rounded the corner of the building, he suddenly knew the answer. There in its parking lane was ol' number four, totally transformed. Around the headlights, a black Batman like mask gleamed in the sun, the paint still drying. The grill now resembled a smile thanks to some cosmetic touches of paint, and the entire body of the bus was striped with black and yellow bands of color. The back of the bus was jet black with a stinger on the emergency door.

"Behold, the Bat Bus!" said the young cleric, obviously pleased with his work. The senior pastor gasped in astonishment and wondered how he would explain this to the trustees. He imagined what criticism would come his way when the congregation got a look at the unique paint job. Within a few weeks, however, Mike would be well prepared for any negativity. You see, every kid in town wanted to ride in the Bat Bus. Parents were calling the church as early as 6 am, hoping to get their child a seat on the black and yellow "wonder bus" that day. The "Bat" normally did two "runs" through the neighborhoods on a Sunday morning. After the transformation to a semi-super hero, the Bat Bus was pressed into even greater duty, managing four or five trips before Sunday school opened. The bus was always full and soon the Sunday school was also.

I mentioned that this story stuck with me—and well it did. A number of years after hearing this account, I was pastoring a growing church in New England. One Sunday morning, I shared the account of the Bat Bus. Shortly after the service ended, two of my youth workers approached me. "You know the van parked out behind the parsonage?" I knew just where this was going… "Well, we want to receive permission to paint it, like they did with the Bat Bus." It was one of the easiest answers I ever imparted as a pastor. And thus, the Gecko Van was born. I believe that tired old van appreciated its second shot at life, for it ran well for nearly ten years after the paisley, rainbow and gecko paint job was applied. And yes, it worked. Kids came. Parents called. And, God smiled.

Father God, I want to make you famous so I will do my part to bring others to church. I will even offer them a ride! Amen

Dropping Anchor: *Old vision gives way to new ideas - often with dynamic results.*

___

___

___

___

Unrequited

"Wine is a mocker, strong drink is raging: and whosoever is deceived thereby is not wise."
Proverbs 20:1

I have a friend that drinks... too much. He is a wonderful person but he is slowly giving away the wonder of his life to the harsh predictability of alcohol. When he was but a teenager, he told me that he loved alcohol. "Well, it doesn't love you back," was my reply. And, like all unrequited love, it is tearing him apart. Alcohol will spend time with you. It will warm you like a lover. But its heart is cold and as empty as the bottle it came in. It will toss you aside in the morning and leave you to clean up the mess.

Booze picks its affairs with hooker-like precision. When the drinks are poured, my friend will swallow two. He needs to forget a few things and the temptation in a glass will help. They go down easy but soon she whispers in his ear, "Let's go..." and he leaves the party, succumbing to the false promise of her charms. He takes her home and tries to hide her from the family... but they know. They plead and pray that he will break up with this heartless tramp, but he claims they don't understand him... not like she does.

She is the first thing my friend thinks about in the morning. She has long gone away, leaving neither note nor gift from the night before. An empty bed is all he has—but, he tells himself she will return. "Yes! Tonight she will be mine again." They will do their lover's dance and maybe tonight, he thinks, maybe she will stay. But she does not stay this night or any other. Cruelly, she steals from him as she leaves before the morning light. Money disappears. Valuables are gone. He buries his head in the pillow and laments the losses. But what can he do? He is a man in love.

My friend has a brotherhood that shares his pain, but they are ashamed and stay hidden. They too, have romanced with alcohol, or her cousin morphine, or her host of suffocating relatives who come for a visit and never leave. One sister named Pornography is so pretty, but she never comes with the rest of the family. She just sends photos, videos and empty promises. She is the most hard hearted of the bunch. She takes your attention and then your heart but gives nothing in return, reminding you again and again that you're on your own.

My friend is alone and on his own. It was a self-imposed prison at first. But now, he can't get away. There is but one escape route and it is a narrow way. He must brave it alone, for "she" cannot come. One has gone before however and is calling… calling. "Follow me as The Way, and True Love. Exchange the lie for life." It is one or the other I tell him, but he doesn't hear me. He is alone again… with her.

> *Father God, my prayer today is for all of those who are bound by addiction. I pray for their families who suffer with them. May true love destroy the lie. Amen*

Dropping Anchor: *The life of moderation is generous with its love and never claims a victim. Addiction is Death by a slow violence that snatches hearts and tortures them with promises of freedom.*

___

___

___

___

Peace Signs

"When thou comest nigh unto a city to fight against it, then proclaim peace unto it."
Deuteronomy 20:10

As much as it depends on you—live at peace with all men. That is from the Bible. I'm so glad that God put the primary clause in that little verse. It is brilliant. The Author knows his creation well. He understands that we don't always get along... hardly ever, in fact. But there it is, sitting pretty in the Scriptures, as much as it depends on you... live at peace with everyone (Romans 12:18).

In order for this little sentence to function—a few things need to happen. First we must allow for the fact that not everyone wants to be at peace with us. Some don't even like us. Petty jealousies, or past unforgiven hurts, block the way of love and affection. Often, these things are held on to like coins in a counting house, adding up so that someone feels justified in their negative opinions. We probably all have someone in our lives who is stacking against us, amounting to a genuine tower of dislike. So, it is dependent on us to ask for forgiveness. It is never wrong to do the right thing. Take the low road (which happens to be the Humility Highway.) If we have caused hurt—own up to it and apologize. It won't kill us. On second thought, Jesus calls us to die to self—so it may well do us in. But, this is good. It is dependent on us to treat those who don't enjoy our company, nothing but nicely. Get over our reactionary posturing and love them. Proactively! Genuinely! Yes, despite the fact that they still don't seem to like you much. You have asked for forgiveness, so live like you have it. God has you on a clean slate—so roll with that. If someone is slow to forgive—that is outside of the primary category of "as much as it depends on you."

Also, in order for this lesson to work in our lives, we must value peace. Many have abandoned any real hope for peace, thinking it an impossibility—a fairy tale. The world we live in rails against peace. Many of us grew up in homes where there was no peace. Even when there was quiet, there was no peace. We just waited for the next bomb to go off. We walked on eggshells. To you I say that peace is possible. True peace is not an absence of conflict. It's one of the results (or fruits) of being a container for the Holy Spirit and His inner peace that you carry with you. Where the Spirit of the Lord is—there is peace. So, invite Him into your life and your relationships. This brings about a peace that transcends circumstances. That is why the Bible calls it, "Peace that passes understanding." It makes no sense, but there it is.

Peacemaking in this fashion is a noble cause. Jesus said that peacemakers who plant seeds of peace will harvest peace. Imagine a full harvest of peace filling our houses and barns. It's possible—but we have to start planting. That much depends on us. Leave the rest to God. You can't force someone to change. If you have no peace in a relationship, you are probably letting someone steal it from you. It would be one thing if you let them borrow it so that they might enjoy a bit of peace themselves, but that is not how it goes. They usually take your peace and toss it on the scrap pile, considering it useless. These types of folks have no respect for peace. Here's why...

Some frankly have never known peace. Within and without they have been buffeted and beaten over time, pulled far out to sea—away from any safe port of peace. They have no standard of measure by which to recognize peace. For them, we must model peace. Go out in a rescue boat and show the way to safety. That much depends on us. Make sure the docks are open and clear when they finally sail in. Don't harbor a grudge.

Don't expect to find peace automatically occurring, even in church. We haven't done too well in the peace department over the years. Not even at first. Well, at the very beginning, the birth of the church in Acts chapter two, everyone got along famously. But, a lot of things that start smoothly don't sustain. Many marriages offer proof of this fact. The church was no different. By the time the Epistles were written to the First Century Church, there were factions, disagreements and doctrinal divisions. It didn't take long to go off kilter in the peace department.

So, although it sounds like an oxymoron—fight for peace. Work for it. It takes time. Years of dysfunction cannot be cured with a conversation. It requires more than just talk. But, in the end, it passes understanding by and conquers all its foes.

Father God, I pray for peace… in my heart, in my home, in my world. Amen

Dropping Anchor: *Peace is a beautiful thing. Let it reign.*

Nathaniel

"And they lifted up their voices,
and said, Jesus, Master, have mercy on us."
Luke 17:13

He waved to his parents from a distance. It was always this way. Their visits, such as they were, broke his heart each time. "Hardly a visit at all..." he muttered as he sat at the stone barrier that marked the boundary he dare not pass.

His parents made the once a week trek to see him from their home on the shores of Lake Galilee, a place he knew well. He had been a boy there, playing on the shore, fishing in the eddies. Now, his home was a frightening place of pain and death. His name was Nathaniel and he was a leper.

He rarely got the food they would leave for him. Ruffians, desperate for sustenance, would beat him to the basket his parents would place at the colony gate. He never told his mom and dad that he was yet hungry after their brief stay. Their sadness was too great already.

With a deep sigh, he watched his family disappear around the bend in the road. No sooner had they gone, when out of the crevices and holes sprang horrid looking men and women. In various stages of the disease, they all wore bloody rags. They all hid their faces. With hands like clubs they tore at the basket of bread and meat. "So, this is my lot..." Nathaniel cried aloud as he returned to the hole in the rocks where he slept at night. There he buried his swollen face in his hands and wept. His aching body forced sleep to take him. He slept as much as possible for in his dreams, he did not have leprosy. He was still a boy by the Lake. While he slept, he was free.

He awoke at nightfall and went to check on his uncle. Close to death, his only family member he could touch was nearly a corpse already. The smell of rot turned Nathaniel's stomach as he approached the cave where his uncle lay. "Go away, lad…" the hoarse whisper came through the darkness. "Let me die alone, like a dog, for that is what I am… and worse." "Can I get you anything?" Nathaniel heard a laugh escape his uncle's scabbed lips at the sound of his question. "A cure," came the reply. But it was no laughing matter. "It is my fault you are in this place...for I contracted the illness first," his uncle lamented. "We've been over this," Nathaniel hushed. "You didn't know you carried the disease that summer you stayed with us." "I suspected, though." His uncle began to weep. Deep, uncontrollable sobs escaped from his aching chest. "I did not want to believe it - so I hid the blemishes for weeks! I am so sorry lad, so very sorry."

Nathaniel crawled next to his uncle and wrapped his arms around the dying man. "Shhh," he whispered into his uncle's remaining ear. The other had fallen off days earlier. Together they slept until morning. With the dawn came the sound of voices.

"One is living… I am not sure of the second. Let's have a closer look." Waking to the sounds of a stranger, Nathaniel scrambled to see who the voice belonged to. A man squeezed through the rock opening and dropped down onto the dirt floor of the cave. He was not one of the colonists. Nathaniel had never seen him before. "Get out of here!" Nathaniel covered his face while he screamed his warning. "We are lepers! Are you crazy? Run away! GO!

"Come with me then," said the stranger. "I will walk you home to the lake." "This is my home," sad Nathaniel. "I am a leper."

"Not anymore," said the man who spoke to him. The pile of rags that marked the place where his uncle had slept, suddenly stirred. "What is this?" His uncle's voice was strong and clear. He stepped into the beam of sunlight that came from above and Nathaniel gasped. "Uncle! You are well!" "As are you!" said the man who stood beside both of them. "Now come with me," he said. "You must show yourself at the temple to be declared clean, but we can then go to Galilee where your family will be waiting."

Nathaniel had been afraid to look at his hands. Afraid it was a dream. But now, he held up his clear hands and checked them over... strong fingers, no aching, and no exposed joints! Could it be? A great laugh came forth from his frame. "Gone?" he asked the man. "Completely…" he replied. "But, how can this be?" Nathaniel searched the eyes of this stranger who had set him free. "Shhh, don't tell everyone." The man put his finger against Nathaniel's lips. "Follow me, now."

As they came out of their hiding place, they could see they were not alone. "His name is Jesus," said a woman who Nathaniel barely recognized as a former leper. "He has healed us." "Last one out, close the gate!" called the One named Jesus. Dancing in the morning sunlight, the prisoners went free, all of them! They passed death's cold boundary into life.

Father God, Make me dance with joy for the Healer has come and He has found me. Amen

Dropping Anchor: *Death's gate is forever closed. Disease sneaks under the bars but is no match for the Christ.*

____

____

____

____

Just A Dream

"And it shall come to pass in the last days, saith God,
I will pour out of My Spirit upon all flesh:
and your sons and your daughters shall prophesy,
and your young men shall see visions,
and your old men shall dream dreams:"
Acts 2:17

Last night, I dreamed... I dreamed that mom and dad were both still alive and we were in our old home. They were young again. I was young also, just a child. The years had not taken their toll. Parkinson's was still far in the future for both Dad and me. Dementia had not yet offered even a hint of its cruel arrival to my mother. We were laughing. Perhaps we laughed because we knew the years would never pass in my dream. We were safe there.

There is a simple joy that comes when you have two parents in heaven. They live beyond hurt and age. They are not touched by disease nor dread. They cannot be shaken by the hard news of earth. And they occasionally come for the sweetest of visits—into my dreams. I never know just when to expect them, yet they are always welcome. They make a pathway from out of their safe place and arrive by nightfall while I sleep. They let me see them as they were, and I understand somehow that is how they are again, young and strong, in our old home, laughing. We are safe there, in my dream.

"I go to prepare a place for you," He said one day. It was still far away and yet to come when He made the promise. He, too, had to pass through the pain of this earth. Thirty three years were His fill of heartache and hurt. He often dreamed of home—the Place untouched by the torment of passing time. The very One who dreamed of the beautiful sky full of stars and then spoke them into being is making an eternal home for us. There, in that place, He will be one with the Love and Peace that abide there. In His dream, in His bountiful care for us—He dreamed of us there... at home with Him.

The Dreamer says it will all come true, one day. As I close my eyes, I say that I believe Him. I am laughing. Last night I dreamed…

Father God, I entrust my soul to you each night. My dreams are of your beautiful home - a home where I belong. Amen

Dropping Anchor: *Love lasts beyond a lifetime.*

A Joy Unspeakable

"And God shall wipe away all tears..."
Revelation 21:4

Perhaps it really was just a dream. Or, was it a vision of future things? I don't know. I do know this much is true—it was a deep revelation and it was deeply personal. It was also beautiful and good, so I believe God sent it. Beauty and goodness are only His to share.

I am saddened as I begin this page, as it tells of the deepest pain a family can know. Friends of ours, we will call them the Robinson family, had three beautiful daughters. Their fourth child, a son, died upon birth. It had been a healthy pregnancy and all seemed normal. But, for reasons known only to God, he passed away. Just when the family was preparing to meet him, he left them for heaven. Shock gave way to sadness. The loss seemed unbearable.

That was several years ago. Friends and family shared the burden, but the pain remained. Then just the other night, my wife awoke from a dream. As she described it all to me, we knew it was not for us to keep. It was for the Robinsons. In the dream, our friend, the mom had reached the end of her life's journey and was being ushered by the angels into glorious heaven. The beauty was indescribable and yet somehow familiar. As Jesus approached her, she saw He held a small child in his arms. Placing the babe gently into her waiting embrace, He looked deeply into her tear-filled eyes. With His hands framing her face, He wiped her tears with His thumbs and said, "I saved all your memories for you!" Then, as it can only be in heaven—time was not. A panoramic (words fail me) film or vision played before them. Memories of a childhood not lived on earth, but preserved in perfect heaven, flashed before her as she held her little boy in wonder.

There he was with his red wagon. There he was wrapping his

chubby arms around her knees while she attempted to navigate the kitchen in their home. A scraped knee, prayers at bedtime, they were all there. And they were now inside of her forever. Jesus had kept them for her. Nothing was missing.

As they stepped into their celestial home, the angel choirs sang. She recognized the song. It was the simple lullaby she had always sung for him, her baby. He had heard it, she now knew—it had reached heaven every time. Together, now forever, they laid down their heads in perfect rest.

Father God, today I pray for all of those whose pain never goes away... those who have lost a child. You know their pain. You are their hope; their only hope. Amen

Dropping Anchor: *Heaven holds joy. Only joy awaits us. Joy of the deepest measure and surely beyond words.*

___

___

___

___

Milton's Missing Tooth

Ye are the light of the world.
A city that is set on an hill cannot be hid.
Matthew 5:14

We Christians have become very good at talking to ourselves. In church, that is. Here's what I mean. Church life often becomes our way of life. We get up in the morning and put on our favorite Christian radio station. We may even watch a little Christian TV. If our car won't start we consult the Christian Yellow Pages to find a God-fearing mechanic. Our relationships, social calendar and volunteer time are all wrapped up in church. If things are going well, we talk within our small group studies and telephone our church friends during the week to keep accountable and perhaps to encourage the one who is having a rough week. On the contrary, when things are going poorly, we burn up the phone lines with the "latest" and stay late after small group is over to talk in hushed tones about what is (or who is) wrong.

We can stay busy all week long with church stuff—and never once speak to an unbeliever. What we have created is a subculture; a Christian environment which is one step removed from the world around us. If we so desire, we never really have to come in contact with the world. Oh, maybe we will see some lost folks in line at the grocery store, but we keep to ourselves and move along. Our church problems are very real to us, issues such as retaining visitors, proper Sunday school curriculum, child care, which version of the Bible we should use for our newcomers… pressing and time consuming troubles. But these "inside" issues are not exactly what the world around us is wrestling with. While the world worries about death and disease, terrorism and taxes, we seem to be more concerned with the flow of the Sunday service.

I had a dear friend years ago. Milton Friesen was a frequent guest on my radio program and the two of us hit it off from the start. Milton was the director of a homeless shelter in the heart of Boston. His stories from the street were filled with compassion and humor, and they kept me spellbound over many a dinner. Milton was missing a tooth. When he smiled, which was often, you could see the gap where the missing bicuspid was supposed to be. He once asked me if I ever wondered why he didn't replace the missing tooth. I politely said that I hadn't wondered about it, although his question got me started. Milton went on to tell me the tale of the lost tooth.

When he was a young man just starting out in rescue work, he was often relegated to the late shift at the shelter. One November night a knock came on the kitchen door. He opened it to find a man in rags, cold and hungry, shivering in the alley. He said he had not eaten for three days. Promising him a hot bowl of soup and some leftovers, Milton sat him down and said that before he gave him the late night supper, he first wanted to tell him of God's love. Indignant, the man stood to his feet and punched poor Milton in the mouth. He quickly disappeared into the cold night. The missing tooth was Milton's personal reminder to never presume to tell of God's love without first showing it. That story always reminds me of the African proverb, "Empty bellies have no ears."

We owe the world the Gospel. I recently heard a disturbing statistic. It was shocking. Ninety per cent of people who were born into the church, grew up in church, married and were buried by the church never share the gospel with an unbeliever once in their lifetime. We need to do better. We must speak. But, we must earn the right to be heard, Milton-style. Love first. Demonstrate that love to those who need it most, those outside the walls of our church buildings. We have done enough talking amongst ourselves. No more can we allow the shallow problems of our subculture to consume us. They are beside the point. Jesus did not come to church—He came to a lost world and loved it. The church is what He left behind to love the planet like He did. Say... Let's talk this over in church next Sunday. Just kidding...

Father God, thank you for the "Miltons" that we have known in our lives. We are better because they were good. They were good because you made them better. Amen

Dropping Anchor: *A shared crust of bread is a banquet for the hungry soul.*

Summertime Blues

"Study to shew thyself approved unto God,
a workman that needeth not to be ashamed,
rightly dividing the word of truth."
2nd Timothy 2:15

Whiffle ball was king each summer of my growing up years. As the New England weather warmed and the days grew longer, my friends and I would get the yellow plastic bats out of storage and check our supply of white plastic whiffle balls that would be considered "intact" enough to qualify for the new season. My buddies and I each had a 'stadium' which we considered our home field. We would play both home games and away, keeping records of wins and losses, charting the standings and individual stats, all through the summer months. We played day and night, although, admittedly, the night games were tough. These were only played at my home field—the parsonage adjacent to the Baptist church which featured a fairly well-lit parking lot. I say "fairly well" with regard to the lighting, for the periphery of our playing area quickly faded to black and foul balls were usually not recovered until daylight. More than one morning found us reviewing a foul call from the night before after discovering a lost ball in the weeds and checking the placement.

The summer I turned fourteen however, King Whiffle and our summer fun took a serious hit. My mother announced, on that first glorious day of vacation from school, that this year I was old enough to have a summer job. In fact, she had already inquired at the farm nearby and secured for me, a position as a 'picker of blueberries.' This was difficult news for a teenager to handle and the lads and the league took it hard as well. "Goodbye, summer," they lamented. "Hello, blueberries," I added. Dutifully, the next day I presented myself at the farm, armed only with a Quaker Oats canister hanging around my neck, my mom's contribution to the collection of berries.

Out in the farmer's field of ripening fruit, I was partnered with youths who seemed to be expert pickers. They were from the city. Each day, at crack of dawn, the farmer's 15 passenger van would pick them up and transport them to the blueberry fields. They spoke Portuguese as their native tongue, a language I knew not. I stayed to myself for the most part, marveling at their picking speed. With blueberries by the bucketful hanging from their necks and arms, they would make their way to the counting shed where the berries were poured into pint boxes. In return for the garnered fruit, workers were paid in tickets (red=ten, blue=five, yellow=one) that would be redeemed at the end of the week at the going rate of six cents per pint. I, too, eventually made my way to the shed. The smiling Quaker on my canister brought me no cheer and little to show in the berry department. I would return to picking with payment (three or four yellow tickets,) envious of the blues and reds that my co-workers had stashed in their pockets. I learned my first Portuguese words under this set of circumstances. At week's end, I turned in my total of thirty tickets and walked home with $1.80. Even my mother had to admit it seemed a low sum. Even my jolly friend the Quaker, seemed subdued. I began to look for work that might prove more profitable… and I soon found it. I became the small job guy. Since my dad was a pastor, we had a good supply of congregation members who needed a hand with raking, mowing, scraping, painting or the like. I had hit pay dirt. The thunk-thunk of blueberries in the bottom of my oats can was a distant memory, although I still rehearsed those Portuguese words and occasionally used them to impress my pals.

I began a succession of odd jobs. These were dump runs, basement clean-outs… random jobs that usually took a day or two to complete. Things were really looking up the day one of our church families hired me to paint the trim on their house. My painting experience was limited, no doubt, but my excitement over the proposed pay was such that I found myself on a ladder the following Monday morning, dipping my brush in a bucket of blue paint—blueberry blue to be exact. The family had left for the day and things were going swimmingly until I had to extend the ladder completely and ascend to the peak. At that lofty height, I thought having a hand free for balance was crucial, so I rigged a holder for my paint can out of a metal clothes hanger and hooked my can carefully over the top rung. On the third dip she let go. I watched the can of blueberry blue paint drop like a bomb, down, down until it met the metal bulkhead doors that covered the entrance to the cellar. It hit with a bang like you can't imagine, causing the neighborhood dogs to howl and bark at this summer disturbance. The bulkhead doors, which once were red, now resembled modern art: Blue on red... A lot of blue. I began my hasty descent and once back on ground level, contemplated the disaster. Breathing one of my savored Portuguese words, I could only imagine the explanation I would need for the homeowner. And then, it occurred to me—why not paint the bulkhead blue to match the trim? Marveling at my own ingenuity, I began spreading the paint with a vengeance, covering the disaster with a thick coat of blueberry blue. In thirty minutes I was back on my ladder, holding the brush in one hand and the bucket in the other, occasionally looking down below at the now-blue cellar doors, drying in the warm sun.

"Nice touch—the cellar doors," said the gentleman upon his return home. "The blue looks good." "No extra charge..." I managed. "Happy you like it." The road to responsibility had brought me a lesson. Sometimes a foul ball, upon further investigation, really does land fair.

Father God, I thank you for all the life-lessons I have learned from working to earn a living and to be a dependable, trustworthy employee. I know you are building my character and I am grateful for every job I have held and the lessons they have taught me. Amen

Dropping Anchor: *Responsibility has its own curriculum.*

____

____

____

____

Short Story

"And David girded his sword upon his armour,
and he assayed to go;
for he had not proved it. And David said unto Saul,
'I cannot go with these; for I have not proved them.'"
1 Samuel 17:39

Getting a three year old dressed can be a challenge. In fact, clothing and kids can be a tough chore for parents right through the high school years and beyond. Let it be known... I am a big fan of school uniforms. They cut down on a great number of decisions in the average teenager's morning. But the clothing angst can start early; way before school clothes are even an issue.

The other morning, my wife was dressing True, who is presently three. The weather forecast was for a sunny day and the spring temperatures were finally going to climb into the mid-seventies. It had been rainy and chilly for weeks it seemed, but on this morning, the promise of summer was in the air. So, Amanda dug into the wardrobe and found some nice, blue shorts for little True to wear. She slipped them on easily enough. But as soon as she buttoned them, True began to sob. "They don't fit me!" he cried. "These are Rory's pants. They're too small for me." Rory is two, and he was going to be breaking out his own pair of shorts on this day as well, with some help from Mom, of course. True, however, did not remember shorts from the previous summer, (a whole year ago), when he was two. He just couldn't comprehend why his legs should be sticking so far out of his pants. He sank to the floor in a heap, crying in desperate hope that we might also see that these pants just did not fit. We could hardly hold back a smile - despite our son's plight of feeling so misunderstood. Couldn't we realize that his pants were "too small?" No amount of encouragement seemed to reach True that morning. He was bluer than the shorts themselves.

Amanda thought of a plan and threw a pair of shorts on unsuspecting Rory. "Look True," she said. "Rory's pants are just like yours." Slowly, one teary eye peeked out from behind his hands.

True witnessed his brother, Rory running around the living room like the proverbial Spring chicken. That was enough to get him over the hump, and soon both boys were enjoying the freedom of their short pants.

You know, we are a lot like my son, True. Our Heavenly Father breaks out new and unfamiliar things for us and asks that we give them a try. But, we are not accustomed to the new look of things. We don't like change. But, Abba Father encourages us that this new thing is for our benefit… even though it pushes us beyond our comfort zone. We fuss and cry in protest, but He is persistent and knows what is best. He has our interests at heart. And, if we look to where his people are, we will see that we have brothers in the same "shorts" as us. We can handle things better when we know we are not alone.

So, take a short lesson from a three year olds wardrobe. If you are moving into a new season, your Father will see to it that you are equipped with the right pants. Just take your eyes off yourself and see the freedom that your brother has found. Try running alongside him for a time.

Father God, thank you for being such a good father that you know just my size. I trust you to put me in places and situations that cause me to grow. In all of these places, be they pleasant or painful, it's my desire to make your name known. Amen

Dropping Anchor: *Your Father in heaven knows your right size.*

___

___

___

___

Bubble Boy

"That our sons may be as plants grown up in their youth..."
Psalm 144:12

Growing up in a small New England town kept me safely secluded in a small town bubble. Not much was going on in the place of my birth. Nothing out of the ordinary was ever expected to occur. The stories that made it onto the televised evening news were all, it seemed, happening in the big cities. There wasn't much news to report from my farming community, featuring dairy barns and green pastures. My grandparents however, were a doorway to excitement. They lived just outside the city of Boston, in a suburban village that featured pizza shops and restaurants, real sidewalks, a twenty-four hour convenience store and a train station. It was the first community where I was ever served a bagel for breakfast. There were no bagels in my little town. There was one coffee shop, but they served donuts, not the more esteemed bagel. And, donuts in my hometown were not fancy or sugar glazed. They were for dunking in your coffee, period.

Whenever I stayed overnight at my grandparents' home, I would lay awake in the spare bedroom and listen in the dark for the lonely blast of the whistle coming from commuter rail "Number Nine" as it approached the crossing at Route 16. The sound seemed otherworldly to my young mind. I could close my eyes and imagine the exotic people on board, coming from faraway places to conduct their business in the big city that lay just up the highway.

My grandmother grew up within just a few miles of where she and my grandfather eventually settled. As a young girl she played on the green hills of Brighton, outside of Boston and watched the trains carrying cattle into South Station. I imagine she was enchanted by the bustle and noise of the cows, which came in boxcars from the Midwestern farms outside Chicago, Illinois. A daughter of Swedish immigrants, Edith Peterson (who went by her middle name of 'Olga,') was a free spirited girl who caught the eye of an

Irishman from Portsmouth, New Hampshire. Several years after a chance meeting, a marriage occurred and soon after, my mother was born. Years later, after graduating college, mom was 'set up' on a date with a young minister and the two fell in love. Mom moved to our small town to live with Dad, the pastor, and thus, she said her goodbye to suburban life.

My home was the rambling parsonage. It was once an inn, run by Joe and Mary Davis. I was quite familiar with old Joe and his wife as their painted portraits hung in the front hall of our old house. The unknown artist portrayed Mr. Davis as dour, stiff and unsmiling. I stared at Joe Davis many times, wondering what kind of man he was behind his long, gray beard. There was not one bright color in the painting; just olive greens and grays. Not a happy man, I supposed, for he had to have approved the picture and thought it had captured his essence well. There, in the long hallway, at first glance Joe stared at nothing. His dark eyes however, had a way of following you, no matter where in the hallway one stood. All things considered, I am surprised my parents did not replace the portrait with something more scenic in nature.

Mary Davis, also captured in oils, had a half smile in her picture. Life with Joe couldn't have been all bad. Tradition was that Mary was a great cook—especially her seafood recipes. The driveway up to the side porch was covered in white clamshells, crushed and broken, a timeless testimony to the fine dining that the Davis family served their guests. On rare occasion during my time at the house, a complete shell half would be found in the drive, leaving one to wonder about whose meal it had been a part of, a half century before. I would sometimes save such a discovery. Other times, I would skip the flat shell across the surface of the small pond that bordered our property.

My grandfather found it difficult to be Irish and not be stereotyped by some. As a result, he never drank alcohol, (his father had reportedly been a drinker) and he worked long hours at the lumber yard amassing a small fortune along with a good reputation for honesty and fairness. He became owner of the company in his later years and piloted it through multi-million dollar lumber deals. He was a meticulous man, and a tough boss. He never came home until after ten at night as he would remain after the five pm whistle and go from desk to desk, checking over every employee's work from that day. Once home, it was a late supper, a cigar, and off to bed. Mornings were a peek at the newspaper, a half of a grapefruit and a spoonful of cod liver oil. His daily dose of fish oil from Sweden came on a spoon held by my grandmother. He pinched his nose and made a face, but dutifully swallowed the treatment. He lived this daily routine for many years until death interrupted him at one hundred years of age.

My grandmother was nothing like her husband. She was a naturalist and a Red Cross volunteer. She spent her time caring for others. She doted over all living things, be they animal or grandchild. I would watch in amazement whenever she would grab a bag of peanuts from the cabinet in the kitchen and open her back door. With one word, "Come!" the creatures would appear: the chipmunk from under the stone wall, the pigeons from their nests, a stray dog or two from who knows where; she fed them all from her open hand. Later that same hand would offer me a lunch of tomato soup and an egg salad sandwich.

'Olga' was a crocheter of rugs and warm sweaters. She listened faithfully to the Sunday morning service coming from Boston's Park Street Church, her old Westinghouse radio tuned and ready to receive the Good News as it came from the Reverend Dr. Harold John Ockenga. She did not drive. She never had a license. Her world came to her, and I was delighted to be part of it. She passed away in her nineties, full of good things.

My home growing up was nothing like the home my grandparents shared. We carried little of our Irish ancestry and only a small bit of our Swedish roots into the mid-nineteen hundreds. My mom was well known as a maker of Swedish meatballs but my dad did most of the cooking. My mom hovered over her paintings (watercolors mostly, no portraits) while my dad studied for Sunday's messages. I was a good boy for the most part. However, on the rare occasions when I received a spanking, it was the Swedes I had to thank for the pain. Hanging in the kitchen of our parsonage home was a thin, pine breadboard carrying the Swedish engraving, "Butter and bread make children's cheeks red."

When I was still a youngster, my mom convinced my reluctant father to take the family into Boston for an excursion. We were sitting at my grandmother's kitchen table and discussing what we would do with the day that stretched out before us. It was settled when Olga said she would go "into town" with us. The whole lot of us climbed on board the inbound train on the 'Green Line' and headed for the city, not unlike the cattle some six decades earlier. We spent the day there, where news was born, staring up at buildings, riding on the swan boats in the park and naturally, feeding the pigeons.

We were wrapping up our outing as evening came to the city. Street lights flickered on (there were no street lights where I came from) as we ventured into a department store, our last stop. Grandmother wanted to purchase a gift for me. I selected a trinket and we stood at the checkout awaiting our turn in line. A woman's scream at the next register snapped our attention to a shocking scene. A young man with a gun was filling a sack with money from the day's earnings while the clerk stood, hands in the air. She was obviously terrified. I was transfixed. With a leap and a bound the gunman cleared the counter and dashed through the exit and into the subway. "He robbed me!" the distraught clerk repeated over and over—in disbelief herself. My grandmother took me by the hand and said to my family, "Follow me." Dutifully, we followed, looking as we went, for a man with a gun on a getaway.

Later on that same night, just before I fell asleep, I heard the whistle blast of ol' Number Nine. As the clackety-clack of the rail cars echoed in the night, I drifted toward sleep, my mind filled with images of cattle cars and subways, commuters and robbers. My small town bubble had burst. I was growing up. The lonely cry of the train whistle triggered a new loneliness within me. It was not a sad loneliness, but more of a personal singularity that the world brings to each of us over time. I never had known just how big the world was until that day. And, I had never felt as small as I did right then laying on the cot in the spare room. Downstairs the grownups could be heard talking. Their conversation filtered up through the heating ducts, rising and falling… occasionally bursts of laughter broke the droning flow of lowered voices. "Butter and bread make children's cheeks red," I said aloud. I wasn't sure why I said it—but it was comforting to me in an odd way. I was part of a family. I was safe. And, I realized, just how fortunate I was. I was a small town boy in a very big world.

Father God, You are the peace that reigns in me. I have often been unsettled by the world as it comes running rampant in my direction, but I find you to be my refuge and my strength. Thank you for my family, whose boundaries keep many unknown, unseen and unwanted guests at bay. Amen

Dropping Anchor: *A dose of discipline is like cod liver oil for the soul.*

Grace Train

"That in the ages to come
He might shew the exceeding riches of His grace
in His kindness toward us through Christ Jesus."
Ephesians 2:7

I am riding the grace train as far as it will take me. I have been on board the other rides, and found them to be going nowhere fast. Grace, I am certain, will bring me home. Any other destination would be meaningless for grace is where God is. It was His idea. He owns grace. It is His gift to us. That means, God sorted through the treasures of heaven, and he pulled out grace to give us, first and foremost. He demonstrated that gift of grace when He willed Jesus to take the punishment we deserve, and placed it squarely on His shoulders. That was the transaction that saves us. That transforms us. That makes us a new creation, with old things passed away (dead) and a new life in its place... a life of grace.

When our original parents sinned, they blew it in sizeable fashion. They were surrounded by grace... living in paradise. Only one rule existed—"do not eat from the tree of the knowledge of good and evil." There was only one mistake they could make—and they made it. In a situation where failure was hardly possible, they failed. Now, the One who placed them in paradise had every right to be fuming. Instead the Response was more grace. Surely, He allowed for some consequences but He covered their shame and restored the broken relationship—even forecasting that this error would result in Grace galore—a Savior would come and conquer the sin problem once and for all.

So why do believers in Jesus frequently miss the grace factor? It looms large and is impossible to avoid when you look at Him. That is, if you look at the true Jesus. There are other forms of Jesus that portray Him as angry and opposed to the people He created. But this is a poor representation of the Truth. God so loved the world... we all know that verse. Consider another one, "God was in Christ, not counting men's sins against them". How can sin not count against us? In a word—Grace.

Where we fall short is in our desire that sin should still count; tallied as it were, awaiting punishment. We subtly want people to pay for their mistakes—especially if they have wronged us. But Jesus has a grace answer for that condition as well—forgive 70 times 7.

Certainly we need discipline. God provides that for those that He loves. But His correction is guiding us toward grace. Maturity is His goal for us, resulting in our final, forever state, which will be to show forth His grace for the ages to come. Grace is the goal of discipline. It is why we can rejoice in hardship. We are headed for grace. It is not something we work around. Grace is what we work within. It's the point. Its why Scripture leaves correction squarely in the lap of the Spiritual ones. (If a brother be overtaken by a fault, you who are spiritual, restore him…) The Godly understand grace. That is why they are authorized to discipline. Children run to parents crying "I'm telling on you" Parents must not discipline based on childish complaints. Parents need patience, wisdom and grace to sort out the facts and to mete out discipline appropriately. They cannot react in knee jerk fashion to every issue raised in complaint. The truth is what they must be after. Grace is partnered with truth and expressed through maturity.

Grace is also closely tied to love. Love produces grace. Recently, I had a person come to me and express that they knew "dirt" or bad things about certain members of our church. They told me that they wanted to fill me in on what I, apparently, was missing, I replied that what was missing was love. I love the people they were ready to malign, and love covers sin. Paul wrote that love hopes for the best—not brings out the worst. Love does not keep a record of wrongs. It bears all things. It is gracious. "From now on, we consider no man from a pre-grace condition," (according to flesh) Scripture points out. Grace has come and saved the day.

When the Apostle Paul began his ministry, he considered himself the "least of the apostles." Later he wrote that he was "less than the least of all the saints." Just before he died, he considered himself the "chief of sinners." His need for grace grew as his life progressed… until that final moment when he was face to face with Grace. On that last day—if you look to point out sin—you will find it a useless exercise. It always has been that... pointless. We know we are sinners—saved by grace. Sin is covered over; removed; Gone and nailed to a cross. Why try to pull it off those wooden beams and throw it around a bit? That job is already taken. There is an accuser. He knows nothing of grace—except for what he sees in us.

Grace seems like 'getting off easy," but actually it is just the opposite. It is the hardest thing we have to do. Paul told the church at Galatia that they had been bewitched—having turned away from grace. The grace life is hard work. And, if you slip away from it—you wind up somewhere you don't want to be… maybe forever. It's that serious. Children of the King bear a family resemblance. Jesus is full of grace and truth. The next time you bring a case against someone, and you want to have others believe it is true, ask yourself—is this accusation balanced with much grace? I am riding the grace train all the way home.

Father God, I am nothing without grace. Correction. I am one thing without grace - doomed. Help me to offer the hope and healing grace brings to those who need it most. Amen

Dropping Anchor: *Truth and grace do not arrive in separate packages.*

Lunch Brigade

"But Jesus said unto them, 'They need not depart; give ye them to eat.'"
Matthew 14:16

Peter was the first one in the boat. Grabbing the cord for the mainsail he muttered, "The Master is really upset with us this time." John, the second to board echoed the sentiment. "He didn't even ask us to come and pray with Him," he observed. "I think He really wanted us to leave Him alone." As the rest of the Twelve climbed into the now crowded vessel, they got busy with the oars and cast off from the dock. It had been a long day. Now they faced the evening task of crossing the Galilean Sea.

Back on shore, Jesus watched them from a distance. He was tired. He was hungry. And, He needed to pray. He climbed up a bluff and headed for the high cliff that overlooked the sea. It was there that He finally sat down and unpacked his satchel. Taking a deep breath, He let His body relax. He smiled when He pulled some bread from the leather bag. Holding it up to His mouth, He thought of the little boy who had brought this bread to the large green field where they had spent the day. It all began that morning with an impromptu crowd begging to hear Him preach. He had obliged willingly, however His disciples had resented the intrusion. "Send them away!" they had demanded.

The band of twelve had been hoping for some down time. They had many questions for the rabbi and they were eager for answers. As long as there were crowds around, they knew their questions would have to wait. Now, after a particularly demanding week of ministry, they had finally convinced Jesus to come away for a private session, but when Sunday morning broke, they saw the throng headed for them. Jesus seemed to welcome them and spoke for hours while the Twelve had fumed on the edges of the crowd.

The grass on the hillside had been covered with a sea of blankets and makeshift canopies while the thousands listened to the wisdom and wit of Jesus. As the evening hours drew closer, restlessness had overtaken most of the listeners. They were scrounging for food, but there was none. That's when the Twelve spoke up. "You have got to send them home," said Thomas. "They all need to leave." "No," Jesus had countered. "You feed them." That produced a cynical laugh in Thomas' throat. "Feed them what?" he queried. "Is it not obvious to you that we are miles from anywhere?" Jesus looked patiently at His friends and simply said, "See what you can find."

Peter had been a little rough with the lad that he found was carrying a lunch in his bag. "Give it to me," he had barked. Reluctant, the boy held on to his bread and fish. "I'll bring it back in a few minutes," Peter said. Turning to James, who was by his side, he grabbed the little basket from the boy's hands and said, "This is all the food there is. Run this to Jesus and prove there is nothing here for the crowd to eat. That should convince Him. Bring it back after He sees it. I'll stay here with the boy."

James cut through the throng and brought the little basket to Jesus who was just finishing a story from Jewish literature about a widow who was poor and needy. A prophet had asked her to pour out the little oil she had left into a cup—and a miracle had occurred. "She just kept pouring." Jesus laughed. "She filled every vessel she could find." Taking the basket from James he turned back to the delighted group at his feet. "Here," he said. "Let me show you..." He thanked His Father in heaven for the food and began passing it out to the hungry multitude. Each time He reached into the basket, more fish and bread came out. It did not stop until everyone had their fill. The Twelve had been ordered to serve and then clean up.

"Leftovers," said Jesus now as He tasted the bread He had saved in His bag. The bread was sweet and made for a good supper for Him now. As He finished the last crumbs He turned His attention to the sea. The disciples' boat was barely visible through the gathering mist of evening. In the western sky, where the sun was setting, Jesus could clearly see a storm forming over the lake.

He was worried about the Twelve. They had been so hesitant to serve lunch and had complained about cleaning up afterward. It seemed as though the miracle had been lost on them. But, when the well fed crowd began to call for Jesus to be their king, Peter and the others stood close to the Master, garnering as much of the attention and praise as they could. "You are missing the point," Jesus had told them. He had then sent them off with orders to meet Him next on the far side of the great lake.

On board the disciple's ship all was misery. "We are going to get drenched," said Peter to his companions, and he nodded toward the western sky. The storm had fully formed now and was to be on them soon. "Perfect way to end a great day," said Judas cynically. Night fell and with it came the rain. It poured out of the sky in torrents. "Take down the sails before the wind takes them down for us!" Peter called from the stern. The wind was blowing hard now as the disciples leaned into the oars and pulled against the gale. "We are getting nowhere," moaned Peter.

About four hours later they were still at their task. They had made little progress and were still far from the opposite shore. The storm raged on. A dread had overtaken them. It seemed as though Death itself was in the storm with jaws wide open wanting to swallow their ship. "This is no normal night storm," one of the Twelve had stated. Everyone agreed and prayed for morning to arrive. They were soaked to the skin, they were exhausted, and they were plenty frightened.

Peter had stopped rowing when the rest noticed he was staring at the dark water. His mouth was open wide in apparent amazement. "Grab your oar, Peter!" John had hollered. Peter did not move. "Guys," he finally said. "A ghost just walked past the ship. I saw it." No one doubted that this rough and tumble fisherman had just seen something. He was obviously spooked. They all strained their eyes against the weather and darkness, looking for something… anything. "There! Over starboard! What's that?" cried Matthew. Peter stood and stared. Without a doubt, a lone figure stood thirty yards away, barely discernible in the dark rain but no doubt real. "Name yourself," Peter stammered. "Are you friend or foe?"

"Peter, it is I," the voice came across the open water. "Jesus?" asked Peter, amazed. "Yes," came the calm reply. "But how... how... how can this be?" Peter was at a loss for any more words. "Come to Me and see," Jesus called. Quickly but gingerly Peter swung his legs over the starboard side. He was battered by the strong wind and needed to hold on tight to the oarlock, lest he be blown over. He held his breath and jumped into the tempest driven waves. But, what was this? His feet hit the water as though hitting a solid rock. Peter didn't sink nor did he need to swim. He took a step, then another. He was walking. And as he neared Jesus, he could definitely recognize his friend, who was walking toward him, arms outstretched. Feeling more than a little confident now, Peter turned and looked back at the dumbfounded disciples. "Look guys..." he called back to the boat. "I am walking on water!" No sooner had the words escaped his mouth, he went down into the waves. Coming up coughing and gasping for air, the fisherman treaded water, barely managing to keep his nose above the stormy surface.

"Would you like a hand?" Jesus was leaning over him. "Pull me up!" cried Peter. Jesus extended his strong arm and pulled soggy Peter out of the water. Together they crossed the span of waves between them and the ship. Hands reached over the side and pulled the pair on board. As soon as Jesus stepped into the boat the storm abated. Instantly it had gone, and ceased. And as they looked about in wonder, they found that they were at the dock on the western side of the lake. "Who is this man who feeds many with little and stills the wind and waves?" "Anyone for breakfast?" asked Jesus with a smile. With the Twelve gathered around, He reached into his satchel and pulled out some leftovers. "Pass it around," Jesus said after He had blessed it. "It's going to be another long day."

Father God, You took twelve men and instructed them to serve. Eventually they became servants. It is always hard to serve others. It must be like carrying a cross or carrying a brother. Walking on water seems more likely to occur than finding a true servant. May I be one, I promise... no complaints. Amen

Dropping Anchor: *Serving others may be more difficult than walking on water. Christ can help us do both.*

Bus Ride

"...before the Lord is your way wherein ye go."
Judges 18:6

I am not one for conferences. I avoid them like the plague. I don't like to network. And, I think I know why. It harkens back to a winter bus ride that I took as a teenager to a large gathering of Christian young adults in the Midwest. The purpose of the youth conference was to motivate and inspire hundreds of young people to go forth and evangelize the globe. I'm not certain that the experience inspired me much, but it did motivate me to stay clear of conferences for a while. Here's how it all unfolded...

On the chilly morning of our departure, my parents drove me to a big parking lot at the University of Rhode Island where we were to board a bus for our long journey. I saw many busses in the lot, big streamlined coaches designed for passenger comfort over long distances. "This won't be so bad," I considered. A small group of us were stamping our feet against the cold February air, awaiting the arrival of our transport. When it finally pulled up, we registered something between shock and woe. It was a yellow school bus with a noisy engine, bluish exhaust pouring out of its rattling tailpipe, and not much to offer in the way of creature comforts, such as heat. Throwing my gear onto the front bench seat, I meandered toward the rear of the rickety school bus. Our driver told us to get comfortable. We were going to be together for five hundred and fifty miles so we had better "settle in," he advised. I was a gangly teenager and my frame did not settle in well. I put my knees up against the seat in front of me and slouched down as low as I could. Pulling my hat low over my eyes, I wondered if it was possible to sleep for an entire twelve hour journey. I soon learned that sleeping would be next to impossible. Every bump in the road bounced and jostled us, mercilessly banging my sore knees against the metal back of the seat in front of me.

We got lost toward evening somewhere in Pennsylvania. These were the days before cell phones, and GPS was relegated to sci-fi films. Our driver had a big red road atlas which he consulted often. He would routinely pull over onto the roadside and flip through the pages, giving a low whistle, then, placing his hand on his forehead he would moan, "Aye, yae, yae!" We didn't have to guess that we were off course. Night was falling and a snowstorm was right behind it. As dusk turned to dark, we could see the white snowflakes in rapid descent, illuminated by the bus's headlights. Soon we could only see a wall of white as the road we were currently lost on was quickly becoming covered with a blanket of powdery snow. Our driver slowed to about twenty miles per hour and aimed for the center of the quickly disappearing roadway. It had been a long time since we last saw any signs of civilization.

The frosty bus plodded along until it could take no more of winter. With a cough and a bang, it rolled to a stop. "Are we there?" called out one wisecracker. "Aye, yae, yae…" said our driver. We were somewhere near the Pennsylvania/Ohio border, but just where we were was anybody's guess. From the sound of it, it didn't seem likely that our old yellow school bus was going to take us any further. The snow was falling at a furious pace. Our tires were already half buried in drifts. "I've gotta go find some help," said our driver. "In the middle of nowhere?" questioned the twenty five or so youths on board the stricken bus. "There must be a gas station or something nearby," he replied. As he went out the door, we heard him whistle "Aye, yae, yae…" In a matter of seconds he was invisible, lost in the falling snow as he and his flashlight trudged away from the bus, onward to "who knows where." As the wind came up, we teens huddled together in the back of the broken down bus, now with no driver, no lights, no heat and no guarantee of anything anytime soon. My watch said it was nearly ten o'clock. It read nearly two in the morning when I was awakened by a shout, "Hallooo bus!" I peered out the ice covered windows and there I beheld a wonder.

Our rescue had come in the form of a huge, flat, logging sleigh, pulled through the snow by two large horses. The storm had passed and a bright moon shone silver over the icy landscape. Our bus driver sat atop the sleigh bench, looking for all the world like he was running for governor. Sitting next to him and holding the reigns was the farmer who had graciously agreed to get out of his warm bed in order to rescue us. We learned later that the bus driver had hiked more than two miles in the deep drifts before seeing a light. He headed for it, across fields and forest and upon reaching the farmhouse; he pounded on the front door until he woke the old couple who lived there. Through frozen lips he managed to convey the urgency of his broken down bus carrying two dozen teenagers stranded in the snow. Out to the barn went the kindly farmer while his wife got busy in the kitchen. As our driver thawed for a moment by the wood stove, the farmer hitched up his team and pulled the sleigh out of the big barn. Together they headed east through the falling snow and about an hour later, they had us spotted. Grabbing our gear, we gratefully climbed aboard the huge wooden sleigh. We sat silently as we skimmed through the snow to the farmhouse. There we were treated to hot cocoa and blueberry muffins, fresh out of the oven. The farmer's wife clucked about, passing out quilts and pillows and finding sleeping room on the floor or in an overstuffed chair. I grabbed a blanket and headed for the staircase where a window with a wide sill offered a cozy perch. There I spent the rest of the night, happy to be warm and dry.

The next morning, our yellow bus was towed to another farm where the resident farmer was an ace mechanic and by noontime we were back on the freshly plowed road, headed again for the youth conference. We had our stomachs full of a real farmhouse breakfast, and enough cheese and bread provisions to last a week thanks to the farmer's good wife. "Go with God," she had chirped as we waved goodbye. "Better late than never," the driver said as we disembarked at the conference site later that same evening…

In the perspective of passing years, the arduous trip was made memorable due to the warm hospitality of an old farmer and his wife. They simply shared what they had with those in need—kindness, caring, and hospitality. At the end of the day, that is the best way to evangelize the globe.

Father God, teach me things along life's journey that will fit me for your heaven. I hope to please you today with my attitude and actions. I am grateful for the road ahead. I promise to remember the lessons you provided on the road that is behind me. Amen

Dropping Anchor: *Most of what we hope for in the end comes unexpecedly, along the way.*

____

____

____

____

Brothers

"and it came to pass, when they were in the field,
that Cain rose up against Abel his brother, and slew him."
Genesis 4:8

The morning dew felt cool on their bare feet as the two boys scurried through the lush, green underbrush of the forest. They had not been in this part of the woods for some time, yet they knew the way they took. They were headed for the Garden, or what was left of it. Eden lay under a curse, a sentence of death; and now, the thorns that tore at their calloused feet were living proof of it. Once a beautiful paradisiacal home to their parents, it presently was guarded day and night by a powerful spirit-being with a flaming sword in his hand. A posted sign read "No One Enters," and the strong warrior angel with the sword of flaming fire was there to see to it. Behind the heavy iron gate, the pair could clearly see the ruins of the original home of mankind. They well knew they were not allowed to enter the former paradise, yet curiosity often drove them close to where it lay, in the low valley between two grand mountains A river ran through the overgrown terraces, but it's waters, once pure and clear as crystal, now flowed a muddy brown.

The older of the two, Cain, stopped to wait for his brother, Abel. "C'mon Slowpoke," he chided. "We are very close now." Abel stopped to catch his breath. "We shouldn't be here," he said. "The Lord God forbids it." "He forbids everything," came the retort from Cain. "I'm tired of it." "Careful brother," said Abel wisely. "He has been good to our family." "Oh, is that why we live by the sweat of our brow trying to scratch a living out of the cursed soil? We are banished from the only home where life was beautiful. How good can that be?"

Abel looked to the horizon, his thoughts far away. He considered the story that his parents often told around the night fire...of the sin, the disobedience, and the punishment. He recalled how his father had told him of the sacrifice that God initiated to cover their shameful failure. Adam had described how, after the Serpent's deception, the Lord had taken an animal, culled from the finest herd. Taking Adam's hand, He placed it on the head of the beast. Furnishing a sharp knife, the Lord placed it firmly in Adam's free hand and guided his trembling fingers as the animal's throat was slit wide open. Blood covered Adam and his wife Eve as they recoiled in horror, having watched the first death on the planet. Turning to them, the Lord spoke quietly. "The animal gave his life for yours," He had stated, "To sin is to die."

"To sin is to die," he heard himself say aloud to his brother. "We must not enter the forbidden area." "Do as you like," spat Cain. "I am going in. The guard stands far from here and we can enter easily."

Inside the cursed Garden of Eden, Cain shouted to his brother. "It's fine!" he called. But it was not as he said it was. A creeping, cold darkness seemed to enter into him. Cain shook his head clear and tried to get his bearings. He felt confused and his head was full of voices. He pressed on and stumbled upon the ruins of a stone wall. Behind it was the remnant of a garden that his father Adam, had planted, many years ago. There was still fruit and produce springing forth from the once tilled earth. Amazed by their size and color, Cain picked some of the finest of the vegetables and fruit and stuffed them into his shoulder bag. He had not noticed before, but the sky was becoming overcast, a storm was brewing. He dashed from the fallen Garden of Eden and ran as fast as he could for home.

As he entered the family compound east of Eden, he saw at once there was company. It was the Lord. Since the great sin of Adam, His visits were less frequent, but not unexpected. "Where have you been?" the Lord asked him. Cain shot an angry glance at his brother. "You told?" he barked. "He already knew!" Abel replied. "Cain," said the Lord. "Sin is crouching at your door and it desires to possess you." Cain's mind immediately recalled the creeping chill and taunting voices he felt and heard in the forbidden Garden. He understood the darkness of sin. "You must master it!" the Lord finished. Thinking quickly, Cain pulled some of the produce from the bag on his shoulder. "An offering for you…" he stated flatly. "It's the finest fruit in the land."

The Lord God was not impressed. "If you do what is right, you will be accepted," the Lord continued. "See what Abel brought to me?" The Heavenly Visitor pointed to the animal roasting on the hearth. "He repented for the consideration, yes, the very thought of entering the forbidden Garden. His heart is not in rebellion, but is instead humble."

Cain rose to his feet in anger and headed for the doorway. "Abel is always right, isn't he?" "No, replied the Lord, "but he does what is right when he errs. To sin is to die. Remember the sacrifice?" "Then, I must be a dead man…" Cain shot the words back over his shoulder as he ran outside. "The darkness of the fallen Garden now lives within him," the Lord said quietly. "It will cost much to rescue him from this darkness." Turning to Abel, He said firmly, "A great cost, indeed and I will pay it personally." "You will change the darkness within my brother to be light again?" Abel had a tear in his eye as he spoke the question. "Yes. I will do that for Cain and for anyone who comes after him. I will remove the darkness for anyone who believes I can do this." "I believe," said Abel. "I know, my son." replied the Lord.

"Then I must tell Cain! I want him to find this light within," Abel grabbed his bag and went out the door to find his older brother. He did not know that Cain lay in wait for him, his hand clutching the knife from the family sacrifice. No one had noticed him take it. Soon, no one would ever forget that he had. What was intended for sacrifice would instead be used for violence and murder. And, so it goes.

Father God, You warn us of the dangers of sin, but sometimes we still turn away from you. It is a great shame that, over the centuries, some have used the sacred to sacrifice to self. May my heart be pleasing to you. May my footsteps lead others closer to you. May my eyes always look to you. Amen

Dropping Anchor: *Beware the poison fruit of Eden's dark garden.*

___

___

___

___

The Collection

"...remember the words of the Lord Jesus, how He said, 'It is more blessed to give than to receive.'"
Acts 20:35

It was Halloween night and I was going to miss it. That very afternoon, I had come home from school early with chills and a fever. My ten-year-old heart was crushed when I learned that there would be no trick-or-treating that night for me. I was going to have to stay in and go to bed early.

Back in the '60's, trick or treating was not the commercial enterprise it is today. It amazes me, in this day and age, to see Halloween specialty stores open up at summer's end and do a booming business right through the end of October. When I was young, we used whatever we could find around the house to transform ourselves into cowboys or princesses. I was to have been Abraham Lincoln on this particular Halloween. However, ol' Abe was going to remain on the shelf until next year. I was housebound.

I remember my mom made me a perch in the kitchen, where I could watch the neighbors bring their children to our door. My dad passed out candy like it was going out of style, while I sat in the big rocking chair wrapped in a warm quilt. "It isn't fair," I remember thinking. Being ill is bad enough, but being sick and missing out on all that candy? I was wallowing in self-pity. It only got worse when my sister returned home like a triumphant bounty hunter, a full bag of candy clutched in her hands. I moaned as she began digging through her sack, looking over her full cache. She offered to share a box of Good 'n Plenty with me. "You know I don't like those." I replied. I couldn't help but notice she was loaded with chocolate bars and lollipops but she was holding on to those. Twenty minutes later, I was put in my bed with a hot water bottle next to me to keep the chills away. I had just drifted off to sleep when my father came in my room and woke me up. "C'mon out here," he said. "You'll want to see this!" Curious, I put on my slippers and followed him to the kitchen.

Billy, my teenage neighbor, was a bit older than my sister, and he delivered our newspaper every day. He was too grown up to go out trick-or-treating, but that was not what brought him to our door. He hadn't come to get candy, he came to give it. He emptied out his newspaper sack on our kitchen floor, pouring a huge mound of candies. "Billy heard you were sick, so he went door-to-door and collected for you," my parents said. "All yours, my man!" said Billy. I was grateful beyond words.

In the end, it's the little things that matter most. Nearly a half-century after that night, I can still see Billy in my memory, smiling at me while he poured out a candy miracle on my kitchen floor. When we live in the "get" mode, we generally consume whatever comes our way. However, when we "give" we share something that will last into eternity. All the candy from that Halloween night was gone in a week. The kindness shown by a fifteen year old newspaper carrier remains to this day.

Father God, thank you for the example set by glad and gracious people I have known. I recall their kindnesses and observe you in each of their deeds of service. Amen

Dropping Anchor: *When we give, we touch eternity.*

Boomtown

"Let not the wise man glory in his wisdom,
neither let the mighty man glory in his might,
let not the rich man glory in his riches:"
Jeremiah 9:23

It was a television program just for kids, and at nine years old, I was hooked. "Boomtown," was king of the Saturday morning broadcasts in the Greater Boston area during the 1960's. Starring the smiling cowboy, Rex Trailer, and his trusty sidekick Pablo, Boomtown was a fanciful slice of the Wild West that came to the old black and white Zenith television in our living room straight from the studios of channel four in Boston. I was reared in the New Bedford area, some sixty miles to the south, so at that distance, I was forced to endure the video snowstorm and electronic static on the small, black and white screen. Despite my best tuning efforts, the picture routinely faded, much like the long-gone days of the true cowboy adventures of the American West. I was left to squint and squirm, searching for the best viewing angle in order to see Rex and Pablo triumph from week to week in their three-hour-long televised escapades.

I was mesmerized by the action and adventure as ol' Rex and his trusty steed, Goldrush chased outlaws and sought to capture the elusive villain of the week, who was pictured in disguise, on a wanted poster for all to see. There came the climactic moment during each episode when all the children who were lucky enough to be in the studio audience were paraded by the even luckier youths who had been selected to be Sheriff and Deputy Sheriff of Boomtown for the day. The job of these two children-turned-lawmen was to recognize and apprehend the 'bad guy' (hidden in the studio audience) using only the wanted poster as their guide. Back at home, I would strain through the interference on my television, studying each face as it passed by the camera, trying hard to spot the outlaw. It was glorious fun.

Afterward, I would always dress the cowboy's part, trying my best to look like Rex Trailer himself. My Schwinn bicycle served as a worthy, though imaginary substitute for the mighty Goldrush. I would take to the great outdoors at the show's signoff, with cap guns blasting and a ten gallon hat, rummage sale reclamation, drooping down over my eyes. My backyard became the open prairie for the rest of the day.

My best Boomtown adventures were on those occasions when we would visit my Grandparents who lived just outside of the city of Boston. We would often arrive on Friday evening and stay through most of Saturday. To me this arrangement meant but one thing... Boomtown would be clearly visible on the color television in their sitting room on Saturday morning! I could practically shake hands with Rex and Pablo, they were so alive in primitive hues, due to the clear broadcast signal from the nearby towers and antennas of channel four.

On one such trip, my parents suggested I bring my best cowboy outfit on the weekend excursion to the grandparents' house. On that following Saturday morning, I was awakened early by my family standing in the doorway of the spare room where I slept, my dad holding my cowboy outfit complete with a new holster and belt. "Let's get ready, we are going to Boomtown!" he said with a merry grin. I could hardly believe my ears, and yet, moments later, we were packed into the station wagon, headed for the fabled studios of channel four. I never looked more natty as that day, and the living proof of that came when I was selected to be Deputy Sheriff for that week's live show. I guess I looked the part with my red hat and leather vest. Indeed, I had been chosen to help ol' Rex Trailer himself in his noble campaign for law and order that day. Along with the youngster who was appointed as Sheriff for the day, I was ushered into the corral area where I stood in awe before the mighty Goldrush. Then, there came the pep talk and words of welcome from Rex. I was in cowboy heaven.

Our dutiful search for the wanted villain didn't go so well. On the first pass of the audience of children through the "Sheriff's office," where no lawbreaker ever wanted to be, the Sheriff and I kept vigilant, but picked no one as the wanted man. So, we tried a second run through. One husky fellow kept whispering under his breath, "It's me. I'm the bad guy." For reasons I know not, we eventually believed him and thus, slapped the plastic handcuffs on his wrists. It was the wrong guy. We had fallen for an obvious ruse. On live television, in our moment of could-be cowboy glory we blew it, the sheriff and I. My moment of fame faded with the realization that I was a duped deputy.

I had learned a life lesson though, one that has served me over the years of being a pastor. Rarely, if ever, does a true villain reveal whom he really is. If someone is grabbing your attention with grand scale claims of poor behavior, you can be pretty sure it's not really them you need to watch for. The real problem is another guy in the shadows with a better disguise. Deception comes up from lowly headquarters. Old Slew-foot doesn't want your attention. But he is the real bad guy. He would rather operate under cover. He doesn't broadcast his intentions. He won't be obvious. You've got to smoke him out.

And then, this: our view of heaven (cowboy or otherwise) may suffer because we are in a far off place. The closer we get to the Source, however, the lesser the interference and the clearer the picture. However close we come, though, there is nothing like being there in person. So, here is your new outfit; put it on! We are going to the place where pictures, deteriorated by distance, come to life in vibrant color. This time, there will be no disappointment or failure. No bad guys, either. Our moment of glory will last for all eternity… "In Boom, Boom, Boomtown!"

Father God, teach me to look behind the masks people wear. May I listen to your voice and not the distracting noise of those who seek not the truth - but want only to be noticed. Amen

Dropping Anchor: *Rarely does the true villian show his face.*

____

____

____

____

The Wood Pile

"And, ye fathers, provoke not your children to wrath: but bring them up in the nurture and admonition of the Lord."
Ephesians 6:4

I was asked to speak at a charter school for teenagers in a nearby city. The school was the educational home for students who had been expelled from the downtown, public high school. Ranging in ages from fourteen to eighteen, these were primarily local youths with family in the region. The nearby public high school was known for violent altercations, drug abuse and gang activity. The students at the charter school were considered to be the worst of the worst. They had been given many chances, and had now been bounced to their last possible stop, and on this particular morning they were sitting before me in a lecture hall.

I looked out over their faces, and in doing so, noted the hardened features of the nearly fifty students. Not one smile could be seen in the group. I looked at my notes, and made a quick decision to toss them away. I decided I would listen instead of speak. I figured this could be far more informational for me—rather than for them. I opened the session with a question or two, and soon found their interest level high and their responses well thought out and sincere.

One young man, however, sat near the back and managed to look as disengaged as possible. As the ninety minute presentation progressed, I noticed that he was growing more and more uncomfortable. He squirmed in his seat, doodled on paper and stared out the window. I desperately wanted to hear his story. Approximately sixteen years old, he was a handsome boy—one you may expect to see on a debate team and not in a charter school for disciplinary problems. He did not raise his hand to speak, but I called on him anyway with the next question. "How can you improve your relationships within your family circle," I asked him. There was an awkward silence that followed. After what seemed like an eternity, he spoke. What followed was something I will never forget.

"I hate my dad," he began. "Hate is a strong word," I answered back. "Are you sure it's the word you mean to use?" "I'm positive," came the reply. With that, he shared a story which I will try to relate just as I heard it that morning.

"My dad works construction, you know? He has his own company. All growing up, I thought he was the coolest. Putting up homes, hospitals or whatever, he could build anything. My dad was my hero. All I ever wanted was to work for him some day. Well, when I was thirteen, my dad asked me if I wanted to go to work with him one morning. It was during summer vacation and he told me I could help him out on a job site. I was so excited."

"We got to the job and he pulled up in his pickup. 'See that big pile of boards?' he asked. 'I want you to stack that neatly over by the trailer.' I told him okay and he left to go check on a job across town. He said he would be back in an hour or two. Well, I got out and started stacking wood. I worked like a dog. I busted my butt. I got the whole pile stacked in about a half an hour. I was done—but I noticed another pile of wood over at the dumpsters, so I figured I would stack that one too. I kept thinking he was going to be so proud of me. I finished the second pile, stacking it by the trailer, just as he pulled in. 'Look!' I said. Well, he looked alright and he got ripping mad. He called me an idiot and just about every other name he could come up with, screaming at me—right in my face. He said he only asked me to stack the one pile—that the other was throw away stuff and now it was all mixed together. I didn't know! I thought he would be happy. He drove me straight home—telling me I was useless. I never want to work for him again. I hate him."

"You know, he was an A-student until the 8th grade…" the school principal told me afterward. "Then, he just mentally dropped out. He doesn't seem to care anymore. That is the first time I ever heard that story, but now we know why."

What a different life story would have transpired if the father, upon seeing his son's mistake, had gently corrected him and helped him fix the error? He instead, broke his son's heart over a pile of wood. Our children are God's gracious gifts to us. They are to be handled with care. The Heavenly Father dispenses much grace. He is patient and gentle with us, His children, and, He covers our mistakes with a cross made of wood. They were just some old boards, really, but they make all the difference in the world.

> *Father God, make me an encourager. I want to build my family up - not tear it down with anger. Anger, like DNA, is passed from generation to generation. With your help; I will end its destructive hold on my home. Amen*

Dropping Anchor: *A son who learns to hate his father, will rarely believe in a heavenly one.*

____

____

____

____

Thin Ice

"Thy word is a lamp unto my feet..."
Psalm 119:105

Having the right information is always important. Having correct information and applying it is even more important. In fact, I am convinced, that is what determines the major difference between a believer and a non-believer. A believer lives by the written word. A non-believer doesn't "heed the creed."

I can remember ice skating on Mr. Goodmore's pond when I was a boy. My mother was an excellent figure skater. Wanting to pass down her love for such traditional winter fun to her children, she had us skating as soon as we could walk. She would throw several layers of warm clothes on us small Deckers and then lead us, like so many penguins, the short distance to the frozen pond. Once there, she laced us into each year's edition of our second hand, rummage sale figure skates. They weren't always a perfect fit and I can still hear her encouraging us to "Push!" She had a nickname for me on those times when I tried to fit my double-socked foot into my "double runner skates." My knees would often buckle, causing her to say, "C'mon Spaghetti Legs."

As I got older, I wanted to wear hockey skates, instead of the black figure skates that she produced for me to wear almost every winter. "Hockey skates have less ankle support," she would remind me. We Deckers were known for weak ankles. They were not quite "spaghetti ankles," but I am certain the thought of expanding the soggy pasta nickname crossed my mother's mind. So, she would comb through yard sales all summer long, looking for boys black figure skates, which were not always easy to find. I recall some winters when I was relegated to wearing white, girls' skates that my mom had spray painted black.

When I was about twelve however, I hit hockey pay dirt. My older cousin made the ice hockey team at his high school, and that began a regular supply of second hand equipment coming down the family pipeline as he outgrew his used gear each season. All that I needed on those winter afternoons was to gather a few pals and we had all the makings of a game of ice hockey. The pond where we learned our "figure eights" now became our hockey rink. My days of figure skating were behind me. With a "Be careful, dear," from my mom, we local boys would grab our secondhand gear and tumble out the door, headed for Goodmore's farm for an afternoon of sport and fun.

There was a sign posted at the far end of the pond. It read, "Flowing water. Thin Ice," and we all knew that the "deep end" was to be avoided. The ice was never as thick there as it was on the rest of the pond, due to the outlet spring that flowed into the running brook at the edge of Mr. Goodmore's property.

One day, in my early teen years (and several sizes of hand me down hockey skates later) we had a pickup game of hockey under way when an errant shot whizzed past the goal and skidded all the way to the far end where the "Thin Ice" sign was posted. We all stood looking at the distant puck, unsure of what to do. Finally, one of our number, Steve, said "I'll get it." Slowly he skated toward the far end. He was almost to the wayward puck when a thunderous crack resounded, sending all of us rushing headlong for the shore. I am pretty sure Steve passed all of us on the way to safety.

Written warnings are good information, but only if you heed them. Just the other day we visited a yard sale, an inherited behavior from dear ol' Mom, no doubt. Yes, they had hockey skates but my days of lacing up the boots and blades are long over. We did purchase a thousand piece jigsaw puzzle that looked like fun to put together. When we got home however, we noticed the writing on the back of the box. In small letters it read "One piece missing." Disappointed, we tossed it away.

Therein is the believer's advantage. As Christians, we have God's Word to follow that keeps us posted and warns us that the road ahead is uncertain. It offers a light for our path along the narrow way that leads to life. The non-believer ignores the signposts. He eventually arrives at the end of life's puzzle only to discover then, that something was missing all along. If that describes you, hurry! "Heed the creed!"

Father God, may I heed the warnings you have posted along the way, found written plainly in your book. These admonitions will keep me from danger. Thank you for caring for me so lovingly. Amen

Dropping Anchor: *There's still time to rush for the safety of the shore.*

___

___

___

___

Chris

*"But when he was yet a great way off,
his father saw him, and had compassion,
and ran, and fell on his neck, and kissed him."*
Luke 15:20

His name is Chris and he is a friend of mine. Chris is an ex-con, having served time in the County Jail. I have known him since he was twelve. It's not like we couldn't see trouble coming his way. We knew early on that he would likely struggle in life, but what we didn't realize was that the church would shoulder much of the blame.

As a boy, Chris went to church every Sunday with his mom. He loved the times of singing the hymns best of all. He would stand tall next to his mother, a shared songbook between them, singing the sacred gospel truth; his clear voice rising and falling with the anthem's notes. Sometimes he would hear his mother's voice adding harmony to his. Chris lived for those moments of musical bliss. He would glance up at her singing with her eyes tightly shut and a half smile framing her countenance. During these times he would silently breathe a prayer of thanks to God above for allowing him this place of peace and serenity. He felt at home.

At age thirteen, he joined the church choir. From his place in the front row, his tenor voice could make the rafters ring. It seemed everyone loved him… that is, everyone but his dad. His father had little involvement in Chris's life. He rarely came home, and when he did, he was usually drunk. Chris would hide upstairs in his room during his visits, trying to avoid the usual beatings. There would always be a shouting match between his parents—and Chris could hear every word from his bedroom over the kitchen. He knew when the escalating war of words was about to get physical and he would fly down the stairs and stand between his mom and dad in an attempt to stop the violence. His dad, furious and out of control would then turn his attention from Chris's mother and unleash his drunken fury onto his son. Chris would take it. He stood tall and would cry through tears of pain and sorrow, "Is that all? C'mon tough guy..." He learned to take a punch the hardest way of all.

One day, I was sitting on the bleachers at the Pony League baseball diamond watching my son, Ash, on the field of play. I noticed Chris was there, leaning against the fence, taking in the action. As he turned and waved to me, I couldn't help but notice the huge shiner that covered most of the left side of his face. "Wow," I whistled as I took my place beside him. "That's quite the black eye." "It's nothin'," he replied, his face turned downward. I told him that he shouldn't fight, and that there were better ways to settle disputes. "Awww, Mr. Decker... I gotta stand up for what's right," he countered. I had thought he had been in a fist-fight with another kid from the block. I never imagined that he had been defending his own mother.

The following Sunday, Chris was not allowed to sing in the choir. "You look awful," said the director. "No singing for you until that swelling on your face goes down. We can't condone fisticuffs here at our assembly." Over time, the swelling and discoloration faded, but with it, his smile started to fade as well. Chris was alone in his stress. He would sit in his room for hours, trying to read the King James Bible he had received as an award for memorizing verses in Sunday school when he was ten. Once, many years later when I visited him in prison, he told me how much that Bible meant to him. "It was a real leather, red letter edition, with gold on the edges of the pages. It had my name on the front cover and everything." He had never forgotten that Bible. I made a promise to replace it someday with a new one.

The dam broke in Chris's life the following summer. He had just turned fourteen, and some well-meaning parishioner from church offered to pay his way for a week at summer Bible camp. Chris got away from the city, and found himself loving the wonders of nature. He made some new friends, but as Chris's luck would have it—he made one enemy as well. It so happened that on the first day of camp, Chris chose a bottom bunk bed—not knowing that another boy, who was a veteran of many summers, had claimed that spot as his. Not one to back down, Chris instead pushed by the irate boy and told him he wasn't moving. That led to the Camp Director being summoned. Assuming Chris to be the troublemaker, the director placed a call to the pastor at Chris's home church. A day or two later, as Chris was walking up to his cabin after free swim, the director whistled for him to come over and talk by the lodge. "I know all about you, now," the director began. "I talked with the pastor of your church. I heard you got removed from choir due to a fight, so you had better keep your nose clean. You may like to get into fights back home, but we will have no black eyes here. I'll send you home to your mother in a heartbeat. I hear your dad's a no-good drunk. Well, you are going to be just like him, aren't you?"

Chris felt his heart melt in his pounding chest. A small gang of campers had been listening to the whole thing. He turned and ran. He didn't stop until he reached the interstate, where he hitchhiked the seventy five miles back to his home. He made up a story to his questioning mother, and then ran to the church. He had no plan. He didn't go in. He was too sad and afraid, so he picked up a rock and threw it at the wooden door. The rock bounced off somewhere, and so did Chris. He never went back. He is still running today.

The other day I stopped in at the restaurant where he works. I brought him a present of a real leather, red letter edition, gold leaf Bible. I had his name engraved on the cover... and as I handed it to him, I knew beyond doubt that his name is also engraved upon my heart. Of all the punches Chris ever took, the hardest blow of all came from the mouth of a pastor. Come home, my friend. Come home. The Father truly loves you and so do I.

> *Father God, help me never to judge but make me a champion for the cause of those who have been wrongly judged already. Amen*

Dropping Anchor: *Sometimes the worst punches are words.*

___

___

___

___

The Mile Man

"...they shall run, and not be weary..."
Isaiah 40:31

"I could have been the best miler in the county," my father would often tell me as I was growing up. That was no empty boast as it was exactly what the varsity coach at his high school had told him. "Give me a few more runners like that and we could win the regionals, hands down," the coach had said after watching my dad run ten laps around the cinder track behind the school. Dad never took the coach's offer of being trained to run the mile, but I can recall how he could outdistance everyone at church picnics or when running the long driveway dash from mailbox to the kitchen. There was once a time, I know, when he needed to run a mile and to run it fast.

It was Christmas Eve. The year was 1936 as far as I can tell. My dad was a young teenager, about fifteen years old. The family was all tucked into their beds; mom and dad and six children, of which my father was the oldest. He was asleep in the upstairs bedroom which he shared with his two younger brothers. It was after midnight when the youngest boy shook my dad awake. "I smell smoke," he said in an earnest tone. Suddenly being awake and alert, my father ran down the flight of stairs. He could hear the whoosh and roar of the fire before he saw it. What he saw upon arriving on the first floor was beyond frightening.

The living room with the Christmas tree and presents was engulfed in a raging fire. The tree itself was like a burning torch, crackling with heat and flame. "Go wake up mom and dad!" he shouted to his two brothers who had followed him down stairs. "I'll wake the other kids!" He ran past the searing flames and into the girls' bedroom. "Fire!" he screamed, waking the sisters. "Hang on to me," he hollered above the sound of the now spreading fire. He led them through the smoke and flame and out onto the front porch where his father was frantically trying to rescue valuables before they were lost to the inferno. His mother was lining up the children, calling names and counting heads. The one telephone the family had was hopelessly beyond reach in the spreading flames and smoke. Turning to my dad, his mother shouted, "Run to the neighbor's house and call the fire department." My dad knew the closest neighbor was a mile away. He bounded off the porch and ran in his bare feet through the icy puddles, following the dirt road that would bring him to the neighbors on the hill.

Over his shoulder, he could see the orange glow from the house fire in the night sky. In front of him there was only the dark of the starless night. The 'could be' mile man ran faster than he ever had on tracks of cinder. He reached the home of the neighbors in less than five minutes. He pounded and shouted until a light came on. The fire could be heard despite the distance and the woods were yielding to the fire's glow, looking like an eerie sunrise as it rose into the night sky.

The volunteer fire department was summoned, but by the time they arrived, the house was a total loss. The family was huddled like refugees on the lawn at a safe distance from the falling timbers. The littlest ones were crying. I reckon refugees were exactly what they were, burned out of their home as the dawn broke on Christmas Day.

In later years, my father would tell the story of the Christmas fire. He would recall the kindness of the community as people made room in their homes for the eight Deckers. A local merchant unlocked his store on Christmas Day and selected a present for each of the six children. Meals were provided and the local Credit Union offered an interest free loan to help the family rebuild and get back on its feet. Oddly, the memory of that fire that remained the clearest to my dad, even in his dotage, was that of his dad, my grandfather, going back and searching through the ruins and rubble for his set of false teeth. They were never found.

So my dad may have been the fastest miler in the county after all. But, I can see why he never enjoyed running for his coach. He had run at record speed one night for his family home and that was enough for him.

> *Father God, thank you for your daily watchcare over us. We will face dangers and uncertainties in life. We know this is true, but we also know these hard places will bring out the best in us. We can run the race before us with your encouragement ringing in our spiritual ears. Amen*

Dropping Anchor: *Family is precious oil that fuels our life's pace.*

____

____

____

____

Bicentennial Bell

"For a thousand years in Thy sight are but as yesterday when it is past..."
Psalm 90:4

The building which I called my home church in my youth was an ancient edifice in the town of Acushnet, Massachusetts. It was a typical white New England wooden frame with a steeple and bell. It had stood through the dark years of America's Civil War, and survived the hurricanes of 1938 and 1960. What it couldn't outlast was time.

I was a "walker" in my elementary school years. My old school house was just a quarter of a mile from my home and the hike there took me right past the old church. I would always pass by at a slow pace, gazing at the tall windows framed with black shutters. The huge double doors at the top of the front steps were never locked and so, on occasion, on the walk home after school, I would push one open and spend a few moments of solitude in one of the pews. The plaster walls seemed to speak to me in those afternoon times of quiet musings. I had a telling sense of years gone by, of people who were no longer with us. I felt a part of something larger... a member of an historical line of true believers.

On the back wall of the old church hung an old print of a painting featuring Jesus as a youth. For some reason I always thought the painting was an image of the Old Testament prophet Samuel, whose name the Lord called one night in the temple. I guess the Old Testament served as the framework for my thoughts, for I was sitting in the oldest place that I knew. Everything was old. Even God seemed old as I sat there in the silence, half expecting to hear my own name called, just as Samuel had at my age. To me, the church seemed as timeless as the very books of the Old Testament, and not unlike the sacred Scriptures, it would always remain. It would survive—it seemed eternal.

The steeple was the first to go. The enormous bell in the belfry was more weight than the old-dry rotted timbers could stand, and after a particularly strong nor'easter one winter we looked atop the old structure, only to find the bell tower listing precariously to one side. A steeplejack was summoned and after carefully looking over the damage it was determined that the tall spire should, indeed, come down. Thus, the bell was removed from its place aloft and placed on a patch of grass behind the old parsonage. There it sat like a silent sentry, summoning no one. Until 1976…

The nation's Bicentennial year, celebrating our independence from British rule, arrived with much fanfare. Red, white, and blue bunting hung from doorways and windows everywhere. Parades and fireworks displays were plentiful, and my hometown was no exception. A parade was planned for the 4th of July and our congregation saw an opportunity for outreach, and perhaps a bit of fun. A flatbed truck was rented for the occasion and our church folks covered it with historical tableaus depicting memorable milestones from our nation's infancy. At the center, the old bell was secured on a wooden platform, and one of our youth dressed up like Paul Revere and rang the old bell along the parade route as if the British were indeed, coming again. The old bell certainly had its finest day.

The old church came down with a wrecking ball a few years after the loss of her steeple. I could not watch the demolition; it seemed as if life itself was crumbling. I felt a sadness I couldn't explain. Perhaps one reason for my sorrow could be uncovered in those times sitting in silent fellowship with the imagined memories of years gone by. It was as if my own life's old testament was coming down in a heap. Memories were now to be replaced with prophecies. The new had begun, with all its uncertainties and mysteries. Going back was no option. The future was upon me.

A new facility now houses the congregants of my old home church. Its modern look appeals to a new generation. On the side lawn there sits the old bell… a monument now. It no longer rings. But, in my mind I can still hear it peal as it did one fall night in

1960 when the winds of Hurricane Donna sent it swaying. And, I can hear it aboard the Bicentennial float of 1976, ringing as if it were the very Liberty Bell itself. As for me, if I can find a place of quiet solitude, I still wait in wonder for the Lord to call my name...

Father God, may we move from our comfortable places in the church and carry the good news to the streets. Let it ring like a bell and never let it be silenced. Freedom! Amen

Dropping Anchor: *The future unfolds before us like a highway but there are no roads leading back from whence we came.*

Bob The Strongman

"For which cause we faint not;
but though our outward man perish,
yet the inward man is renewed day by day..."
2 Corinthians 4:16

I have a friend who is going to heaven; it seems, a little at a time. Bob is my age... but he looks older. He has struggled physically for many years, and the battle scars are clearly seen. He is weary of the conflict, but he fights on. He is not a workout kind of guy—but despite his average build—he just may be the strongest person that I know.

It began twenty five years ago with kidney failure, transplant list, and dialysis. Finally, after much prayer and a long wait, a donor match was found. Bob received his new kidneys. Transplant work was not as refined nearly three decades ago, and so my friend was told the new organs may last five years. He kept them nearly twenty.

Then, circulation issues came knocking and Bob lost a foot, then a leg, then the other leg. With each loss came the adjustment to life without a limb. Prosthetic devices can be cumbersome and awkward, especially at first. Bob lives alone and so he has little help getting ready each day. I should correct that last statement. Bob lives by himself when he is home, for despite his handicaps he is often out and about, paying visits to others, attending church or teaching at the Bible study he has led for years. His careful instruction in the Scriptures attracts eager learners both young and old. He keeps a busy schedule despite having to go to the clinic three days out every five. The kidney dialysis machine is hooked up to my weary friend and he remains attached for hours.

For those of us who have never undergone a dialysis treatment, we just don't comprehend the effort required. It is painful.

It is dangerous. It wears you out. Each week, Bob is driven to the clinic where he is hooked up to the machine that will cleanse his blood. Cheery on the way—content while there—sleepy on the way back home, Bob plugs on in the struggle to live.

The other day, a raging infection in his hand meant the doctors took another piece of Bob. This time it was a finger. But, you see—with each loss, Bob does not weaken; instead he grows stronger. I think God must still need most of Bob here on planet earth... I know I do. He is the strongest man I know.

> *Father God, I pray for all those who, like Bob, have suffered loss. Many people have minimum care and help provided for them - Please use me to encourage someone who is lonely and afraid, no matter how strong they are. Amen*

Dropping Anchor: *Physical strength can lift a great weight. Inner strength can lift a spirit.*

___

___

___

___

Simon Of Samaria

"So when the Samaritans were come unto Him,
they besought Him that He would tarry with them:
and He abode there two days.
And many more believed because of His own word;
And said unto the woman, 'Now we believe,
not because of thy saying: for we have heard Him ourselves...'"
John 4:40-42

Simon was a sorcerer and a good one. "The best!" the enthusiastic crowds would exclaim. Indeed, he was considered to be the best and he knew it. People would come from many miles away just to see him defy the laws of nature. Or, so they thought. Inside his own head, the 'magic man' as he was known, knew just how much trickery was involved in his feats of the paranormal. This knowledge troubled him greatly. He felt strangely empty.

As a young man, he had studied the ancient religion of Egypt. He had grown up there in that land, in the shadows of the grand pyramids. His teachers were known for their mystical powers and potions, and Simon was one of their foremost students. He would sit in rapt attention as he was taught the names of Cleopatra, Jobab, and Moshes, three legendary magicians of yore in the Nile region. Long ago, they had baffled large crowds with feats of wonder. It was said of them that Cleopatra was centuries old, but at the cost of her soul, had been gifted with the smooth skin and fine features of a young woman. Jobab had great wealth and was one who talked with the gods in person. Moshes was a prophet who once parted the great southern sea.

Simon desired the fame and influence that his teachers spoke of. Much of his time was spent alone, honing his craft and calling upon the gods. His father and mother, Antonius and Rachel, would worry about their son. His character and his countenance seemed to grow darker by the day. The once playful boy had become a strange and spiritual young man. So, when the time came for the family to leave Egypt and move to a small town to the north called Getta, they quickly seized the opportunity. "A change will be good for Simon," they considered. It was there, in Getta however, that the young man became known as Simon Magnus. All of his sophisticated training seemed to find a home in the simple folk of the region. Simon was an instant celebrity. At times, he still struggled with the fakery involved in his craft; nonetheless, he continued to dazzle the masses with his gravity defying tricks and schemes. His magic shows grew more and more popular.

Samaria would be his next move. After the passing of his beloved mother, Rachel, Simon relocated to Samaria with Antonius. His aunt, a spry woman named Josephine lived alone there. She had sent word to her brother and his son that she had a spare room for them to reside in. It was agreed that she would help care for Antonius in his feeble years. Simon would help pay the bills. The Samaritans received the sorcerer with open arms and his fame grew far and wide. Year after year, the magician practiced his craft in Samaria. To the villagers, he was their own. "Simon is great like a god!" they called out to him in the marketplace. Shopkeepers would beckon him into their stores along the main thoroughfare for they understood that a crowd always followed Simon wherever he went. In short, he was good for business.

Business was good for Simon Magnus. His sleight of hand maneuvers and his "levitation" abilities were the talk of the town; and beyond. Some locals even claimed they had seen him fly. Simon loved that kind of talk. He denied no rumors as to his greatness. The only place of contradiction was in his heart, for he knew his own limitations, even if the public considered him to be a god.

One evening, Simon went for a stroll through the village. He often walked late in the day in an attempt to clear his thoughts. As he neared the town well, he noticed a small crowd had gathered and some Jewish men were coming up from the well in his direction. They obviously felt out of place. Samaritans and Jews did not get along. He brushed by the group with his eyes focused on the setting sun on the distant horizon. None of the Jews made eye contact with Simon as they passed by him, none except the rabbi in the middle of the group. His eyes met Simon's and held him captive for what seemed like an eternity. It actually was over in a few seconds, but Simon knew he had never seen a countenance like that one.

"Who was that rabbi?" he asked a woman who stood watching the Jews walk away along the road out of town. Simon recognized the woman who now stood, mouth agape, in the street. She had a poor reputation in the town. She was one of loose morals and had been tied by rumor and innuendo to many men. Normally, Simon would give her a wide berth, but on this occasion, he felt compelled to speak. Slowly, the woman drew her eyes away from the band of Jews and acknowledged Simon, standing before her. "That man is a prophet, no... even more than a prophet!" The woman was speaking dreamily and yet there was no doubt that she knew exactly what she was saying. "He told me things about myself that I have never told anyone," she said, looking squarely at Simon. "I know who you are, Simon Magnus. But who is this rabbi that met me at the town well?" "That is what I am going to find out," breathed the sorcerer.

Over the following weeks, Simon spent more time in Jerusalem than in Samaria. He studied Jewish writings and visited the temple in hopes of finding more information about the strange rabbi who had captured his gaze and captured his soul with it. Jesus the Nazarene as he was called, had gone to the north up beyond the sea, and was clearly having an impact. Stories of miraculous healings and feats of natural wonder drifted back to the capital city. It was rumored that the rabbi had even walked across the sea on a stormy night. "Impossible..." muttered Simon when the story reached his ears. And, so he went home to Samaria.

Antonius was dying. His days would certainly be few. Josephine tended to him with love and care, but the old man's condition worsened daily. Simon would sit by the bedside of his dying father, wishing, hoping that his luck would change. He prayed earnestly to the gods he learned of as a boy in Egypt, but to no avail. Before many days passed, Antonius breathed his last. Simon Magnus, despite his fame and fortune was alone in the world. The emptiness he had known for years was now all around him. It pressed in from all sides. He could not free himself of the pain in his soul. Simon Magnus went into seclusion.

There were no reports of Simon flying from rooftop to rooftop. There were no magic shows in the amphitheater. For many months, Simon the Sorcerer kept out of the public eye. He just could not find the pleasure in performing any more. What he sought was an end to the restlessness and loneliness he felt inside. His only lifeline was Josephine. She made sure Simon ate and washed regularly, but even his beloved aunt grew more and more worried. Weeks passed. Still, Simon stayed in his self-imposed cocoon.

Then, one evening, Josephine came home from the market. "I met a man," she told Simon. "He told me all about new life… abundant life. His name is Phillip and I invited him here for dinner." "Bah!" said Simon, scowling. "He has seven daughters with him, lovely ladies indeed," Josephine added. Upon hearing that news, Simon considered that maybe a guest or two for dinner may not be so bad. An hour later, the house was full of bustle and laughter as Phillip and his daughters took over the kitchen. "I often cook for the believers in Jerusalem," Phillip announced. Simon questioned, "Believers... Believers in what?" questioned Simon. The guest answered "Those who follow The Way." "We follow the rabbi, or rather the Messiah, Jesus of Nazareth."

Suddenly, Simon flashed back many months to the incident in the village square. He recalled the look of wonder on the face of the woman at the well. He remembered the intense gaze of the rabbi as he had passed by Simon. Looking now in the face of Philip the Evangelist, he saw the same divine look in his eyes. "Simon," said Phillip, "you are chosen to follow with us. That is why I came."

Over dinner, Simon and Josephine listened as Philip shared the good news of the Christ. As he spoke, Simon felt a strange wonder capturing his soul. The fatigue and loneliness, the false bravado, all seemed to melt away from Simon's cold heart. Kneeling before his house guest, Simon believed. "I saw him that day at the well," Simon told the small gathering. "His eyes spoke of love, a love that I now know within." After dinner was over, Philip baptized two new believers, Josephine and Simon Magnus. The Sorcerer had found the truth that changes everything. Instead of using trickery, this power to change a man's heart from gloom to joy flowed from person to person like a gift from on high. Simon would seek now to share it with everyone. "Jesus is great! He is God!" he proclaimed, as it were, from the rooftops.

Father God, thank you for telling us the truth, so that we don't spend our lives seeking answers in secretive religion. May we remember how simple you made it when you sent Jesus and showed us the way. Amen

Dropping Anchor: *Truth needs no magic to astound.*

Me And Mr. Addison

"'Be not afraid, only believe.'"
Mark 5:36

He was a product of my childhood imagination - a complete fabrication, but oh!... he was more than real enough to me. I called him Mr. Addison. That was the name I assigned to the ferocious eight hundred pound gorilla that lived under the stairs in the front hall of my parsonage home. I never actually saw this monster but I was certain he was there alright, hiding out in his under-the-stairs lair.

My biggest problem navigating the dark and narrow front hall came at night. Our big, rambling parsonage home had but one bathroom and that was located upstairs. Those stairs—home to Mr. Addison—eater of little boys who had to pee. During those years, I often wet the bed at night. I guess I figured the shame was more bearable than the fear. Passage through that hallway was nerve wracking to say the least. Long shadows formed in front of and behind me as I timidly tiptoed in the feeble beam of light cast by my trustworthy Boys Brigade, RAY-O-VAC flashlight.

How did an imaginary gorilla end up with a formal name like "Mister Addison?" My parents thought my naming of the beast was a result of growing up in the sheltered environs of the church where my dad was pastor. For many years, the church's Sunday school superintendent was Joan Addison. She and her four children were regular congregants of the little house of worship. Mrs. Addison sang in the adult choir in addition to holding down her Sunday school duties. She was in church every time the door opened. But, not Mr. Addison—He never came. "He stays home to watch the news," Mrs. Addison explained once to a curious deacon many years later. As a child, I never wondered about Mr. Addison's reasons for avoiding the church fellowship. He was absent. This much I knew. He became enshrouded in mystery in my young mind. I had never seen Mr. Addison, and I had never seen the gorilla in the hallway... but I was certain they both were real. Over time they became one in the same.

Often I would awaken in the middle of the night with a full bladder. Not wanting to deal with damp sheets—I would go to my parents' room and stand by my dad's side of the bed. I would clear my throat a few times in an effort to wake him. Opening one eye, he would always say the same thing… "Don't be afraid. There is nothing to be afraid of." His words had little calming effect, because to my way of thinking, there certainly was one very big thing to be afraid of—and his name was Mr. Addison. The bravery my dad displayed on such nights was epic. He would take my hand and walk with me down the hall, to the bottom of the winding staircase, where he would wait for me while I went to the bathroom. Sometimes, on the way back to my room, we would detour to the kitchen for a glass of milk and to see "what sort of goodies mom has laying around for us." Often, we would find a slice of pie or a couple of cookies which made a perfect midnight snack for a boy and his very brave father. By the time I was tucked back into my bed I was no longer gripped with fear. I was filled with the stuff of my dad the hero, not hallway shadows or noises in the night.

Fear is a controlling factor and it cripples us. Fear keeps us from enjoying life because we are too afraid of losing it to a ravenous disease, or an imagined eight hundred pound animal. Fear lives within us but it is most often irrational. Most of what we fear is not real. However, we go through our days as though we were treading on eggshells, trying not to awaken the gorilla under the stairs. We imagine the worst, and the worst thing a seven year old could come up with was a huge, hungry primate.

My fear of Mr. Addison hung around me for years, but it was many more years after when I heard the news that Joan Addison had passed away. The funeral was on a crisp New England autumn day. I took the time off from my duties and drove the distance to my boyhood hometown. Once there, I made my way to the local cemetery. It was there that I saw him for the very first time, standing with his grown children. Sad and worn, and bent over his cane, frail old Mr. Addison approached me and introduced himself. "I'm Pastor Loren," I replied. "You knew my dad," I added. "Yes, I remember him," his words were hardly more than breath in his mouth. "Would you say a prayer for her, Reverend?" He nodded toward the casket. "I will, Mr. Addison," I answered. He started to walk toward the grave and then turned back to me. "Will you walk with me, Reverend?" he asked with tears in his eyes. "Don't be afraid," I told him softly and then took his arm in mine as together we walked to the graveside, me and Mr. Addison.

Father God, help me overcome fear and replace it with compassion. Help me to operate in the truth and not in the anxieties that live only in my thoughts. Amen

Dropping Anchor: *Fear of the imaginary misshapes our reality.*

____

____

____

____

Tiger Fan

"Thus shall ye do in the fear of the Lord,
faithfully, and with a perfect heart."
2nd Chronicles 19:9

My father was a Detroit Tigers fan. His allegiance to the major league ball club from the Motor City was unflappable. Some of my earliest memories are of warm summer nights, with the windows open throughout the house, the sounds from the old Philco radio floating into my bedroom from the kitchen. There, my father would sit in the wooden rocking chair, creaking back and forth while he endured the AM radio signal that came from Tiger Stadium.

WLS in Detroit would broadcast the sounds of the ballgame over hill and dale, bouncing off the atmospheric cloud cover and skipping across the Great Lakes to my house in Acushnet, Massachusetts, to my dad's awaiting ears. The distant signal carrying the voice of legendary sportscaster Ernie Harwell was rarely clear by the time it reached our home. The whoop and hum of frequency interference rose and fell like the luck of the Detroit nine. A distant thunderstorm somewhere over Pennsylvania or New York would cause static to drown out the action as the electric crackle of lightning burst across the AM dial. If the inning was late and the game was close, Dad's rocking chair would stop its creaking. All would be silent, with just the crickets in our yard producing their own natural sounds of static; all I could hear beyond the drone of the distant broadcast play by play. However, there were some nights when the conditions were just right, and the call of the ballgame came through crystal clear, without any interference at all. Those were fine nights, indeed, nights to live for.

Tucked in my bed, in the converted pantry, which became my room, I could listen in and imagine the game being played so far away in Michigan or perhaps, at the home city of one of the

Tiger's American League rivals. The sound of the static and buzz that battled old Ernie's call of the game drifted to my ears like so much crowd noise. The creak and groan of my dad's rocker kept pace with the game while singing me into sleep with its wooden lullaby.

My dad became a Tiger fan in odd fashion. He wasn't from Detroit, not even close. He hailed from upstate New York where baseball was defined in Yankee terms… Lou Gehrig, Babe Ruth and the boys were kings in my father's hometown. But, at my dad's address, baseball was low on the list of topics to consider. Thus, when a high school classmate asked him which team would win the World Series that summer, he had no ready answer. "There must be a team called the Tigers," he thought on the fly. That became his answer in 1938 and it remained his answer for the rest of his life. Interestingly, the Detroit Tigers went on to win the World Series that year. My father was hooked and the lifetime of allegiance had begun. It lasted through the many summers of wins and losses. Dad's heroes were the ball players. Names like Bill Freehan, Norm Cash, Al Kaline and Dick McAuliffe frequented his conversation during my growing up years. In later times, I would bring up those old timers and get my dad going on the reminiscing pathway as he looked back through the years. He passed away, many decades later, with a Detroit Tigers cap firmly on his head.

My dad listened to yet another frequency all those Tiger years. The sound came from far away… Over the landscape it travelled, skipping through the atmosphere of earth's interference, news from a distant—yet drawing ever closer—land. The inning grew late and the score was close. The creaks and groans of earth would grow still one last time—this time for good. Yet, if I listen closely I can still match the rise and fall of that far signal in my own bed at night, as the static lessens and one Voice becomes crystal clear. The crowd is cheering. It must be a win. I think I will wear dad's old Tigers cap in the morning. He left it behind for me.

Father God, You know us intimately and well. You make us joyful with simple pleasures… family, rocking chairs… long summer nights. These things and more make us long for the home you are preparing for us. It must be incredible. Amen

Dropping Anchor: *Heaven pours forth speech on a divine frequency. How is our reception?*

____

____

____

____

Lazarus

"Now Jesus loved Martha, and her sister, and Lazarus."
John 11:5

"Lazarus, my friend, come out here!" The voice calling for him was familiar, but it seemed oddly distant. Jesus, whose voice he now recognized, had called his name a hundred times from the portico outside his home near Nazareth. The two men had been friends since childhood. They had spent countless hours together, usually with their fishing lines in the water. Lazarus loved to fish. It was one activity he could easily do. Rough games played by other boys were not possible for Lazarus. He was lame in both legs ever since birth. While many children in the neighborhood teased him, Jesus was always kind and understanding. Lazarus had something wrong with his breathing also. Often, after only a few steps, he would lean over his crutches, trying desperately to catch his breath. Jesus had fashioned the wooden crutches for his friend in his father's carpentry shop. He had also made a wooden push cart to transport Lazarus to the village on their many excursions into town. They were quite a sight together, disappearing down the gravel road. "Slow down," would cluck Martha, Lazarus' older sister. "Don't worry Martha!" the young Jesus would call back over his shoulder. With a knowing wink at Lazarus, the pair would be off for the day, nearly tipping at every turn. Their laughter could still be heard when they were well out of sight. "I'll have supper on the table when you return," Martha would call to the wind.

One such day, Jesus and his friend happened to find a bird lying on the path in the woods. "Is it dead?" Lazarus asked. "It would appear so," replied Jesus, taking the bird into His hands. Jesus cradled the pitiful creature and then seemed to whisper something as he held it up to the blue sky above. After a moment, the little creature spread its wings and flew away. "I guess it wasn't dead after all," said Lazarus. Jesus smiled and looked straight into his eyes, as Jesus drew close to His friend, "Perhaps not... but there are things that are stronger than death." They both knew this was a conversation to remember. "Death is not the end," Jesus spoke with authority..."Dead things come alive!" Watching the bird fly out of sight, Jesus again turned to face his astonished friend. "You will need to remember that one day." There was seriousness to the sound of Jesus' voice.

Their friendship grew as the years went by. Boyhood games were traded for adult discussions around the dinner table. Lame Lazarus would sit for hours talking with his friend. His younger sister Mary would join the group at the table, always quiet and listening. Martha would bustle about, always on her feet... always serving. As time went by, the discussions deepened to cover some amazing occurrences involving Jesus. It seems he was claiming now to be the Son of God and he was working miracles to back up the claim. Lazarus would study his friend's face on evenings like this, looking intently—trying to measure the sincerity of Jesus. He wanted to believe, but it seemed impossible. Jesus had no friends in the power structure and his only companions were a rough and tumble group of fishermen and zealots. Occasionally, one or two of these disciples would come to the house with Jesus. These were intense times and Lazarus lamented that his condition kept him increasingly house-bound. He was worsening with time, that much was obvious, yet he still leaned in and listened carefully to the dinner talks until..."Off to bed for you Lazarus." It would always be Martha sending him off to his bedroom in the back of the house. "Oh, Sister, it's early yet," he would protest. "You need to get stronger and sleep will help with that!" she would counter. He knew arguing was pointless. Martha ran a tight ship. "I will be back to visit soon," Jesus would say to his tired friend. "Sleep well."

"Why won't you heal him?" Mary asked Jesus one night after her brother had retired to his room. "I know you can do this thing. He is getting sicker by the day. Can't you help him?" "Oh, Mary..." breathed Jesus. "Sometimes our questions have no answers until the Father in Heaven reveals them." "Will he never be well then?" Mary's question hung in the air. Finally Jesus spoke. "Lazarus will be more than just well. There will be a day when he will be made more alive than he has ever been." Mary sighed and stated, "I believe in the resurrection of the dead on that final day. But I hate to see him suffer so." "The darker the night, the brighter dawns light," replied Jesus. Everyone around the table nodded in agreement.

One morning, Lazarus was too weak to leave his room. "His fever is high," fussed Martha. "I'm going to call the doctor. "I am worried about our brother." Mary brought a cool, damp cloth and laid it on Lazarus' brow. "I will send for Jesus," she said, not taking her eyes off her brother. A deep cough rattled in the sick man's chest. He gasped for air. He was laboring for each breath. "I don't think that Jesus is nearby," replied Martha. "He was travelling north last we knew." A messenger was dispatched nonetheless. Hope against hope, the sisters watched at the bedside of Lazarus. Each breath came more slowly than the last. And then there were none.

"I must have been more tired than I thought," considered Lazarus. "Did I really dream of angels?" He heard the voice of Jesus calling again. But where was he? He tried to call back to his friend, but there was something covering his mouth. Peeling it away he managed a response. "Coming, Jesus!" Where were his crutches? Why could he not see? This was not his room in the back of their house.

"Here, let me help you with those wrappings." The voice belonged to a man dressed in white. He had a glowing inner light that radiated around the place where Lazarus lay. "This is a tomb!" Lazarus whispered the words. "Yes, it is," said the one helping him unwind the cloth strips that were wrapped around him. "Am I dead, then?" asked Lazarus. "You were," replied the glowing man. "But our Lord has called you back to earth life. Now go forth." "Are you an angel?" Lazarus asked the question as he was led to the mouth of the burial cave. The man just smiled and said, "You won't recall where you have been, but you will see it again in time." "I remember it was beautiful." Lazarus was trying to clear his thoughts. "That it is," said the man. "I am returning there now."

As Lazarus stepped out of the tomb, he realized he had left his crutches behind. He had no need of them. He took a deep gulp of fresh air and fell into the embrace of his friend. Jesus and Lazarus were beyond happy. The two began walking arm in arm the mile or so to the house, leaving the astonished sisters and the disciples to stand and wonder. Their laughter could still be heard when they were well out of sight.

From that day forth, Lazarus was constantly by his friend's side. He stood with his sisters on Golgotha's lonely hill while nails were driven into the hands that had fashioned the old crutches that he had once owned. Three days later, he had greeted Jesus with indescribable joy on the morning He awoke from His own grave. Lazarus had never given up hope that there would be a resurrection of his friend, for after all, he had experienced one himself. And after Jesus ascended into heaven, Lazarus walked alone as an evangelist, carrying the message of the Christ. "Death is swallowed up by life!" he would say.

It is said that in his elder years, old Lazarus was brought up on charges by those seeking to snuff out the early church. Threatened with execution if he continued proclaiming the new gospel, Lazarus laughed. He could be heard laughing still, as he walked out of sight. "Dead things become alive." they heard him say as his words floated back on the wind.

Father God, may my heart always treasure the truth that death is swallowed up by life. Amen

Dropping Anchor: *You will live - Again!*

Dinner With Billy

"And in this mountain shall the Lord of hosts
make unto all people a feast of fat things,
a feast of wines on the lees,
of fat things full of marrow,
of wines on the lees well refined."
Isaiah 25:6

This story unfolds in Columbia, South Carolina. I travelled to that city to cover the Billy Graham Crusade event for the Christian radio network for which I worked. I was there to collect interviews, produce a daily one hour broadcast and to report on what was occurring at the crusade site. These trips were always exciting and rewarding. In places like Sacramento, Hartford, Rochester, Newark and New York City, I had journeyed to be a part of history; with microphone in hand, as I recounted the phenomena of Dr. Graham's mission to the world.

I landed in the South Carolina heat, and took a taxi to the hotel. My companion was to meet me there. Steve was a police officer. He had volunteered to spend a week at the crusade and to help me with the 'heavy lifting.' Steve was an earnest fellow and I was looking forward to his arrival. His 'beat' was the graveyard shift in a high crime area which made for some incredible street level stories. He was due to arrive later that evening, so I grabbed a quick nap and then headed for the hotel restaurant for a bite of dinner. I left a message at the front desk instructing Officer Steve to meet me in the dining room.

When I entered the small dining area, I passed by a table of gentlemen, casually dressed and faces buried in their menus. A few steps beyond the group, I felt a hand on my shoulder and a familiar voice said, "Hello, buddy!" I turned to see Michael W. Smith, the well-known musician. I knew Michael from past encounters in New England. Our mutual friend, Dan Russell often brought Michael to the Northeast for concert events. He was now in town for the Graham Crusade. There in the restaurant, we exchanged pleasantries and a hearty hug. I then continued to my seat at a small booth nearby.

A few minutes later, my own menu before me, I heard a gentle voice say, "Do you mind if I join you?" Expecting my friend, Steve, I looked up to see Dr. Graham standing there, smiling. He had gotten up from his seat at the table I had passed upon entering the restaurant and had come over to my booth. "Please..." I stammered. "Have a seat." That began my dinner with Billy Graham. We shared a meal and conversation. I told him about my work and what a privilege it was to be able to be at the crusade. We talked of radio, ministry and family. He also shared stories from the many countries he had visited. He was humble and gracious. He asked if I had accepted Jesus as my Savior with the same sincerity he employed when speaking to stadium crowds. I told him that I had, as a small boy. He grinned in genuine happiness. I felt the wonder of his salvation question with an intensity and newness that bore witness to the millions of souls across the planet that had responded to that same question by leaving their seats in arenas and ballparks, just to come forward and give their hearts away at the altar. I promise you, I gave my heart to Jesus all over again, at the moment I heard his question.

Steve arrived some thirty minutes later, only to find his seat occupied by Billy Graham. A bit stunned, he grabbed a nearby chair and pulled it up to the booth. The evangelist was very interested in Steve's police work. Steve drew out his most interesting tales from the city streets. The time flew by. When Dr. Graham finally returned to his former seat, we stared in disbelief, awed by the blessing of our private dinner with such an incredible man.

Dr. Graham knew Jesus well, and he behaved like Him too. Jesus is humble and gracious. I know now why thousands of people have responded to the evangelist's offer for salvation by coming to know Jesus personally. His humble heart and gracious manner were not an act put on for the masses of people gathered in massive stadiums. Billy Graham would have reached out for just one. This much I know is true... He did for me.

Father God, I praise you for the gift you gave the world in a country boy turned evangelist. Mr. Graham has passed and we are poorer for his loss. But heaven is richer - for the many saints who have gone before us. Thank you for Godly examples. Amen

Dropping Anchor: *Evangelism is always personal, at a restaurant or in a stadium.*

Boni

"...His countenance was as the sun shineth in His strength."
Revelation 1:16

I was refereeing a Town League basketball game in the old, run down gym that the local boys' high school division used on Monday nights during the harsh New England winters. The two teams on the floor that night were locked in a close game. Tensions were running high as playoff berths were at stake. The team that I coached was seated in the tiered stands, waiting to play the next game. That was how we ran things in the league; we had one paid 'official' referee and the other whistle was worn by a volunteer—usually the coach who had 'next game.' That night it was my turn to wear the ref's whistle and I used it plenty. The action was rough and getting rougher.

Late in the second half, during a time-out, I walked over to talk with my point guard who was observing all the action from the third row of seats. He was a kid from the streets, familiar with tension and he coolly scanned the floor as if it were a church picnic. "Boni, the lid may blow off before this is over," I said. "I know, Coach," came his reply. Boni was blessed with great talent and true leadership skills... but me being a pastor; it was his name I liked best about him. Boni's full name was Bonifacio de Jesus, which translates to 'the beautiful face of Jesus.' Boni came from tough stock. His dad was mainly a stranger to him. His mom worked hard to keep the family together. It was clear; Boni had the heart of a champion. He just needed a break. I had him close to my heart, and tried my best to keep him close to my side; how I loved that boy. 'Keep an eye on the blonde kid, number eleven," he said as I returned to the court at the blare of the timekeeper's horn. "I can see that!" I called over my shoulder to Boni.

Then it happened. A hard foul knocked a player to the floor. A wild swing connected with the young man who had committed the foul and he went down in a heap. Suddenly, everyone was fighting. I glanced at the stands **only to see an empty space**. Suddenly he was beside me, pulling players apart, separating them with his calm voice. I did the same wherever I could, dodging some flying fists in the process. As order slowly returned, Boni glanced my way and smiled. I was certain he had done a noble job of preventing an escalation in the violence and saved more than one player from serious injury. He was returning to his seat when the official pointed at him from the center of the court and loudly announced that Boni was being thrown out of the gym facility. "I saw you come out of the stands," the ref went on. "To help... not to hurt!" I protested, "He was helping me restore order." "That's not how I saw it," the official replied. "Well, then you saw it all wrong," I countered. "Never mind arguing with me," he said, a little too closely. "I'll throw you out too." I thought I heard a racial slur escape his lips as he nodded in Boni's direction. "That's right, De Jesus. You are out!" Boni's face turned blood red and I thought he was going to cry.

I then watched as the beautiful face of Jesus, trying to hide his embarrassment and tears, ran out of the gym and into the cold night. Tossing my whistle to my assistant, I ran after him, but he was long gone. It was days before I saw him again. "Boni, that whole scene wasn't fair," I managed. "It hardly ever is," he answered, "I'm used to it."

The idea is centuries old, as old as the Old Testament itself. Eliminate the threat before it threatens. Pharaoh didn't try to get rid of Moses as a child because of what he was. He was no challenge for the throne as a baby. No, Pharaoh feared what the child would become. The enemy knows what Boni carries. I always considered him to be the "tipping point kid." If he would dedicate himself to God and to good—certainly a large number of youth would follow his lead. Like Moses himself, Boni was the chosen one to lead his contemporaries out of the slavery of addiction and crime. But, since the enemy feared his tomorrow, he fought hard to discourage and disarm him at a young age. It's a tactic often used on our future leaders to this day. Take them out of the game early, even before birth, before the child becomes a man.

Boni is a man now. I am still coaching in the Town League. When my need for an assistant coach arose, I knew just who to recruit. Boni and I were together again, and he was so excited to become a positive role model. Helping, not harming had always been Boni's choice. Public perception kept him prisoner however and Boni struggled to find his way. It seemed there was a target on his back. Despite his earnest desire to be a good man, many seemed unwilling to give him the benefit of the doubt. Doubt brings discouragement and it took its toll on Boni. He only found acceptance in the underside of society and there he drifted.

The night Boni was arrested I am told there were a number of young men at the scene, but only he wore the handcuffs. He was taken out of the game—again. He calls me from the prison where he is locked away. We talk about the old days and that night of the big fight. We talk about the future and what he will do when he is released. He still smiles a bit when we talk, but just like his namesake, the beautiful face of Jesus has grown weary. I'm out here, waiting for his release...not just from prison—his true and final release, when God will wipe away all tears and call him by his true name. Yes, the beautiful face of Jesus. How I love that man.

> *Father God, be with all those who are locked in prison and yet look to you for their freedom. Grant them patience and strength and May we never forget them in our prayers. Amen*

Dropping Anchor: *Prison bars do not an instant captive make. Evil turns the key in the lock slowly over time.*

____

____

____

____

Through The Fog

"For now we see through a glass, darkly;
but then face to face: now I know in part;
but then shall I know even as also I am known."
1 Corinthians 13:12

When I was working in the radio broadcast media, travel was part of my job. We would pack up the portable studio and hit the road not unlike Charles Kuralt, broadcasting from various locations where our program was heard. It was a fine way to discover the beauty and diversity of our native land. As long as there was electricity and a phone line, we were on the air. One of our favorite areas to visit was Lancaster, Pennsylvania, home to WDAC radio and our friends Paul Hollinger and John Ebe. It was also the home of the Willow Valley Inn, featuring the finest oatmeal anywhere and vanilla buns that were simply legendary. The Amish were many in number in Lancaster as well, and we always enjoyed their cautious interaction with us.

As inviting as Lancaster was, it was a long way from home. Getting there by automobile was grueling and so we began to fly on our frequent visits. A small four seater airplane, owned by a friend was made available for our trips, and a pilot who worked out of Cape Cod was always willing to handle the aircraft controls for us.

One morning, before sunrise, we were to board the ready Cessna in Norwood, Massachusetts, then fly to Pennsylvania where a fundraiser banquet was being hosted at Willow Valley. As we drove to the airstrip we encountered a thick fog that hugged the ground like a blanket. It was certainly a growing concern as we crept along back roads toward the waiting plane. Visibility was zero in the predawn hours. As first light broke we boarded the airplane and took our seats. Scott, our pilot began running the checks on gauges and meters, while we nervously peered out the windows. Nothing could be seen before us or behind us, just thick grey fog. "It's a day for instrument flying," announced our pilot with confidence. We were not sure it was a day for flying at all. As we turned the plane and prepared for takeoff, we could barely make out the runway lights marking our path along the tarmac. As we took off, it was pure guesswork as to whether or not our wheels were still on terra firma, or in the air. As we gained altitude, we had no sense of speed or surroundings. It was akin to riding in a small car at 120 miles per hour with a grey blanket covering all of the windows. Scott took his eyes off the dials just long enough to say, "Can't see much of anything, right? Just wait another minute or two and you'll be amazed."

Sure enough, at about three thousand feet the aircraft flew out of the thick ground cover of fog and burst into sunshine and blue skies. Suddenly, we could see. We watched in wonder as the sun burned away the menacing fog and a bright and beautiful day emerged. As we flew over Pennsylvania a couple of hours later, we could see the patchwork of the Amish farms, so neat and orderly from our view on high. The sun had done its job. The fog had vanished.

I always remember that particular flight through the fog. Here's why. We are all living at breakneck speed, forward through the fog of life's uncertainty. We cannot see anything before us, so like our merry band of Lancaster bound travelers, we trust the Pilot who has his eye on the dials and meters. "Just wait," he tells us. And so we wait—anticipating that moment when we will burst forth from the grasp of the mist and see what was there all along—just beyond our vision. It's dramatic and beautiful as it stretches out into the distance. All below us appears neat and orderly from up on high. And, there is to be a feast tonight at the grand tables at the Inn. We are amazed. The Son has done His job.

Father God, help me remember that things are clear from your vantage point. I will trust your direction and guidance, always. Amen

Dropping Anchor: *Gone is the mist of uncertainty. There are blue skies ahead... forever.*

Snow Day

"And when these things begin to come to pass, then look up, and lift up your heads; for your redemption draweth nigh."
Luke 21:28

I currently have a large bowl of popcorn beside my computer. As I write this, the snow is piling up outside my door. It is a regular March Nor'easter, New England style. The forecast is calling for nearly two feet of snow before the storm heads out to sea. Inside, however, we are warm and dry - and well covered in the snack department.

I am working on a sermon outline for Palm Sunday. Holy week is coming soon on the calendar. As I study, I find myself trying to imagine the range of emotions that followed Jesus as he rode into Jerusalem some two thousand years ago. The crowd was surely excited. This was the moment that many had hoped for, ever since Jesus had fed the crowds with a little boy's lunch some months before. Many on that occasion had called for his coronation. He would be the one to break the yoke of Rome and re-establish a free Israel much as it was in the glory days of King David. And yet, since that miracle meal on the green hills of Galilee, Jesus had kept a low profile. "Smart," said old men in taverns and on street corners. "He laid low in the weeds, but now he has momentum... now is the time!" You could see the hope on their faces. You could hear it in their voices as they called, "Hosanna!" They waved their palm branches as though they were regal banners. Afterward, they watched the temple intently, looking for any signs of a takeover. Jesus was surely going to make his move.

Some in the crowd were jealous of his popularity with the people. These were the religious leaders, and they had murder in their hearts. They were plotting to do away with Jesus and this triumphal entry into the ancient city was certain to complicate matters. They were annoyed but determined. Then, there were the city folk; local yokels. They were overwhelmingly happy. People like Zebedee, who had two sons follow the Rabbi Jesus, leaving their family fishing business some three years before. Old Zeb was pleased… perhaps now his boys would gain some prominence in the power structure. Lazarus was there (who was no longer dead) and old Blind Bartimaeus, (who was no longer blind) and their allegiance to Jesus was evident as they danced and sang their way through the gate. There were prostitutes and tax collectors, former lepers and children… swarming children, alive with giddy wonder and heartfelt joy.

Just now, I dropped a piece of my popcorn. My Cocker Spaniel heard it fall to the floor, unfolded himself from his spot on the easy chair (which he frequently occupies) and sauntered over to pick up the fallen morsel. He crunched it quickly and then sat at my feet and stared at the floor. I knew what he was thinking. "Maybe there'll be more…" I found it amusing that he watched the floor, head down, and as if waiting for popcorn to magically appear. He sat, poised and ready. I tossed another piece to him and he gobbled it down - his eyes never leaving floor level. "Just like those first century followers of Jesus," I considered, "Watching ground level activity and forgetting that the real action is up on high."

We still do this kind of thing. We watch Washington and Tokyo, Moscow and Baghdad. But the real action is going to drop from on high. Luke wrote down what Jesus told us… "Look up. Your redemption is coming soon." Again, I look out my frosty window, but this time I do not look at the accumulation of snow on the ground. Instead, I look up at the white crystal flakes coming down from on high. Perfect. Now, if these clouds would just part…

Father God, thank you for your forgiveness that makes my sin as white as snow. May I be as forgiving to others as you have been to me. Amen

Dropping Anchor: *Look up. Always up.*

___

___

___

___

Who Is We

*"Now it came to pass, as they went,
that He entered into a certain village
and a certain woman named Martha
received Him into her house."*
Luke 10:38

I was just sitting down to work on this story, when Amanda asked me to go down cellar and put the wet clothes in the dryer. Now, our cellar is an old New England basement with cobwebs hanging from the beams and dingy lighting from a solitary bulb in the farthest corner. The stairs are rickety and steep. Suffice it to say, laundry duty is an effort at our home. Add a little Parkinson's into the mix and you "up the ante" for real adventure. Nonetheless, as I journeyed to the bowels of the building, I found true happiness in knowing I could assist my wife with the laundry. After completing my task, I came back upstairs and sat down again to write, but Amanda's call from the kitchen told me I was needed to reach the crock pot for her. It is stored in the high cabinet above the stove—beyond her reach. Up again! Perhaps I am growing "up" some. Not because I am tall enough to reach the crock pot—but because it was a pleasure to serve without complaining.

You probably know the story from Luke chapter ten in the Bible. A woman named Martha opened her home to Jesus—a good move by any standard. But then she filled that same home with complaining. It seems her sister was not helping to get dinner on the table. Back in those days, getting a meal together was not a simple feat. Today we can pop open the fridge and grab a ready to heat microwave meal. Poor Martha had to catch chickens, milk cows and build a fire. The Scripture says she was quite distracted by the details. Rickety stairs, dim lighting and cobwebs… I know, Martha. I know...

Jesus is patient with us. He lovingly told Martha to chill. And she did… Later, in John chapter twelve we read of a banquet given to honor Jesus. Three words stand out in that story. "And Martha served." Months before we heard "and Martha complained." This time she simply served. As it was a banquet, there was certainly a lot of preparation to be done. "I know, Martha." No time to sit down when there are crock pots in high cabinets that need a long reach. Parkinson's Shmarkinson's...

Serving is the goal we are shooting for. I have met many people over the years who want to do something significant in the Kingdom. What they really mean is that they want to get out in front where everyone will see them. Meanwhile, Jesus is looking for humility and hard work.

The story is told of a time many years ago, when a world renowned musician came to Tremont Temple in Boston to give a recital on the church's magnificent pipe organ. He thrilled the audience with flourishes of Beethoven, Handel and Mozart. After an hour of musical masterpieces, intermission was announced. These were the days before electricity. The grand organ was powered by pumping air through the giant valves, thus creating the beautiful sounds that emerged from the pipes. The maestro had offered to pay a young boy a nickel if he would pump the needed air supply through the bellows, hidden behind a heavy curtain. At the break in the program, the lad peeked out from behind the drapery and addressed the mighty musician. "Weren't we great?" he chimed. "Who is 'we?'" came the gruff response from the prideful organist.

As the second half of the concert began, the audience was waiting in hushed silence. The silence continued however as the playing began. The organist pressed the keys, but no sound emerged. A second time he raised his hands and struck the first marvelous chord—again nothing happened. A third try brought the same result. No sound whatsoever.

Just then, from behind the curtain, a tiny voice was heard to say, "Now, who is we?"

Jesus doesn't need us out in front of anything. The top spot is His and He deserves it. But, Christ has many tasks that require plenty of effort and little thanks. If you want to be noticed by men, you've got a tough road ahead. If you want to get God's attention… serve lunch. Fetch the laundry. Catch a chicken. Wait! Amanda just called for me again. You turn the page while I see what I can do to help her. Better yet, hop up off your seat and put the laundry in the dryer. I'll meet you back here in five minutes. "And Martha served."

Father God, never should we boast or be prideful. We need others to help us - sometimes the ones we notice least, matter most. May we remember to be thankful. Amen

Dropping Anchor: *Jesus doesn't need us out in front. That's His spot.*

____

____

____

____

Home Security

"...and behold a ladder set up on the earth,
and the top of it reached to heaven:
and behold the angels of God ascending and descending on it"
Genesis 28:12

It was a hectic weekend. Murphy's Law seemed to be in full sway as Amanda and I worked our way through a stretch of shopping runs for groceries, school clothes, and a pet fish. (We had told Prudence that she could get one.) By mid-afternoon, I had started feeling poorly. My old friend, Mr. Parkinson's was acting up and I felt weighted, fatigued and nauseous. I looked over at my wife and she looked pale. "Honey, I feel awful," she said. Never one to complain, Amanda rarely spoke about health issues. I knew that if she considered it worthy of mention, she, no doubt, was feeling very ill. As if on cue, the two youngest Deckers began to cry. For just a moment, both Amanda and I felt very overwhelmed. It was an unusual feeling for both of us.

"This is spiritual," said my wife, and instantly I knew she was correct. There was but one course of defense, and so quickly, we huddled in the kitchen and prayed. I asked Father God to dispatch angels to stand guard over our home. Within minutes, Rory and True were both peaceful and playful and our physical calamity had passed. Feeling so much better, and more than a little relieved, we decided to take an evening drive to watch the sun set over historic New Bedford harbor. Summoning Prudence, who had spent the afternoon with our next door neighbors, we were climbing into the family vehicle as she came running across our backyard. "I just saw an angel," Prudence said matter-of-factly as she buckled her seat belt. "Really, what did it look like?" I asked, looking in my rear view mirror. Prudence went on to describe a beautiful creature, with wings made of "like feathers, but not..." and a purple-bluish glow around its face. She went on to report that she heard the angel say "God has done good things for you; watch, for He will do more."

A half hour later, we were looking in admiration and awe as the sun set over the sea wall and fishing boats in the cove. The sky was awash with colors that only heaven owns. We celebrated with an ice cream cone and slowly made the drive home. After putting the children to bed, Amanda and I sat down in the living room. "Incredible..." we breathed, "God truly cares for our family." A terrible afternoon had been dissolved and dispatched by a lovely evening.

The next day was Sunday. While I was carrying some Sunday school supplies out to our SUV, True lugged his little three-wheeled tricycle out onto the deck. I was leaning in the back of the car and did not know that True had decided to follow me, and that he had chosen the tricycle as his method of transportation. I turned toward the house just in time to see him push the front wheel over the top step. "OH! NO" I cried as he began to tumble down the high steps. I started to run toward the unfolding disaster as True pitched over the handlebars and landed face first on the concrete step at the bottom of the set of stairs. I gathered up my son, expecting to find broken bones, a gash, a scrape—but there was nothing. There was not a mark on him. True didn't even cry. I had never seen one of my children take such a violent fall, and here I was holding him, without a scratch.

Driving to church thirty minutes later, a thought came to me. "Prudence," I asked my daughter seated behind my driver's seat. "Yes, dad?" she replied. "When you saw that angel yesterday, where was he standing?" Her answer sent a shiver through my frame... 'He was standing by the deck, right at the bottom of the stairs."

Indeed, God has done great things and we daily watch for more. I love heaven and what it brings to earth.

Father God, you are the captain of angel armies. I thank you for their attentive care for your children of earth. Amen

Dropping Anchor: *Heaven visits earth every day.*

____

____

____

____

Baseball And The Beast

"... therefore will the Lord wait,
that He may be gracious unto you..."
Isaiah 30:18

It was the first time that God ever spoke to me. I recall where I was and what I was doing... I was ten years of age. That would make the year 1967. All that summer, New England was baseball-crazy. The Boston Red Sox were jockeying for first place, and fan loyalty was at a fever pitch. Everything was baseball... from the actual rush for the American League pennant, to the television commercials featuring the local nine. Do you remember "Big Yaz Bread?" It was regular sandwich fare, but its secret formula was supposed to provide all the nutrients we would ever need to become like Big Yaz himself, Captain Carl Yastrzemski. Loaves flew off the grocery store shelves faster than you could say "Tony Conigliaro."

The Sox were genuine heroes to my way of thinking. I spent hours out behind my house "hitting rocks," and playing imaginary ball games in my head. Rico Petrocelli, Jim Lonborg, Reggie Smith all held hallowed space in my young heart. It was somewhat of a surprise then, that one rainy Saturday; I curled up on the sofa in order to watch a baseball movie about a rival team. The Pride of the Yankees, or the Lou Gehrig story was being broadcast, probably in an effort to capture the baseball audience on a stormy day when the Sox were idle.

I was riveted. As you know, "Sweet Lou" was the Iron Horse of baseball. He never missed a game at first base for the Yankees that is until he contracted ALS, the deadly disease that claimed his life at the age of thirty five. In the film, there is a scene where Lou's neurological symptoms begin to flare up. He struggled to tie his necktie. I had a tear in my eye and I watched this great athlete grow weaker and weaker. That is when I heard God's voice. It was not audible to my physical ears - but my spirit caught every word. "You will struggle like that one day..." A simple phrase - but it never left me. I was reasonably sure that ALS or "Lou Gehrig's disease" was coming in my future.

Loren Paul Decker

I was diagnosed with Parkinson's disease in 2009… The doctors told me that Parkinson's was not a beast, but an "animal we know well." ALS is a beast. I feel fortunate to have one and not the other. I receive great comfort in knowing that my Father whispered a caution into my spirit while I was young. I am grateful that He saw my disease first and allowed it. He knows beginning and end. He knew before there was time. As one who writes stories, I am captivated by the way He is writing mine. I smile now, whenever my lovely wife, Amanda, ties my necktie for me. I know I am much closer to the last chapter of my life than I was in 1967, but I have learned to trust the Author. He has gone before me to the future and He loves me. The next pages hold no beasts… not even the final page. In the words of Lou Gehrig, I consider myself the 'luckiest man on the face of the earth."

On the very last page of the volume of my life story, I want only One Name in the list of credits. The End will be the Beginning.

> *Father God, may I accept whatever you choose to allow in my life. I know if it comes to me - it has passed through nail scarred hands. Those hands are ultimately healing and not harmful. Amen*

Dropping Anchor: *Parkinson's is not a beast - it is an animal we know well.*

A Bad Break

*"And make straight paths for your feet,
lest that which is lame be turned out of the way;
but let it rather be healed"*
Hebrews 12:13

It felt like I broke my ankle. It hurt—a lot. I was just a young teenager at the time, but I knew that the pain was crippling. It happened on a Monday night, the much anticipated night of the week when the Boy's Club met at our church. Nearly twenty lads, all about my age, got together for fun and games along with a Bible lesson. My dad, the pastor, ran the group and I'm certain he loved Monday nights as much as we did. On this particular night, we were playing outdoors in the crisp fall air. The sun had set and the conditions were just right for one of our favorite games. We called it "Sardines" and the object was simple. Find the person who was hiding and when found, hide along with them. We would squish like sardines in a can, trying not to give away the sought for location by excess giggling. The last boy to discover the packed hideout would be forced to go inside and read the Bible lesson for the duration of the game. In retrospect, making Bible study a punishment was not our wisest move.

On this night, the game of "Sardines" was going along swimmingly, and everyone was having fun when I happened to step into a sink hole in the gravel lot behind the church. I felt my ankle give way and the audible snap of my bone breaking was disconcerting to say the least. I went down in a heap and hollered for a time out. "Somebody get my dad!" I called. He was quickly summoned, but his arrival brought little comfort. "Can you stand up?" he asked. I managed to get to an upright position. "Let's walk it off," he said. "Walk it off??" I didn't think it was possible. However, with a friend on each arm, supporting my weight, I hobbled back to the church.

After the night was over and the last club member had gone home, I sat in the kitchen of my home and took off my shoes and socks. My mom gave a low whistle as she and my dad assessed my injury. My ankle had a golf ball sized egg of greenish hue protruding from the joint. "I think I broke my ankle," I said to my mom. "Let's try to walk it off and see if things improve," my dad stated, matter-of-factly. This cavalier attitude was something my father must have picked up as a young man. If one us scraped a knee or an elbow, or got hit by a pitch in a Little League game, his response was always the same, "Rub some dirt in it. It's good, clean dirt. Now, walk it off." Well, try as I might, I could not seem to walk this injury off.

I eventually hobbled in to the Emergency Room at the local hospital and winced my way through a series of X-Rays that were taken. "Just a bad sprain," the doctor announced.

Over the next few years, I struggled with a weak ankle. I attempted to walk it off when I stepped on a sneaker while going for a rebound in basketball. I walked after turning my weakened ankle in a game of beach volleyball. I rolled it over on uneven sidewalks and any number of other missteps, each time hobbling and limping in an effort to "Walk it off..."

Then in the summer of my 18th year, I snapped it good. I heard the crack of the bone breaking as I fell to the gym floor in shock and in pain. The friends that were playing indoor soccer with me gathered around in concern. I was transported to the local hospital, where a round of x-rays was ordered. Painfully, I obliged. An hour or so later, I was waiting for the doctor to return with the results. He came in with x-ray films in hand and proceeded to clip them onto the light bay for review. "You broke it," said the doctor as he pointed to the crack in my bone. Then he paused and looked intently at me, then back at the x-ray. "This can't be you," he stated, taking a closer look at me, and then looking back at the dark film. "Your name is here on the file, but this foot is too small." I looked down at my size 12's and could see the negative image on the film was indeed, a picture of a much smaller foot than mine. After digging around a bit, the good doctor produced a second x-ray with my name clearly written on it—and it was my foot, size 12. A closer look at the first film showed a date of five years before!

It was the x-ray from my Boy's Club days. They had misread (or just missed) the fracture that night, calling it a bad sprain instead. I had been unaware of the break, that is, until a second visit five years later.

Many of us catch a bad break in our early years. Alcoholic parents, an abusive uncle, mistreatment from a bully; there are so many things that can hamper our walk through life. We try to "walk off" the pain, but our wounded spirit just cannot support the weight. As a result, we end up with a break in the center of our existence that remains flimsy and weak. We did not know we were broken. We just hurt a lot. A broken bone is painful, but a wounded spirit hurts even more. It also takes longer to heal. Your first step toward healing however is a journey back to where the pain began. You may have tried to "walk off" a pain that needed to be set and supported, and if you go back and take another look, you may find something that you missed before. That "something" may be all you need to face the problem properly. Once you know that, the healing can truly begin.

In this incident of my broken bone—the original break was actual—the X-ray showed it. But it was mishandled and hidden away for years. There was no help for me until it was brought to light. You may need to go back in your life file and bring an old pain to the light again. How? Tell someone. Share your weak spot. Make sure that "someone" can read an X-ray properly. You won't heal on your own. But the One who made your frame will bring the healing. He knows not to bear weight on an injury while broken. He has someone close by who will share your pain, support you, and help you heal.

Father God, for those today in physical pain or distress - we offer this prayer. Comfort them with your love. Amen

Dropping Anchor: *The Great Physician has an office - We call it Church.*

____

____

____

____

Chevy Heaven

"According to the commandment of the Lord they were numbered by the hand of Moses, every one according to his service, and according to his burden..."
Numbers 4:49

In 1982, Chevrolet introduced the new design of their popular sports car, the Camaro. It was sleek and speedy and since I, in my mid-twenties, was at a sleek and speedy phase of my life, I knew that I had to have one. My dad, living in Brattleboro, Vermont, knew a man who owned a Chevy dealership further north in St. Johnsbury and according to the local buzz, he had a real beauty sitting on his lot. Charcoal metallic in color, gold rims and a tinted T-roof made this brand new Camaro Berlinetta seem like something right out of a Hollywood movie. I test drove it and a few hours later drove it home, on the edge of disbelief that this vehicle was actually mine. Driving home down I-91 South, I turned up the eight speaker stereo system and cruised along, the speedometer hovering just over the posted limit. I was in Chevy heaven.

Once back in Massachusetts, I drove that Camaro everywhere. I picked up friends and took them to the cinema or the mall. We cruised the 'strip' along Nantasket Beach on Saturday nights and showed up late for church on Sunday mornings, making sure to pull into the parking lot with windows open and the radio up loud. The car made a statement and sitting behind the wheel was one of the most incredible feelings I had ever experienced. That is, until winter came.

During the cold weather months, New England roadways become challenging. Hardy souls who live in the region know all about snow tires, chains and four wheel drive. A T-roof is of little use when the snow begins to fly. It was apparent that the "even weight distribution" on my sports car made gripping icy pavement a "free for all." Front tires? Rear? Traction was anybody's guess. Stop signs were mere suggestions as the Chevrolet Limited Edition reached the unwavering limitations of science and stayed in motion despite my valiant effort to apply the brakes.

When the winter snow accumulated, my neighbor Don became an oft-utilized partner for pushing my sporty vehicle. He would get low on the bumper of the Camaro while I spun the tires on the graded hill that led to my driveway. It became customary that whenever he would hear my tires singing in the snow as I was attempting to navigate toward a parking spot, out the door he would come, throwing on his coat and pulling on his galoshes. "Not again!" he would exclaim. "We ought to put a glass case around this vehicle. It's beautiful to look at, but it's useless in foul weather."

Oh, it was a speedy vehicle on the open road. The first weekend that I had the car, I drove to my grandparent's home outside of Boston. Heading home after dinner, I opened up the throttle a little bit and marveled at how the Camaro handled cornering on the back roads. Lost in the bliss of the moment, I pushed the accelerator too hard and flew past a police car parked in a hidden cutout beside the road. He had his radar gun pointed at my sleek sports car as I zoomed past his speed trap. I was snagged—caught speeding I was certain. My speedometer had been hovering close to double the posted speed limit as I zoomed by the officer. I glanced in my rearview mirror, expecting blue lights behind me, but there were none. A mile and minute later—still nothing. "He can't be letting me go, can he?" I asked myself. Another minute passed. I was just about to enter the on-ramp for the highway when the blue lights and siren came up behind me.

I promptly pulled over and rolled my window down. "I thought you were letting me go!" I said as he asked for my license and registration. "I kept looking for you, but I didn't see you for the longest time," I said. "Do you want to know what took me so long?" he asked. "Sure," I offered. "Well, my radar clocked you at just over seventy miles per hour and I thought that it couldn't be correct; my radar gun must be broken. So, I stayed behind to check the next three cars and they each passed by at the proper speed limit, so I said 'That's it! I'm going to get him!'" We couldn't help but share a laugh as he handed me a written warning. "Nice car..." he said as he headed back to his cruiser.

Many of us are overly concerned with appearances. Not unlike my shiny sports car, we look as though we are cruising along life's road in style. But our trials come like winter storms and if we don't have the right equipment—we will surely slip. A friendly neighbor may offer help when we get stuck, but without a true changeover to a proper mode of transportation, we are doomed to slide off the path again and again. Change your wheels for something much more practical. Now, the pace at which the Lord rolls is sometimes maddeningly slow, but it is also steady and sure. He isn't one for flash and flare, but He will never wind up in a ditch, nor will He slide helplessly past a warning sign. With His Spirit as the guide the road becomes manageable no matter what conditions you may have to weather. I recommend a test drive. You won't regret it. Oh! Your new vehicle will come equipped with GPS (God's Plan of Salvation) which will always get you up the hills and safely home.

Father God, man's machines - no matter how sleek, are no comparison to the universe that you designed. I love the complexity of creation. Your heaven is far beyond my ability to imagine. I long to see it. Amen

Dropping Anchor: *When His Spirit is the guide the road becomes manageable.*

____

____

____

____

Of Scars And Such

"...for I bear in my body the marks of the Lord Jesus."
Galatians 6:17

When I was in my early twenties I was hit by a car. A Dodge sedan traveling at about 40mph motored into the same stretch of pavement that I had chosen for an attempt to cross Route 9 east-bound on foot. It was immediately clear that the road was not big enough for the both of us. Now, I am a pretty big guy. (I consider myself to be "husky.") But with one ton of metal, grease and rubber coming along at such a good clip—I was not going to get the better of that collision. The force of the impact knocked me out of my shoes and sent me tumbling down the highway. A gash in my head and a severely broken leg were my takeaways from the encounter.

Today, some thirty years later, I still have a significant scar on my leg. Interestingly, the remnant of that old wound is not there as a result of the impact of the Dodge. No, the scar represents the work that was done by medical professionals in an effort to save my damaged limb. Let me explain...

The brute force of the car hitting my left leg caused trauma to occur underneath my skin. Our leg muscles are held in place by fascia—a sheath of sorts that wraps around the muscle. While muscles will swell significantly when injured—the fascia will only stretch so far. When they reach their limit, they act like a tourniquet and squeeze off the flow of blood to the injured area. Unless corrected quickly, gangrene can occur. That is exactly what happened in my situation. I nearly had to undergo an amputation due to excessive swelling and the resultant choking off of the blood supply to the injured area. Avoiding that radical surgery involved a small miracle of sorts.

The doctor who worked on me in the emergency room experienced a late night due to my injury. He had been wrapping up his shift when I was wheeled into the ER. After spending the extra hours tending to my wounds, he grabbed a few hours of sleep on the sofa in the doctor's lounge area. He was responsible to be back on duty at seven the following morning. He awoke at daybreak and proceeded to put in another long shift, involving yet another emergency operation. Coming out of the medical center at about eleven pm, he was climbing into his vehicle when his pager lit up. On the orthopedics wing where I was hospitalized, the eleven to seven shift was coming on duty and they were in the middle of "rounds." A belligerent young man on the ward was giving his nurse a run for her money. This particular floor was the only wing of the hospital that was still using mercury thermometers. The rest of the hospital had transitioned over to digital thermometers but our rooms were not yet in that mix. Taking the patient's "vitals" is the ordered routine at the beginning of each shift. While taking the temperature of this particular young man, he became combative with the nurse and bit down hard on the glass instrument, causing the mercury within to flow into his mouth. Mercury is toxic and the hospital policy stated that whenever it is accidentally ingested, the patient must be seen by a physician. "Who is his primary?" asked the head nurse. After consulting the chart, it was noted that he had the same physician as I. "He is home now, I am sure. He was in the ER early this morning," said one of the registered nurses. "Try paging him anyway," said another.

Thus it was that my doctor climbed out of his Jeep and re-entered the hospital, dog tired but dutiful. After checking out the mercury in the mouth situation he considered, "I haven't looked in on Loren yet today. While I am up here I may as well see how he is doing." He entered my room, saw the dangerous swelling occurring and within forty five minutes I was in emergency surgery. Had I gone another hour, amputation of my foot would have resulted. Had I gone through the night with the swelling unchecked—my leg would've been lost. Because a young man got uppity and bit his thermometer I have two legs to stand on here and now. They are banged up and knobby but they are both there. The deep trauma within was not able to be seen—but the corrective measures taken in an emergency surgical procedure, are visible on my outward skin to this day...

Many of us are wounded deeply—inside where things can be hidden from sight. But, our Great Physician won't bypass our hurt. He sets about mending the damage—and often this process is clearly visible. So when we see someone going through a rough time, stop and consider; they may be under the scalpel of the Almighty—being healed, not harmed.

Father God, each scar is a testimony of your faithfulness. I have lived through some frightening times and have the marks to show for it. Jesus, your scars are the remnants of love - expressed on a cross. I know they harmed you - but they now bring healing to us. We are grateful. Amen

Dropping Anchor: *The healing scalpel still leaves a scar.*

Sparky

"As the sparks fly upward..."
Job 5:7

We started calling her "Sparky" after the fire. One fine spring day, my daughter, Evangeline accidently burned our storage shed to the ground. It was quite an afternoon of terror for her and her friends, but looking back, we can be very thankful that all we lost were some memories. Let me start at the beginning.

Amanda and I had taken little Prudence for a follow up visit to Children's Hospital in Boston. She is routinely checked there for her progress in the repair of her cleft palate and lip. It was a "clinic day," an all-day event where she is seen by doctors and speech therapists, dentists and a host of other specialists. Evangeline had just graduated from High School and was watching the house for the day. She asked if she could have a few friends over and as they were responsible young adults, it was no problem for us—some sixty miles away. The evening before, most of the same young people had been sitting around our fire pit, guitars strumming and voices rising in song. Sometime around noon, the gang decided to prepare the fire pit for another night of "S'mores" and songs. Evangeline took the ashes from the previous night and carted them over to the clear space behind the storage shed. There she dumped the load. You can see what's coming next, can't you...

A phone call rang in on my cell phone. It was Evangeline. "Dad, the shed is on fire!" She sounded frantic. "Call the fire department and then call Doug," I responded. Doug lives nearby and is a trusted family friend. Within minutes, both fire engine and Jeep were on their way to the scene.

Meanwhile, Evangeline ran to the kitchen for water. She grabbed a mixing bowl and filled it. She ran back for the shed, which was now fully engulfed in flames, sloshing water everywhere as she ran. By the time she got to the smoking shack there was not much water to toss on the flames. She hurried in a panic back for the house and hid under the stairs, not wanting to watch the destruction out in out yard. She later told us that one of her friends had come in our house looking for her and when the door opened; my terrified daughter could hear the whooshing sound of the fire. "Dad," she later explained. "I didn't know fire was so loud! I thought the whole woods were burning from the sound of the roar!"

The fire department soon arrived at the scene, with Doug close on their heels. The firefighters got busy putting out the flames, while my friend comforted my daughter. She felt terrible. "I didn't think the coals were still burning..." she lamented.

Over the next few days we picked through the ruins of our storage shed. Many of my mother's things were stored there, now lost forever to the flames, the smoke, and the soaking water from the fire hoses. We spread out her family artifacts on the lawn. I was particularly looking for an autographed baseball that I had stored away at my mom's apartment for safe keeping. It was signed by Roger Clemens and I had lost track of it when my mother passed away. It was eventually going to belong to my oldest son, Ash, but now I feared it was gone.

Toward evening, I kicked at a box that was barely visible under a pile of charred and soggy kitchen items. To my amazement a ceramic chicken tumbled out followed by a baseball... the baseball, signed by the former Red Sox ace himself. My mother had neatly packed it away when she had to move to assisted living. In her growing dementia she had reasoned that a decorative hen and autographed baseball should be packed away together. It was perfect. They were perfect—untouched by the fire.

It reminded me of the story of the farmer whose barn burned to the ground one night. The following morning he was picking through the sad remains and he nudged a badly burned carcass of one of his hens. To his surprise—out from under the dead bird's wings, four baby chicks scampered into the farmer's open hands. Moms are amazing. I had a great one and my daughter, "Sparky" is destined to be another. She's been tucked under some strong wings over the years.

Ash now has his baseball, Prudence has a lovely smile and all is well at my house. In the end, we lost no memories; we just replaced them with new ones.

Father God, we cannot keep earthly possessions beyond our lifetime. Sometimes they are even lost along life's journey. Only one possession will we carry into heaven. We have your love, and it is all we will need. Amen

Dropping Anchor: *It only takes a spark to set a fire out of control.*

____
____
____
____

Northern Lights - Southern Exposure

Knowest thou the ordinances of heaven?
Job 38:33

Sometimes things don't go as planned. On those occasions when plans go a bit awry, they can offer us humor, if not success.

It was many years ago. I was in my junior year of college. My roommates and I were not the best academic students that Gordon College on the North Shore of Massachusetts, could boast of, but we knew how to have a good time. Or so it seemed...

It was autumn and the campus trees were a beautiful blend of fiery fall colors, mixed with the deep green of the majestic firs that stood tall on the grounds. One memorable week that first semester, the sky above matched the beauty below as for several evenings the Northern Lights appeared above us, drawing much of the student body out onto the "quad" and the adjacent soccer field. There they stood in wonder night after night as the blue green colors of the Aurora Borealis danced in the northern, night skies.

If I failed to mention it, I should do so now... this was the late 1970's. Something called "streaking" was popular on college campuses across the country. This activity involved running through a public place in the nude. I'm not sure how it ever caught on - but two of my roommates decided that this would be an opportune time to try it. And, so - they devised The Plan.

Outside the on-campus apartment building where we lived, there was a shed. This shed was the storage location for our discarded trash. Filled with garbage cans, students in the building had a weekly routine of emptying waste baskets into trash bags and then taking them down to the shed where they were collected on Saturdays. This shed was also selected to serve as the launching pad for my streaking friends who planned to burst out on cue and head, lickety split for the boy's dorm on the far side of the quad. My job was to stand guard at the shed door while my roomies put on, or rather took off, their uniforms for the big event. Thus prepared, into the shed they went. I took my position and whispered a few "Are you ready?" queries in their direction. "Just about," they shot back. "We are getting psyched up for a minute!"

It was then that I saw her. A shy coed who rarely ventured out of her apartment came down the stairs, trash bag in hand and headed for the shed. I quickly considered the mostly bare human contents of the shed and thought to warn them of the young lady who was soon to arrive on the scene. But, I thought better of it and instead, stood back and watched the drama unfold. That it did. The unsuspecting female student opened the door and met two unsuspecting male students who were just about to exit the shed and enter into Gordon College lore. The trash bag hit the ground as the young woman stood, blinking her eyes in disbelief. The lads stood blinking back in their birthday suits. For a moment, no one moved. Then, with speed beyond what my streaking friends could only envy, the trash dropper ran back up the stairs and into the safety of her apartment.

I can only imagine how this story has been told in her circle of family and friends over the ensuing years. As for my friends, they called off the dash across campus and quickly pulled on their blue jeans. Their winning streak ended at one.

We never really saw her again by the way. I kept an eye out for her, but I think she may have transferred to another school. I can't say as I blame her. And I must admit that there is no real applicable lesson to be learned from this story. It is just fun to tell. Sometimes we need to chuckle at ourselves. Recently, a friend of mine happened to say, "I can't remember the last time I saw the Northern Lights." "I can..." I replied. And so, I told the story again.

Father God, thank you for saving me - with all my flaws and fears. You love me despite the crazy things I have done, and you have probably kept me from some that I did not recognize as trouble at the time. You are wise. I am not. You are all knowing. I am not. You are eternal - and thanks to you, so am I. By the way, the Northern Lights are of phenomenal beauty. Amen

Dropping Anchor: *Avoid action in a crowd that would prove embarrassing before just one.*

____

____

____

____

On Board

"...'We will go with our young and with our old
with our sons and with our daughters,
with our flocks and with our herds will we go;
for we must hold a feast unto the Lord."
Exodus 10:9

Thanksgiving - It was almost four hundred years ago that the early settlers from England crossed the ocean and landed in Plymouth. They came on the Mayflower, a tiny ship packed from stem to stern with men, women, children (and a few animals.) There were more than one hundred souls, sailing for months in a space no bigger than a modern one bedroom apartment. They were determined folk, indeed they must have been. They endured sea sickness, fear, loneliness and a general lack of privacy. When they arrived in this new world of America, there were no relatives waiting—no welcoming committee or chamber of commerce. In fact, when they stepped ashore, the hardest part was just beginning. They had to carve a life for themselves out of the rugged and rocky New England landscape. Retreat was no option. So, despite losing nearly half of their number to the harsh elements during that first winter in the new land, they pressed onward with strength, courage and God-given determination.

About fifteen years ago, I launched an idea that became an annual tradition for our youth group at the church where I pastor. I asked the good people at Plymouth Plantation if we could hold a Thanksgiving Eve service aboard the Mayflower II, the exact replica of the original ship that reached the frigid New England coastline in 1620. The channels were graciously cleared and an appreciative group of youth from our church boarded ship at nightfall. We were about thirty in number. As we went below decks, we stooped and shuffled into the cramped quarters. The creaking of the masts and the slapping of the waves were our only music as we sat in awe of our surroundings. We were in the place where Thanksgiving began.

The chilly night air came rushing down the open stairway from up on the main deck as it started to snow. We huddled closer together and tried to ward off the cold ocean breeze. The gusts picked up, pouring through the ports. We served communion. The temperature dropped to below freezing and we found ourselves chilled to the bone. We marveled at the strength of those ancestors aboard the first Mayflower, and wondered how they withstood the elements. We then opened the first law of the New Land—the Bible—and read together. Then as the night settled in around us, we read aloud these words from the Mayflower Compact penned by the first Pilgrims:

"Having undertaken for the Glory of God and advancement of the Christian Faith and Honour of our King and Country, a Voyage to plant the First Colony in the Northern Parts of Virginia, do by these presents solemnly and mutually in the presence of God and one of another, Covenant and Combine ourselves together in a Civil Body Politic, for our better ordering and preservation and furtherance of the ends aforesaid; and by virtue hereof to enact, constitute and frame such just and equal Laws, Ordinances, Acts, Constitutions and Offices from time to time, as shall be thought most meet and convenient for the general good of the Colony, unto which we promise all due submission and obedience."

The reading of those ancient words enables one to realize these adventurers had indeed left everything behind and were looking only forward, despite the hardships and dangers. They were "all in." No looking back longingly at the comforts of the old world. Clearly—they were together… bound by a purpose.

Today, the ship sails on, no, not the Mayflower. It is rather, the unseen ship that steers through the centuries. It carried the first settlers and carries us—their descendants. It is the ship of Faith and it is headed for a New World. The journey is hard, but the hand of the Almighty is making us strong enough to endure. Blow chilly wind! We will open our mainsail fully and bounce across the waves of open sea before us. We too, are together—bound by purpose.

When we all finally step on shore, we will look in awe at the place prepared for us. Then the hardship will be forever behind us… Press on, Pilgrim—I can see land from here. A Promised Land lies dead ahead. We will enter its gate with thanksgiving, a place carved out of Glory by the master hand of The Carpenter.

Father God, You have been faithful through the centuries and a blessing to every generation. I'm thankful for your constant love. Amen

Dropping Anchor: *The Promised Land awaits and the report of the pilgrims is good.*

Conner Pond

"A good man out of the good treasure of his heart bringeth forth that which is good..."
Luke 6:45

He was "Uncle John" to me. He was no blood relation, but his wife and my mother were dear friends, so we saw each other quite often. John Moore was a gentle man. His rich, deep voice was as soothing as a storybook at bedtime. In fact, it was his voice that I knew best.

Uncle John was an outdoorsman. He had a cabin on a lake in the heart of the mountains of New Hampshire. Fishing and canoe trips were the way of life on Conner Pond. Uncle John also had four daughters. I reckon they preferred fashion to fishing. So, my "Uncle" took an interest in my young life. He taught me a thing or two about life in the woods and on the water.

But, his voice... that was indeed what I knew best. On my 10th birthday, my parents got me a cassette recorder. It was a standard issue recorder and player with a condenser microphone built in. Immediately, I loaded one of the blank cassette tapes into the machine and quickly filled up the 15 minutes of side one with a description of my birthday and the amazing tape recorder that I now owned. A week or so later, we were due for a visit to see Uncle John and his family in their year 'round home in the suburbs of Boston. I brought along my new electronic sidekick to document the journey.

Uncle John had a cassette recorder as well. It was part of a stereo system from Sears that featured a record player and an 8 track function, and the cassette deck, complete with auto reverse. I marveled at the smooth operating cassette tray that glided noiselessly open and closed with the push of a button. My portable player had an eject lever that clickety-clacked the cassette out of the machine. Uncle John dropped my c30 tape (15 minutes per side) into his state of the art system and soon my description of my 10th birthday was filling the Moore living room from the wood grained, cabinet speakers. Amazingly, Uncle John found my tape to be interesting.

A few weeks later, I received a package in the US Mail. It was a c30 cassette tape in a plastic case. The label read, "News from Conner Pond," and it contained a wonderful audio visit to that beloved New Hampshire retreat. That initial mailing began several years of cassette exchanges between Uncle John and me. I would routinely run to the mailbox to see if the postman had left any small box wrapped in brown paper, with my name on the address line. On those days when the cassettes arrived, I would run to my room and spend some time alone, listening to my Uncle's voice. He would always include questions for me to answer in my return tape.

One summer, my family piled into our station wagon and we headed north… destination, Conner Pond. We had been invited in audio fashion via cassette and on the long trip up, I repeated the recorded invitation that featured Uncle John's description of the route and what to expect upon arrival. When we did arrive, we discovered things were even better than we had imagined. We slept in hammocks and paddled the length of the lake in sturdy canoes. We fished and swam. The days hung lazily, like so many lifejackets, spread out on the tree branches, drying in the warm sun. Everything seemed just right at the camp. Behind all of the adventure was the steady voice of Uncle John. He was a most generous host. We all felt at home.

These days, I listen to another voice. It comes to me from Scripture and the ever-present Holy Spirit. It arrives in my listening heart and brings me the Good News that I have been invited to a beautiful northern camp on a crystal lake. The voice that beckons is soothing and sweet. The One to whom it belongs tells me of the road through the mountains that ends on Heaven's shores. The fish are biting and the sunrise carries the scent of the campfire. When I arrive, it will be better than imagined. The morning mist will clear and I will be home. I am sure my Uncle John is already there.

Father God, I am so grateful for the men and women who helped shape my life. They were coloring in a picture of you… filling in the blanks. I know You now, thanks to them. Amen

Dropping Anchor: *Does the sound of your voice soothe the listener?*

____

____

____

____

Faking It

"...whatsoever things are true, whatsoever things are honest,
whatsoever things are just, whatsoever things are pure,
whatsoever things are lovely,
whatsoever things are of good report;
if there be any virtue, and if there be any praise,
think on these things."
Philippians 4:8

As I was growing up, I was pretty sheltered. Not much of the outside world crept into my small town. Of course, there were rare moments of excitement, like when the bull got loose from the local dairy farm and proceeded to take over Main Street. He was none too friendly and definitely in a foul mood. I don't recall how he was returned to his proper environs, but I'm pretty sure it involved the police and a dented squad car. Then, there was the time two motorcycles collided head on, just outside my house. Both riders were amazingly alright, but the bikes burst into flame and were total losses. These were rare moments. I soon discovered that when the norm of life is sedate, one's imagination often comes into play as the only source of available excitement. The most treacherous situations of my growing up years did not occur in my hometown; no... they occurred in my own vivid, boyhood imagination. In there, I was destined to be a hero.

My dad was no adventurer. He truly appreciated the slow pace of our hometown. Settled as he was, my father didn't look to make much happen. It was my mother who finally planned a family vacation... a drive in our old station wagon to the nation's capital, Washington, DC. "It'll be educational for the kids," she remarked to my reluctant father. "It's a violent city," he replied. "We're likely to get caught in a crossfire." I was unsure as to what a crossfire was, but I knew we wanted to stay away from any that may occur during our week's stay.

The drive down the Eastern Seaboard was uneventful and we finally arrived at our destination, an old Washington hotel where our reservations had been made. We looked for all the world like country bumpkins. Every time we ventured from the safety of the hotel, my mother would point out the sites, while my dad looked nervously one way then the next, expecting any minute for the gunfire to erupt. "Be careful of the traffic," offered Mom. "We are in a prime location for a crossfire," muttered Dad.

There were no shootouts that week. No gun play. We saw monuments and historical buildings. We saw where history happened. But at my age, I thought more about making history than visiting it! In my active imagination I dared to rescue a family, like mine, that had unfortunately been in the wrong place at the wrong time... and were, in my dad's words, caught in a crossfire. Instead, and in reality, I found I had a sense of boredom as we headed home for New England.

Back at home, I recounted the story of our trip to my friends, making sure to include the parts where we ALMOST got caught in a crossfire, but managed NOT TO. It gave us boys a thirst for action, and since there was none, we embarked on our "faking phase." This involved several options... the bicycle wreck, the fist fight and the sports injury. Whenever we arranged for the bicycle wreck, we would scramble two of our bikes into a twist of tires and handlebars, and then lay nearby in a twist ourselves – hoping to look as though we had been thrown onto the lawn upon impact. The object was to lay there moaning until some poor passerby would see our plight and come to our needed rescue. The problem arose when no one stopped—a rare automobile would pass by arousing our hopes, but as the hours ticked by, we began to snore, lying as we were, in the summer sun. As I mentioned, it was a quiet town.

The fake sports injury never worked either. There was only so much damage one could receive from a whiffle ball. Since we lived next door to the church (and its windows) the plastic sports equipment was pretty much our limit. We would occasionally sub in a tennis ball, but that didn't cause much damage or alarm to my parents. On top of limiting our play to the fairly harmless playthings, my mother also kept an eagle eye on the back yard. She was usually well aware when we had ceased pitching and hitting and had started plotting instead. She knew it would be a matter of moments before one of us ran in claiming that a freak foul ball had dislocated an arm or a leg. "Hmmhmm" she would say. "Be more careful, dear." That was my mom's name for me… "Dear." Not exactly the kind of nickname that a rescuer-of-those-caught-in-a-crossfire would carry.

The third ploy actually achieved a modicum of success… the fake fist fight. One of my pals was a bit of a gymnast. He could throw himself around pretty well, without injuring himself. So, on evenings when we hit the mall or an ice cream parlor, we would exchange knowing glances and pretend to start arguing. The noise level would escalate—summoning an impromptu crowd. Then with high drama and a fake smack to the head, my pal on the receiving end of the "punch" would do a back flip and toss himself in the bushes. The rest of us would gather around to act the part of the crowd of shocked onlookers. This third phase of foolery ended abruptly when a woman exited her vehicle and dashed inside the restaurant stating that she was going to call the cops. That did it for us. We didn't want any real trouble. We would have to admit however, we felt pretty good about coming so close to the real thing that we actually fooled someone and spawned ACTION.

We often react to things that appear real, but are not. My dad's conjured imagery of the crossfire never occurred. The bike wrecks, the sports injuries, the fights—all imaginary. Many of us carry these fantasy worlds within us. The problem occurs when we live in reaction to the imaginary, as though it were real life. For example, let's say at your place of employment, there is an issue between you and a co-worker. We 'suppose' that we know what they are thinking about us—we even create 'fake' conversations in our minds… "I'd like to tell them ___________" And I know their response would be "_____________________________". We allow these fabricated arguments to affect our real life attitudes - yet the confrontations have never actually happened! They are as imagined as my dad's crossfire in the capital—as phony as a staged bicycle accident. Holding onto a poor attitude born out of an assumed offense is as silly as laying on the lawn, hoping some passerby will take pity on your plight. No one else lives in your inner land of make believe. They won't be stopping by.

There are, sadly, places in the world where crossfires really do occur. There are real wrecks and there are true-life fist fights. There are plenty of them as a matter of fact… too many. Perhaps there would be fewer actual fights and firearms if we learned how to control the conjured arguments that we create all on our own, in our minds. Imagine that.

Father God, may I never fake my relationship to you. You see through my pretense - so there is little use in employing it. May I live, love and minister based on truth. My thoughts are only a wisp of smoke that is gone with the breeze. But, your word is eternal and your truth never changes. I love you - nothing fake in that. Amen

Dropping Anchor: *Reality offers enough to handle in one day.*

____

____

____

____

Awake

"Awake up, my glory; awake, psaltery and harp
I myself will awake early."
Psalm 57:8

A household awakens a little at a time, much the same as it settled down the night before. The little ones are first to greet the new day. In the wee hours of morning, the baby stirs in his cradle and begins the cooing and gurgling which will soon become a full cry for mother's milk. The patter of small feet will tumble down the hallway above, signaling the imminent arrival of a two year old in the parent's big bed. Mom and dad are now "awake." We are not yet "up," however, but that is coming.

"I want cereal," means up and at 'em, Dad. The night is over. Let the day begin. Breathing a prayer of gratitude for the soon to be sunrise, you make your way to the kitchen. "Cereal coming right up," you tell your small son. Pouring a bowl full of kid's breakfast cereal can cause something to trigger within a parent. The colors, the crunch, and the sugary coating entice you, so you grab a second bowl and fill it for yourself. The two of you sit content in the predawn darkness and munch. One must admit that you make quite a pair… father and son, staring at the back of the cereal box, mouths full of fun shapes of flavor. When finished, the bowls go to the sink for rinsing because there is no adhesive in the world that can match the stickiness of dried cereal in a non-rinsed bowl. It is easier to scrape barnacles off a boat in dry dock than to mess with hardened cereal on a ceramic bowl.

Finding the Binky is next on the list of early morning pursuits. Your job is to track down one of the dozen or so pacifiers that you have purchased in the last six months. The intent of your search is to keep Junior quiet so that his mother and his siblings can sleep for ten more minutes. I am quite certain that the Almighty has an angel brigade, solely in charge of handling all requests for lost binkies. There are surely thousands of them daily… Stepping on a lost binky means you have found one. Grateful, you pop it in your child's mouth—remembering too late that it should be washed. So you quickly pop the pacifier in your own mouth and then re-insert the plastic peacemaker into your waiting child's mouth. This is considered proper parenting.

By this time, those who were merely "awake," are now also "up." A cry goes up for coffee, and the resounding echo is heard throughout the house. Teenagers emerge from under piles of blankets—their first words uttered go something like, "black with two sugars." For a split second, you are taken aback, for what seemed to be a pile of laundry now moves and speaks. This is how teenagers spend the night. They curl up on the couch to watch a movie, usually falling asleep before the final credits and then, 'come to' in the morning, in desperate need of caffeine. Having received the coffee mandate you grab a twenty dollar bill off the kitchen counter, (that was for the babysitter!) and head for the coffee shop. Not just any shop will do. You must journey to the trendy cafe which features the latte of choice. Not just any latte will do. You drive on with purpose, passing lesser coffee shops and wondering just what makes a latte a latte. How did you manage these fifty plus years without the latte? You have settled for coffee all this time. You have even tasted the dreaded 'instant' coffee which comes in crystal form and brews in your cup. You must be a coffee survivor. Thus, you are the hearty veteran on the caffeine quest for your family this morning. They must not be made to suffer as you have in the past. Lattes it will be!

Once you arrive at the trendy cafe, you immediately realize that there are many others in search of liquid caffeine. You wait your turn while standing in a line of stylish folks which passes directly in front of the counter featuring scrumptious looking chocolate items which you now MUST HAVE. You DESERVE such a treat. You are the one who made the early morning journey to latte-land, so you should be rewarded. Besides, you will have eaten it before you arrive back at home, and none will be the wiser.

You return from your travels with a cardboard carrier filled with barely balanced cups of latte. Returning from a snowy hunt with a dead moose in tow could not be more difficult. You stand on your porch kicking at the door (the foot being the only free appendage with which to knock) however everyone is now showering or getting dressed and so you balance the precious liquid on the porch railing while you quickly open the door. You then enter the kitchen, hoping for a hero's welcome, much like your Viking ancestors would have known upon returning from conquests and such.

Alas, you are by-passed completely as the caffeine crowd assembles and your wife and children get busy reading cryptic labeling and doling out the treats. Three year old True well knows this routine, and he exults in one of our favorite expressions that he utilizes "Our family is all for-gether." For-gether indeed. As for you, you sit down in your favorite chair, listening to the coffee talk and considering yourself the luckiest man on earth. You are awake and up on this gift of a new day. You have saved your chocolate bakery item in your pocket for later. For now, life is sweet enough.

Father God, may I serve others, beginning with my own family. I want to be a hero to those that I live with. Amen

Dropping Anchor: *An everyday hero is still a hero to his family.*

____

____

____

____

Reunion

"...it doth not yet appear what we shall be:
but we know that, when He shall appear,
we shall be like Him..."
1 John 3:2

I have often wondered what heaven will be like. Now, I think I know.

It happened at Christmastime. My oldest daughter Evangeline was spending her first Christmas away from home. She had taken a position at a church in Florida earlier that year and despite being surrounded by a loving ecclesiastical family, as the holiday drew near, it was apparent she wanted to be "home." Phone calls were nice, but they only seemed to accentuate the distance between us.

One particular night a few weeks prior, Evangeline called us in tears. She was really emotional about missing her siblings and the family Christmas traditions that we enjoy each year. We had taken her with us (electronically) on the night we picked out our Christmas tree. Always one of Evangeline's favorite events, the choosing of the tree is a Decker tradition where every member of the family has to agree that this is the "one"—not too tall, not too short, not too fat and not too thin. We had Evangeline looking in on the live stream video feed from my cell phone. She settled on the same one that we liked, a shapely seven footer that seemed perfect for our living room, but as we brought it home to decorate—her image flickered off our tiny screens and she was left to imagine the rest of the evening from far away Florida. We had no choice but to proceed at our home in Massachusetts without her.

Some very kind members of LifeHouse church learned of my oldest daughter's sadness and unbeknownst to us, they purchased an airline ticket for Evangeline to fly home three days before Christmas. Standing in our living room they told both Amanda and me to close our eyes. "We have an early present for you," they said. On the count of three, we opened our eyes and there stood my daughter, Evangeline! She had completely surprised us. We laughed and hugged and cried. Then, we laughed and cried and hugged. We were now all together for Christmas! (Three year old True calls it our family being all "for-gether").

I mentioned that I think I know now what heaven will be like. We are separated from Home by a great distance. Prayer, like phone calls, keeps us in touch—yet it is not quite the same as in person, face to face communication. But someone paid the price to get us home. And someday when we close our eyes—we will open them to see the One we love standing before us. And, then, the family will all be "for-gether" for every Christmas thereafter. Amen.

Father God, bless my family - both far and near. I love them. Amen

Dropping Anchor: *Earthly breezes carry the celestial scent of heaven.*

____

____

____

____

Missed Opportunity

"A friend loveth at all times..."
Proverbs 17:17

We all miss the boat some days. Despite our best efforts, we all fall short. It's just who we are. We are human and humans make mistakes. On occasion, those mistakes can really sting. As we all know, time has a way of healing the hurts and can even produce a chuckle or two when we stop and consider a particularly grand scale "missing of the boat." One such blunder is etched upon my memory, and although I initially winced, I now have to laugh.

It was summertime and I was still a young man. It was a wonderful season of life. I had my own small apartment just outside the city of Boston. My good friend Ken had insider access to Fenway Park, home of the Red Sox, allowing him to get seats for low (or no) cost, and he frequently passed on the blessings. I watched a lot of baseball that year. The ballpark was just minutes away down Beacon Street, a drive I would often make with the T-roof open on my new Camaro, sunshine splashing on my face as it began to sink low behind the city's skyscrapers. It seemed as though everything was going swimmingly. I was even flush with cash.

Ken had a deejay business and he began to get so busy that he offered to cut me in on the action if I wanted to help. I was happy to oblige and thus, spent many nights spinning records for high school dances or private parties. My favorite duty was aboard the Boston Harbor cruises that sailed out each night. We would be the musical entertainment for the evening as the cruise ship coasted lazily through the waves, the shimmering city of Boston in full view behind us. As the moon would rise above the Hancock Tower, I would often find myself thinking "It doesn't get much better than this."

So, now comes the blunder. One August afternoon, Ken left me a message on my answering machine (remember those?). There were no cell phones in those days. People made telephone calls from the office or their home. After that there was no mode of communication other than a public phone booth. I got home from work and checked the messages on my 'incoming' cassette tape, and there was Ken's call—only it was a poor recording due to a bad connection. I hit 'rewind' and listened again and again but all I could gather through the static was that we had a booking for a cruise that night and that I should meet him at six o'clock to assist. The location he gave sounded like Rowe's Wharf, a place I knew well. Try as I might, I could not make out exactly where he said to meet but I threw on a tie, headed for Rowe's Wharf and figured I would find him easily enough.

Pulling into a parking spot twenty minutes later, I saw no sign of Ken. I was early, so I figured I would just wait until he arrived. As the clock drifted past six, I turned on the local news station to check the traffic report. There was a jam downtown on the expressway the radio reported. I assumed Ken was delayed due to traffic. Cruises usually depart at seven each evening, but as the seven o'clock hour drew near, I began to grow concerned. I walked down to the dock, but there was no sign of Ken. Seven fifteen came and still no Ken. As the clock on my car's dashboard read eight pm, I reluctantly turned the key in the ignition and headed home.

At about eleven pm, my telephone rang. It was Ken. "Buddy, where were you tonight?" he asked. "That was my question for you!" I said to my friend. "Long Wharf, just like I told you," he said. "Ohhh, I thought you said Rowe's Wharf," I replied. "That explains that. Did I miss a good time?" Ken then began to tell me of his evening on the water.

He got to the wharf at about six o'clock and since I was nowhere to be found, he loaded all of the equipment on board ship and set up the portable sound system. He kept checking his watch, wondering where I was. About six-thirty the first guests began to arrive on deck. Ken thought that there were fewer in number than for a usual Friday night, but he continued his preparations. As he did, he noticed a few celebrities were coming up the steps and climbing aboard. "Where is Loren?" he wondered, thinking I would enjoy this gathering of stars.

About seven, there was still no sign of me, and the ship was about to pull away from Long Wharf. Ken started the entertainment with a very popular song by an internationally known singer who had local roots in Boston. "Nice choice," said a voice behind him. He turned and found himself face to face with the musician himself.

He had rented the cruise ship for a private party for his dad's seventieth birthday. I won't mention the star by name, but you would know him well, and it was enough to make my jaw drop. "We hung out together all night long," crooned Ken. "Dude, you missed the best boat ride ever!" This was a colossal blunder.

So, why am I laughing about it now? Because I learned that when you miss the boat and mess something up, having a friend who really hopes you are going to make it is a great gift. The best things in life are not brief encounters with rock stars. Much better than that are friends who see your mistakes and truly feel empathy for you. They are the kind that cut you in on a good thing and share the best they have. A cruise around Boston lasts only a few hours. My friend Ken has been there for four decades. We don't deejay any longer, but if he needed me tonight, I would be there—or at least in the vicinity.

> *Father God, my prayer is simple... may I be in the right place at the right time so that I do not miss the boat that takes me to you. Amen*

Dropping Anchor: *While you are missing the boat, having a friend who hopes you'll make it is a gift, indeed.*

____

____

____

____

Damascus

" As for Saul, he made havock of the church..."
Acts 8:3

The first few stones missed their mark. It was almost as if no one had the stomach to carry out the execution. Each hurled missile flew wide and high, past the kneeling man named Steven. He was praying and that was obvious. His face was serene, a sharp contrast to the menacing looks of his executioners.

"Is nobody able to do this thing?" The voice belonged to Saul, the ringleader who was in charge of this deadly affair. "Is anybody going to hit the target? Do I have to do it myself?" Up until this moment, Saul of the order of the Sanhedrin had been holding the cloaks of the mob who stood around the doomed man at the top of the temple terrace. Saul had charged a hefty fee from each man who wanted a part in the execution. They had seemed eager enough to pay for the privilege, and yet now, they appeared hesitant. With a sigh, Saul tossed the coats aside and picked up a rock. Marching closer, he stood about fifteen feet from the condemned man. Without a second thought, Saul released a savage throw. It found its mark with a sickening thud. The force of the rock knocked Steven down into the dust. The blood flowed from the deep gash opened above his ear. Seeing that, the tidal wave of evil crested in the heart of each man. One by one, the rocks began to find their mark as the dying man became sport to the killers. Saul, back at his perch with the cloaks, fingered the coins in his pocket and smiled.

This was a strategic execution. Steven had been a leader in the renegade religious movement called The Way. Their growing numbers offended the keen Jewish dogma that Saul espoused. The Way claimed that Jesus of Nazareth was the fulfillment of the Scriptures, the prophesied Messiah. They claimed that after his crucifixion he had laid in a borrowed tomb for three days. The common punch line amongst his followers went something like this... 'He only borrowed the grave because he wasn't going to need it for long!' Saul bristled at the thought. Looking at the corpse of the dead man lying where he fell in the bloody dust, he mused, "You gonna rise up too? I doubt that," and with a chuckle he mounted his horse and rode away.

He went straight to his favorite tavern, where the talk was plentiful and the drink flowed freely. Saul was a bit of a local celebrity in this kind of environ. The area Jews appreciated his efforts to quell the ranks of the upstart Sunday worshippers, even the Romans allowed him free reign in dealing with the Christ followers. The last thing governing Rome wanted was a religious firestorm, pitting passionate factions against each other. This kind of thing had occurred in the past, with deadly results. Zealots of the Jewish faith had attacked soldiers of the Roman army on numerous occasions. As far as Saul was concerned, Jesus of Nazareth was just another misguided enemy of Rome and the Jewish power structure. Rome and Zion would both like an end to the growing group of Christians, as they had become known. And, Saul was their man to bring down the final curtain on the sect. No one was safe from his deadly pursuits—not if they believed that Jesus was indeed, the Messiah. Women, children, the elderly—all were fair game… Now, Saul had some more momentum. The stoning of Steven had taken out a ringleader of the church, and surely, there would be those who were now frightened. "We are driving them underground and then into oblivion," Saul announced to the group of men at the bar where he stood. "Just like their Misguided Messiah, underground and soon to be forgotten." Hearty laughter rose from the men and carried out the open windows and into the night.

"There are a growing number of the followers of The Way in Damascus," Saul read the report the next day with interest. A messenger stood in the doorway of the small apartment that Saul had rented in Jerusalem. He used it as a headquarters, but he was rarely there. Now it appeared that the ancient city of Damascus would be his next raid. Saul summoned a few of his trusted men and together they headed for Syria. It would take some time to reach their destination, but their spirits were high and the miles disappeared behind them quickly.

They were close to the border when Saul sensed something was wrong. He heard something first like a buzzing or a hum. It was almost musical. The afternoon air became suddenly alive with flying creatures—beings of great strength and beauty. They flew close to the men, but Saul noticed that his fellow travelers were looking straight ahead, seeming not to notice the heavenly invasion. He was just about to speak, when one of the creatures shoved him from his mount and sent him sprawling onto the dusty road. As he scrambled to his feet, Saul heard a voice like thunder calling his name. "Yes?" he managed to reply. He looked to where the voice had come from and there stood a man like none other. He stood head and shoulders taller than Saul, and he glowed with a white light that seemed to radiate from within. His eyes were like burning coals of fire and his raiment was whiter than new fallen snow. Saul collapsed in the road, speechless. His companions, looking back and seeing Saul on the ground, hurried to his aid.

"Saul...why are you persecuting me?" The glowing man spoke in a whisper but somehow it echoed across the sky like the peal of a great bell. "Who are you?" Saul requested of the stranger. Even as he asked the question he felt he knew the answer. "I am Jesus, the very one whom you persecute," came the reply. "You shall see no more until your spiritual eyes are opened. Until you are ready to lead others to the light, you shall have to be led through the darkness." With that, the man disappeared, taking the flying creatures and Saul's eyesight along with them.

"What happened? Can you see nothing?" One of Saul's men was speaking in his ear. Words were beyond his grasp as he shook his head and tried to rise to his feet. "We must turn back," said another of the band of men. "NO!" shouted Saul. "We will proceed on our mission." Reluctantly, the confused men aided Saul onto his horse and the reins were fastened to the saddle of the lead rider. Saul said not a word for the rest of the journey. Arriving in the city of Damascus, he booked a room in a local inn and sat alone in the darkness. He answered no knocks upon his door. He ate nothing. In his misery, he could only think of one thing. The man on the Damascus road had claimed to be Jesus. "The one that I persecute,"

Saul said aloud. Up until now, he had considered Christ followers to be the objects of his hate and violence. "But, Jesus had said it was him that I am hurting." Saul turned the thought over and over in his head. He settled one idea. If there was such a one who was so close to his devotees… then, "I want to follow The Way." Saul announced to an empty room. If a being so powerful, as wonderful as the one he had seen on the road; who knew him by name, if that One was the Living God, Saul thought he would gladly trade all his religious trappings and ceremonies—just to know Him. "Jesus, help me find you." Saul breathed a simple prayer, but it felt like the first one he had ever said from the heart.

Just then a knock came on his door. "Paul?" a voice from the hallway carried to his ears. "Wrong room," Saul answered. "I am Saul, not Paul." There was a hesitation outside his door, and then, "No, I have the right room, and the name is correct. Jesus has sent me to you, brother Paul."

> *Father God, only you have the power and the capacity to change a man's heart. But, when you do, there is nothing more wonderful than that. Thank you for caring - even for your enemies. Amen*

Dropping Anchor: *Sometimes the church's greatest enemies become its dearest friends.*

____

____

____

____

When Mark Spoke

"...I cry unto Thee, when my heart is overwhelmed..."
Psalm 61:2

I am usually able to come up with words, because, well... I am a writer and a minister. However as I sit down to write about my friend, Mark, I am nearly at a loss.

Mark left this world for heaven in April of 2017. Just as winter was releasing its harsh hold on New England, so too Mark found his release from a body crippled with palsy. He lived fifty one years in his prison of flesh. He could not walk or speak and had limited use of one arm, just enough to guide his electric wheelchair. But, oh! The life he lived...

Mark was apparently a normal baby upon birth. Within a short while however, it was clear that his life would be nothing like normal. As he aged, his limbs atrophied and grew twisted. His verbal communication was a series of grunts and groans, mixed with a ready resemblance of a laugh. He endured feeding tubes and catheters with an acceptance born of a patient spirit. People often unknowingly insulted his intelligence by speaking loudly and slowly, but Mark graciously overlooked the misunderstanding and smiled his crooked smile at everyone he encountered.

He was a beloved member of LifeHouse Church. Over the years that he attended, he helped build our congregation. Every new case worker or caretaker that he employed was scheduled to work on Sunday mornings so they would have to attend church with him. Most of them joined the fellowship.

The church softball team knew him as their assistant coach. During the summer nights when we would play ball, I would frequently check in with Mark on the sidelines to see the game strategy he had, that I was missing. Pulling out a spell board, he would often painstakingly spell out, letter by letter, a detailed plan of how we could accomplish the win.

He was our self-proclaimed worship leader. He zoomed around the auditorium in his electric wheelchair, (often at high speeds), pumping his left arm and fist as a gesture of enthusiasm and praise. Periodically I would hold his feeble arm in the air as high as he could extend it. These were the times when I knew he wanted to lift his hands in worship.

If you were new to the church, Mark sought you out and would purposely roll right up in front of your seat and start swinging away. Sometimes in his exuberance he would run over feet and pocketbooks. No one ever seemed to mind. What he provided was not embarrassment or concern, but a genuine inspiration and an invitation to praise. No matter what kind of a week you had, you knew Mark faced a tougher struggle. If he was able to praise God despite his hardships, well then, what excuse did we have to hold back?

On what was to be his last Sunday with us, he did something he had never done before. He pulled up beside my seat during worship and pointed to the microphone on my chair. It was clear that he wanted me to hold it for him. "You want to speak to the congregation?" I asked. He nodded in a determined fashion.

He had never asked to use the mic before, but I knew this was to be a God moment, so I announced that Mark had something to share. He began with his familiar groans and as he spoke them, awe fell over us. He went on for a short while, clearly working hard to express himself, and then ended with three long sighs that came from the depths of his soul. Silence followed. There wasn't a dry eye in the congregation… Mark was telling us goodbye.

Not two weeks later I held his hand as he left us to be with Jesus. He took his last breath on Earth in perfect peace. He drew in Heaven's celestial air with his very next breath. I am certain that the feeble arm I used to hold high is strong now. His body is well. And, yet I really don't believe his voice has changed much... for it was already perfectly understood.

Father God, bless all those among us who suffer with a disability. We believe you are able to shine very brightly through their condition and you speak loudly through their silence. Amen

Dropping Anchor: *Love is its own language. Speak it!*

Trumpet Sounds

"Blow ye the trumpet in Zion, and sound an alarm in my holy mountain..."
Joel 2:1

I'm certain I had a normal childhood. I had two parents and an older sister. I played Little League Baseball and Cowboys and Indians. I rode my bicycle everywhere. I went to church on Sunday and to trumpet lessons on Monday. Later, in my young teen years, I devoted Saturday mornings to marching band practice.

I never really enjoyed playing a musical instrument. My parents thought it would be a good discipline for me, so after school each day I was mandated to practice my horn for a half an hour. I would blurt and blat my way through the church hymnal or try my valves on some "classics" that were in my music book. Au Clair De Lune and When Johnny Comes Marching Home Again were barely recognizable but my lip was getting stronger and so was my will to master my wind instrument made of brass.

My first music teacher was a high school student who attended our church. I don't remember much about our sessions which we shared on Monday afternoons after school. I do recall that he often said, "And how and how," when I would show some musical promise on a particular song or exercise. I wasn't sure what that phrase meant, but I thought it was "cool," as was he. He had a Beatles style haircut and could play "I Wanna Hold Your Hand." So inspired was I, that I dutifully played through my ascending and descending scales and hoped that my parents would let me grow out my bangs. "Johnny," that was his name, also showed me that by removing the mouthpiece and blowing through that trumpet attachment, you could sound an awful lot like Donald Duck. He and his mouthpiece eventually went off to college however so my parents had to search for a replacement musical instructor. My dad had a pastor friend who knew a pastor friend who had a parishioner who had a brother who was an unemployed cleric, and a trumpet player, who could surely use a little extra income. My lessons therefore continued on with the recommended Reverend from New Bedford. "Call me Roy," he said at our first meeting.

Wednesdays were my lesson days with Roy. New Bedford was the big city and I often felt a bit uneasy there. However, as soon as I arrived at his second floor apartment home, he would set up a music stand in the middle of his living room and make me a glass of chocolate milk. If there was a Mrs. Roy, I never saw her. My instructor would then bring two metal chairs (with foam seats, covered in plastic) from the kitchen and place them "just so" in front of the sheet music on the metal stand. Away we would go. I soon realized that Roy was not so far ahead of me on the trumpet player skill chart. My parents were wise enough to use the thirty minute lesson time to run errands. After all, we didn't sound very good, and Roy was not a fan of the Disney Duck squawking noises that I was quite adept at by this time.

No, Roy was all business. There were no brass-based cover versions of Fab Four songs at these trumpet tune-ups. We stuck to the songs that were included in the Trumpet for Beginners music book. I always left the apartment with a low grade headache. I think the place smelled funny. Anyway, on the way back home to the neighboring town of Acushnet I would lean my head against the cool of the car window ("Open it just a skinch dear," my mother would say) and breathe the fresh air. A jaunt through the drive through lane of Howdy Beef Burgers, where 28 cents would buy you a sizzling burger fresh off the grill, would serve to lighten my mood. For just another quarter, you could add French fries to your meal. And the chocolate shakes were a cheap treat that doubled as a tasty dessert.

I never mastered the horn; however I got good enough to double tongue my way through "I Wanna Hold Your Hand." I lied once, trying to impress Sandy Sousa in the 5th grade and told her I could play all of the *Monkee's* originals. I don't think she bought it but I did manage to sound like Donald Duck enough to make her laugh at recess. I had brought my mouthpiece to school that day, and just for that purpose. I am sure that I thought more about little Miss Souza than my trumpet skills. The proof was in the pudding.

The last time I attempted to make music with my trumpet was at a sunrise service on Easter about twenty years ago. One of my church deacons also played the trumpet and we decided to perform a duet to open the gathering of hearty, dawn breaking Christian souls. The hour was early and the music difficult, but we launched into "Christ Arose" nonetheless. About half way through, I began to laugh, thinking it sounded more like "I Wanna Hold Your Hand," than any Easter hymn. Laughing is not conducive to trumpeting and so the two of us botched the duet pretty badly. The thing is, when you mess up an Easter service, the Donald Duck mouthpiece voice is not a second option. So, as we finished the song, I put down my trumpet and turned to the congregation who appeared appreciative of our effort if not the end results, and simply said, "And how and how..." The cleverness of the catchphrase had not diminished, despite the passing of years.

The book of Revelation says that at the end of the age, an angel will blow a trumpet call for all the earth to hear. I don't know how much practice time that heavenly herald puts in. It's a pretty big gig after all, announcing the Lord's return. You don't want it to sound like the Beatles, circa 1964. But, if it goes that way, he can always pull off the mouthpiece... I plan on being all smiles when Christ returns... and how and how.

Father God, it is the sound we wait for... the trumpet sounding your return to earth as king. May it happen soon. We need you here. Amen

Dropping Anchor: *One day - everything will change. Plan to rejoice!*

____

____

____

____

Intervention At The Intersection

"...Blessed are they whose iniquities are forgiven, and whose sins are covered..."
Romans 4:7

Life comes at us at a pretty good clip. There just isn't a lot of time to catch your breath. In our rearview mirror, the fading horizon falls farther and farther away. In that retrospect, we can sometimes say, "Ah! So that's what happened." We glance back hurriedly though, and then look straight ahead, making sure to keep our eyes on the road. Navigating the unexpected turns, bumps and intersections takes all our concentration. It is a good thing we are offered Help with the driving.

My wife, Amanda is a community organizer for a nearby town. I guess she did such a fine job organizing my family that she became 'in demand' for bigger projects. She is good at what she does, that's for certain. Much of her work, funded by government grants, involves battling against the woes of underage drinking and drug abuse, two problems that are moving fast in our direction. Recently, she put together a drug awareness event at a local high school. It was a night for those in need of help to be made aware of the support and treatment which was readily available. The community came out in force, filling the auditorium to capacity. There, they listened as experts shared help and hope. One gentleman who spoke represented a faith-based program which was known for having great success in saving lives.

After the presentation was completed, tables were set up in the corridor for more information. It was at such a table that a distraught woman approached the man from the faith centered organization. In tears, she shared how her teenage son was addicted to heroin. "I've never heard of your program," she offered. "Could you help us? I've nearly lost my son three times to overdoses." The representative took her aside and said a prayer, asking God to move in the situation. "Even tonight, Lord, may we see a miracle occur for this teen."

Later that same night, everyone was back in their own homes. At the rehabilitation center, the team that had been at my wife's program was pretty hungry, having missed the supper hour. Raiding the kitchen in search of snacks, one young man ate a cookie which contained nuts. He soon discovered he had an allergy to that kind of nut, and within minutes he was swollen and gasping for air. Quickly, he was helped into a van and the leader of the group hopped in and drove the five blocks to the hospital. There, in the ER the young man was treated and then held for observation. As the pair waited in their curtained cubicle, they heard commotion in the next treatment area. Although they couldn't see what was happening, the sound of voices made it clear that it was a drug overdose involving a young man. He had been given emergency treatment in the field and was now being stabilized.

When it became apparent that he was coherent and communicating, the pair from the rehab struck up a conversation with the teenager on the other side of the curtain. They learned this was not his first overdose; in fact it was his fourth. Telling him that they could relate, they explained that there was hope. They invited him to come to their facility. They opened the curtain, joined hands and prayed with him. They encouraged him to press on. He agreed that he desperately needed help and promised to sign in that very next morning. Just then, his mother was escorted into the emergency room. The two men from the rehabilitation center looked at her in amazement; it was the same woman who had met them at the school some four hours before. They had prayed for a miracle to happen that night and they got one. God had arranged for a peanut allergy to intersect with a drug overdose and His will was accomplished in a young man's life.

Yes, life comes at us pretty quickly. We aren't able to see what is coming up ahead. God knows the way we should take. When you are on the right road, you find some pretty amazing things occur at the intersections.

Yes, my wife does good work for a good cause. Occasionally, she receives assistance from the government. Sometimes, help comes from an even higher Source.

Father God, thank you for arranging all the circumstances that look to many like coincidences. I see your hands at work - shaping my life. Amen

Dropping Anchor: *When you glance in life's rearview mirror, you realize you have travelled best with your hands off the wheel.*

____

____

____

____

Provision

"Hast thou commanded the morning since thy days and caused the dayspring to know his place?"
Job 38:12

It's like a game of cat and mouse. Each morning, Tyler the Cocker Spaniel lays listening for the sound of me. That is, if I turn over or reach for my cell phone to see what time it is, and I manage to make the bed creak—even just a bit—Tyler is up, figuring that I am now available. My availability in a pup's world means two things. One, it means a trip outdoors and two, it means breakfast. His eagerness for both is inspiring. When I pick up the human end of his leash and move toward the front door, he quivers and leaps with genuine canine excitement. Every morning, it is the same way. The door is like a portal to Grand Things for Tyler. He cannot wait; his anticipation is so great that he can hardly hold himself in check.

Out we go! Into the yard where sights and sounds await our discovery. Tyler explores the familiar environs as if we were seeing them for the first time. I attempt to mimic his curiosity and listen carefully for the noises of my early morning world. The sun is not up yet, but the highway is alive, nearly two miles from where Tyler and I stand. The low murmur of traffic breaks through the closer sounds of my neighbor's clucking birds in the hen house. Further away, the rumble of an eighteen wheeler tells me that a trucker is leaving the business park with a full load. A mile and a half to our south, the early morning stillness allows me to follow him through the progression of gears until he reaches the on-ramp for the highway and gets swallowed up by the steady traffic hum.

Back inside the house, duty done, Tyler is all about breakfast. He knows the routine and it's almost more than he can take. He quivers anew and dances around his bowl, just knowing it will soon be full. I am amazing in his eyes. I am the Provider. I bring out delicious doggie treats. The tidbits tumble into the bowl while he sits by and sniffs the air. It smells like his breakfast; there can be no doubt. There will be provision for him this morning.

Today, as he eats, I find myself back at the front door. Touching the brass handle, I pause to wonder what my Provider has in store for me this day. I venture out into the yard again. "I will walk on familiar pathways today, Abba," I pray, "Grant me the opportunity and the desire to look for the new within the old, and feed my soul from your storehouse of provision."

The sky is lightening as day breaks. The hen house is in full throttle now, next door. The rooster who lives there lifts his voice in a morning song. The tune isn't much, but the heart behind it cries "Good Morning, world!" I answer him back with a tinge of embarrassment. The two of us play call and response as if we were in church, until I hear human voices; the farmer is coming to spread chicken feed. Provision for my bird friends is on the way.

Back inside, I pick up my Bible and sit down for my soul breakfast. With a glance toward my dog, who is licking his bowl while pushing it across the floor with his nose, I dive in. The excitement of a new day is upon me now. There will be provision for me this morning. "Abba, you are amazing in my eyes. You are my Provider."

Father God, thank you today for my food, both physical and spiritual. I need both. Amen

Dropping Anchor: *Give us this day our daily bread.*

Guilt Edged Grace

There is therefore now no condemnation to them which are in Christ Jesus..."
Romans 8:1

I suppose it is okay to tell these two stories now. Many years have passed by since they occurred; however, it remains fresh in my memory. I think of it from time to time, especially when I need a sermon illustration on the issue of guilt... or grace.

I was a kid who knew about guilt. Reared within a strict, every week (never miss) Sunday school regimen, I was informed early in life that we all sin, and the payback for sin is death. I memorized Bible verses, and even collected memory merit badges that I proudly wore pinned to my shirt; their sheer number, a testament to my memorization accomplishments. As a "PK" (pastor's kid), I didn't have much opportunity for grand scale sinfulness, but I did manage the occasional lie when it seemed convenient. I stole a bit during my early teen years; my grandfather's cigars were my favorite target for thieving. Oh, yes, I smoked too. While my parents were at Wednesday night prayer meeting, I would take one of the Cuban casualties of my corruption from its hiding place and sit on the back porch, puffing away. I wasn't good at hiding my guilt-ridden conscience. Feelings of culpability clung to me like cigar smoke to my clothes.

In this first story, after nearly setting the woods behind my house on fire, fear and guilt kept me wide awake, despite the late hour. Peering at the gentle snow falling outside my window, I called my parents to my bedside and asked if such snow would put out a forest fire; say if one just happened to be in the smoldering stage nearby. With a knowing glance at each other, they hoisted me out of my bed and began the inquisition. I sang like a canary... giving up the whole enchilada. Henry, my friend next door, and I, had tried that day to make a bomb with an old bottle, some gasoline and a box of wooden matches. By the time I got to the "bursting into flames" part of the story, my father had already thrown on his winter parka and galoshes. Through my repentant tears, I watched him head for the woods armed with a bucket of sand and a shovel. "They are lucky they didn't set the whole neighborhood ablaze," he said upon his return. My waiting mother called Henry's parents, despite the late hour. It was going to be awhile before we would be allowed to play together, that much I knew, but back in my bed, I managed to smile. I had come clean. Confession clears away guilt in fine fashion.

Now we go to the other story. It is the story of my familiar, deserved guilt, and an undeserved grace. When I was a young boy, about the same time period as the would-be woods fire, I had a friend whose family was well known in town for their business success. By any standard, they were wealthy. Upon my first arrival at their luxurious home for a playdate with Mark, their son who was my age, I looked about in awe at the beautiful furniture and expensive vases and lamps which filled their home. Sent outside to the big backyard by his mom, we played until suppertime. Summoned by his dad to come eat, we collected the basketballs we had been using and headed through the sliding glass door into the downstairs parlor area. Trying to extend the fun I called to Mark and sent one last pass his way. It was a poor judgment combined with an even poorer throw. Sailing over Mark's head, my errant pass landed with a crash on a beautiful crystal lamp. We both watched in horror as the loose ball also took out a floor vase and a magazine rack before coming to rest, leaving a trail of devastation in its wake. I was horrified. The sound of footsteps on the stairs meant discovery was moments away. I was guilty.

"I did it," said Mark. "What?" I stammered. "I did it," he repeated, this time to his mom who had arrived on the scene. I watched in silence as she gathered up the broken glass. I sat quietly during supper, and throughout the subsequent ride home, I spoke not a word.

To this day, my picture of the grace of God includes an image of a twelve year old boy, calmly looking into my fearful countenance and saying, "I did it." Or perhaps that same grace appears as a dutiful father in galoshes and overcoat, armed with a shovel, heading for the smoldering woods of my transgressions, to put out yet another fire. Either way, I am grateful, not guilty. I can rest in that.

Looking back, I imagine Mark's mom knew what had really happened. I told you, I could never hide my guilt very well. Back at home, when my head hit the pillow, guilt kept its usual knocking upon my conscience. But this night, it could do no damage. Something bigger had taken its place. It had been sublimed by grace. I suppose that was the very night I became a Christian.

Father God, how can I thank you enough for your grace? It is my life - described in a single word. It is you. It is me. It is all in all. Amen

Dropping Anchor: *Grace takes the blame. I am saved by grace.*

____
____
____
____

Herb

"There were giants in the earth in those days..."
Genesis 6:4

Not many folks remember Herbert Henry Ehrenstein, and that's a shame, really... he was a joy to know. I was still a young man when I knew Herb. I am sure he looked upon me much as I see the young men in my congregation today. I had yet to acquire an appreciation for the lifetime we are given. The years stretched out before me like an open prairie—ready to be explored. Most of Herb's life was behind him then, much as mine is now.

Herb was a scholar, a Bible scholar to be exact. He hailed from Philadelphia where he was a staff member at a large church. It was Tenth Presbyterian Church if my memory serves well. I was working in Greater Boston as a producer for a nationally syndicated Christian radio program and every Tuesday was Herbert Henry Ehrenstein day. He would fly up to Boston each Monday, arriving in time to teach a Bible class called The Life of Christ, a series that went on for years and produced many volumes. It was my job to record the lessons and then catalogue them. I always wondered how Herb found so much relatable material to share about Jesus. The answer is a simple one. He just knew Him better than I did. The series was comprehensive and I am certain it would stand today as one of the most exhaustive studies of the person of Jesus Christ, if it were not lost to time.

Thus, Tuesday mornings were Herb's and mine. I would pick him up early, around 6 a.m. at his hotel and we would head for the radio studios where we would go live on air at 7 a.m. The show's founder and regular host would take the day off and leave the broadcasting to us. Callers would ask questions about the Bible and Herb would tackle them one by one as I patched the callers through. I was always amazed at the spiritual acumen of my friend on the other side of the glass in studio one. After the program was over, it was my turn to ask the questions over a hearty breakfast at the Sheraton. We had the same restaurant, same table, and same waitress every week. It was I who was doing the changing. Little by little, broadcast to broadcast, breakfast to breakfast, I was slowly gaining maturity, thanks to Herb and his patient interest in my life.

Time eventually runs out. After many years, Herb found the schedule and travel between the two cities to be burdensome. He retired to his apartment in Philly, where he met his new breakfast companion, dementia, a cruel guest indeed. During his final months, Herb would write me lengthy letters which got more complex and confusing as his mental capabilities left him little by little.

Herbert Henry Ehrenstein died one grey Tuesday morning in Philadelphia, but I know he was not alone when he passed. He had invested his life in the pursuit of knowing Christ. I imagine those two had some pretty good discussions together in Herb's final days. What sounded like gibberish to medical personnel and the rare visitor was no doubt a clever conversation in the language of heaven. Herb's life was hidden in Christ, and as it became less and less recognizable, it eventually faded completely away, as Herb disappeared into Jesus.

Father God, I am grateful for those who have gone before me and have helped show me the path of life. Amen

Dropping Anchor: *Not all great men travel in wide circles.*

Shepherds

"...neither doth God respect any person:
yet doth He devise means,
that his banished be not expelled from Him."
2 Samuel 14:14

He's just a shepherd... nothing to brag about. Sheep herding has always been a low target to aim for when thinking of a career path. And, yet - some of God's best work over the centuries, has been accomplished by lowly keepers of the flocks.

The night Jesus was born in Bethlehem of Judea; the angels appeared to shepherds, to announce the globe-changing, miraculous event. These simple men of the pastures were the first on earth to receive the news of a Savior King, lying in a manger. They were the first missionaries as well, carrying the story of the stable baby to the streets and beyond.

Centuries before, a man called Moses became the person God chose to lead His people out of Egyptian slavery. But before Moses was to be God's point man and leader, he first logged forty years of shepherding in the deserts of Midian. He learned how to lead a nation by starting on the lowest rung of the ladder of life.

And, then there was David. The eighth son of Jesse, he was an outcast and source of shame to his family. The likely result of an adulterous affair, his red hair served as a constant and obvious reminder of his father's shame. Considered an embarrassment, he was hidden on the outskirts of the family farmland, away from the public eye. When the ancient prophet Samuel came to anoint one of Jesse's sons to be the next King of Israel, David was completely overlooked. "In sin I was conceived," he would later write about his starting place in the proud family of Jesse. To this day, historians and theologians have nothing but guesses as to the identity of the woman who gave birth to the future king. While his brothers lined up in legitimate expectation of coming greatness, David tended the sheep on the green pastures of Bethlehem. It would seem he had little else to look forward to.

But, God moves in ways we cannot understand. He chooses losers not winners. He takes shepherds and makes them kings, deliverers, and missionaries. No matter where you are starting from, He has greatness waiting for you. You may feel as though you have been pushed a long way back in the pack, or that you are daily trudging through a barren wilderness. God has not overlooked you. He is devising plans to bring you to Himself. Imagine that? He is making plans in heaven, plans to meet you. He will put love in your pathway so you will stop and gather it up.

The One He sent before us to show the Way was Himself a shepherd. "The good shepherd..." that was how he put it. One who is willing to lay His life down for the sheep. He stooped low and became the defender of the flock. That flock is us... the merry band of followers who know the voice of Love, calling us out of hiding, out from our shame and into the presence of Greatness.

> *Father God, thank you for your love for the lowly and humble among us. You resist the proud, but give grace to the humble of heart. Make me like that. Amen*

Dropping Anchor: *No matter where you are, you cannot escape the cords of His magnificent love.*

____

____

____

____

Disguise

"And when I saw Him, I fell at His feet as dead.
And He laid His right hand upon me,
saying unto me, Fear not; I am the first and the last..."
Revelation 1:17

The other day, Prudence had a question that she posed to her mother and me. It involved gaining permission for something and, as her parents; we needed a minute or two to talk it over. We launched into parent "code mode"—you know how that works. You spell. You point. You nod. You grimace. Prudence has been around for nine years now. This was not her first rodeo. "I know that look!" she announced. "That is the look parents use to communicate when they don't want the kids to know what they're saying." I have to admit… it worked better when she was younger.

We often disguise things that are too complicated for others to comprehend. Recently, I was in the middle of a discussion with my wife, and we were talking about allegiance, allegiance to the church - indeed, allegiance to God. Amanda mentioned that there seems to be a lack of respect for Jesus. We reduce Him to a manageable size. We talk about our relationship to Him with words like, "Me and Jesus." (Notice the "me" comes first.) "Jesus is my buddy" is expressed as a popular sentiment in some circles. There must be a reason why we feel we can bring Him down to our lower, sub-supernal level of operations.

We see Jesus as a man (he walked the planet—found in appearance as a man.) He purposely set aside His awesomeness in order to put on human flesh. He stooped low—on purpose, so that we could relate. But, the 33 year old carpenter on the cross is a divine disguise. God in skin.

Months before the cross, He had revealed a glimpse of His glory on the mountaintop with Elijah and Moses. He glowed brightly there, and for a moment, we caught a fleeting peek at what exactly was contained in that human form. But, the disciples, while appreciating the view, did not comprehend its meaning. Since they had never known Jesus in this heavenly light, they likely considered the two glorified prophets to be the source of the glow that splashed over onto Jesus.

Suppose you were at your child's first soccer game on a Saturday morning and the parent standing next to you was none other than the President of the United States of America. He was there watching his own little one play. The two of you exchange pleasantries. You discuss parenting, youth sports and the weather. After the game you head for the car and home. But, the president leaves the game and resumes his duties as leader of the free world. He laid aside his power for a short while to be a "normal guy," but back in the Oval Office he is authorized to lead the nation.

Jesus set aside His power in order to become like us. He appeared normal. His followers had no idea of the authority He wielded. He had set that aside. As a result, His followers vacillated. They were in—they were out. Just like us. Their perspective on Jesus was colored by the level of their interaction. They met Jesus the carpenter, Jesus the rabbi. His miracles astounded them for they didn't know how an ordinary man could make things happen supernaturally. They had no idea that within the human body was the Creator of the universe, the bright, Morning Star. Therefore, they found their allegiance was thin, and their loyalties were stretched.

Jesus is not attempting to be your buddy. He did not come to increase your swag. He is the Ruler of the Universe. Paul wrote it to the church this way, "Having the eyes of your hearts enlightened, that you may know what is the hope to which He has called you, what are the riches of His glorious inheritance in the saints, and what is the immeasurable greatness of His power toward us who believe, according to the working of his great might that He worked in Christ when He raised Him from the dead and seated Him at His right hand in the heavenly places, far above all rule and authority and power and dominion, and above every name that is named, not only in this age but also in the one to come. And He put all things under His feet and gave Him as head over all things to the church, which is His body, the fullness of Him who fills all in all. (Ephesians 1:18-23 [ESV])

I love this passage of Scripture, for it points out the magnificence of Jesus, but it also tells us that He is ours! The Father placed Jesus in charge of the universe and then gave Him to us—the church. He is ours. We are His. Perhaps if we see Jesus for who He truly is, we will find our allegiance to be rock-steady.

Father God, may my life be open to you today, and may I be as a curious child who listens carefully to the words you speak. Amen

Dropping Anchor: *It's good to have a good king.*

Road Trip

"Have ye not asked them that go by the way? and do ye not know their tokens."
Job 21:29

This morning I woke up in Florida. A twenty two hour drive the day before had landed us here at the home of our friends. We are vacationing. Twenty some hours in a car, covering over twelve hundred miles is an incredible journey. Oh, it isn't like crossing the open prairie in a covered wagon or anything like that. We had the relative luxury of my Ford SUV to carry us along, but with eight of us crammed in the car, ages six months to nearly sixty years, and only making stops for fuel or the occasional 'potty' break, I have to say that I am proud of my crew. My family travels well.

There is something about driving in the darkness over mile after mile of unfamiliar highway that alerts one's senses in a unique way. We pay close attention to the road signs, knowing one wrong turn could put us somewhere we really don't want to be. We could easily end up lost in a strange neighborhood, or an unfamiliar city. We could suddenly be amongst people who do not have our best interests at heart. And so we hurtle along on the main road, family buckled in. We watch the miles slip away, and eventually we are "closer." There are more miles behind us than what lie before; the destination is near.

You know, travelling in a crammed automobile reminds us of truth that we must live by. One cannot be selfish when packed in close and tight. Well, you shouldn't be. One demanding attitude can throw a carload into disarray. One discontented child can send the entire family into whining. When this occurs, everyone is forced to focus on the unhappy traveler. Even the driver must change his concentration from the road ahead to try (along with the others) to pacify the needy child's complaint. This could involve a switching of seats, which is difficult to undertake at sixty five miles per hour. In worse case scenarios we may need to stop the car completely and deal with the problem. Destination is momentarily forgotten in the present effort to settle an inner squabble. In these moments, I am reminded of church.

We in the church have a great set of directions. Jesus left them for us… Love one another as He loved us... Go into the world and make disciples of all nations… we are surely clear on the destination. We are even up to speed on the recommended behavioral practices while on our journey. We have been told to treat others as more important than ourselves. This involves patience and self-control. These are commodities that can run low in close quarters. When the patience gauge is on empty, the only place to fill up is from Heaven's supply. These virtues are in abundance there, but we must choose to yield our cranky spirit over to Divine Nature.

There is bound to be a meltdown or two in any church, just as there was on our twelve hundred mile trek. Somewhere around mile 1,037, Baby Rory was very hungry, but we were out of infant food and there was no place to buy more in Hardeeville, South Carolina at three o'clock in the morning. This lack of necessary formula caused him to cry. Crying babies stress parents, stressed parents can argue with one another, and in a split second, the road was a lost concept and all focus was on handling the crisis in the car. We dispatched an older sibling to attempt to pacify the baby's needs so that we could stay with the flow of traffic, rolling along.

At church, most of the difficulties we handle are once removed from the real threats that surround us. We tend to things inside the 'vehicle,' while outside there is a ten car pileup on the freeway. (For example, musical styles of worship seem to present more of a pressing problem than, say, global famine.) We should be zeroing in on the highway dangers and demands, but we are forced to handle squabbles that break out within the car. This takes our minds off the mission and goal (the destination) and causes us to consume our energies on the situation within. While doing so, we may, perhaps, miss an important road sign. We can even get stuck on a side road we never intended to travel. All the while we are trying to rearrange seating or discipline the wrongdoer, our focus is off the mark. In this manner, many churches have lost their vision for the journey. Just keeping everyone on board happy becomes the new purpose—not arriving at the destination. So consumed with keeping the family happy are we, that contentedness becomes our new goal. Before we know it, we have pulled into a rest area. There, drowsiness overtakes us and we are resting comfortably, but we are also stopped at a standstill. It would have been better to suffer some discomfort, and dispatch an older sibling to deal with the problem for then; we would still be on the road and making headway. The destination would be getting closer, with more roads behind us than before us. Personal crankiness would have been swallowed up in the chorus of excited voices that call out together, "Are we there yet?" Almost, but we have to keep moving, eyes on the road.

Father God, we will travel near and far today. We will board planes, ships and automobiles. Keep us safe and keep us pleasant. Amen

Dropping Anchor: *A good destination requires good directions.*

___

___

___

___

Observations Under Water

"And God said, Let the waters bring forth abundantly the moving creature that hath life...'"
Genesis 1:20

We bought my daughter, Prudence, an aquarium for her eighth birthday. It's not a big tank... just ten gallons of water. But it is a pleasant addition to our living room and we all enjoy peering into this tiny water world, eyeing the antics of the little fish who live there. It is a remarkable place, a completely separate environment from our air breathing world—under water—behind glass. It's an entirely different kind of reality, yet I think we can learn something from these aquatic dwellers of the deep (well, not so deep, actually).

Just like you and me out here breathing the fresh air, my fish live in a fallen world. All of creation groans in its sinful predicament, awaiting the revelation of the King of Kings. That truth is found in Romans chapter eight, and is evident every time we take an honest look at what's really going on. The audible groan is our own as we struggle for better and wait for the Best to come. Yes, even our little aquarium groans within its glass boundaries. In the fallen microcosmic eco-system of this wet world, there is no civility. Food is fought for and devoured in such a greedy fashion that it is, at times, uncomfortable to watch. Several of the fish are true bullies. They chase the little fish into the relative safety of the plastic weeds, where they can seek cover from these tough guys of the tank. This goes on and on. They don't seem to ever work things out. Apparently there is a reluctant acceptance of the way things are in the sea. These creatures are living out the groan shared by all creation, everywhere. I expected peace in my aquarium, but there is no peace.

These swimming fish don't know me, but I am their provider. I plug in the filter and the heater that control their environment. Pure water comes from me. I supply the fish flakes. I had set up the aquarium before any of them ever came to live there. I bought them and I paid a price. They are my possession. Sometimes they sense my presence, usually when they are looking for a meal, but I remain a mystery to them. I am from a different world, a separate dimension. I am outside of their fish-life experience. They are totally dependent upon me for their life and health, yet they remain ignorant of my existence.

The fish maintain a social order to some degree, but that is fallen, too. The little neon guppies school together, as do the bigger orange fish. They each know their own kind and keep close alliances within their little groups. I don't know how much brain power these little fish have, but it obviously doesn't require much cerebral activity to segregate. Segregation, even aquatic style, establishes boundaries that eventually become barriers. We have a clear example of this occurring in two glass bowls on the mantle above our fireplace. Each bowl is home to a single Beta fish. They are banned from aquarium living. They cannot conduct themselves in social situations. If just two are ever put in the same container, they will fight for dominance until one of them is dead. They lead a lonely existence due to their ill temper. I have no idea what original sin caused the Beta Wars to begin, but it is a long standing feud, known to every member of the species. You can spy them for yourself in any pet store—dozens of them—each in a little clear plastic prison no bigger than a coffee mug. Temperament tells the life story for these sad little swimmers.

I could now draw the life comparisons as they relate to us, living in this dimension of the troubled creation, but I fear they are so obvious that I may insult intelligence. Instead, I am going to go and feed the fish in Prudence's aquarium. I will watch as the struggle for the fish flakes plays out yet again. I may even tap the glass sides of their water world to let them know I am watching. But, they will carry on as usual. They do not heed my admonition to be fair, to share, and be kind.

I believe I will go and talk with my Provider, for I am so thankful that "revelation" is in His good nature. That tapping on the glass you hear just beyond the borders of your understanding? It's Him:

Your Provider. He wants you to know He's there and He will go to great lengths to prove it. It sounds as crazy as me climbing into the fish tank and becoming like them, to instruct them that they are cared for—but that is just what Jesus did, and does, and always will. No wonder He first called fishermen to follow.

> *Father God, I invite you into my world. You have made it. You sustain it. So, instead let me thank you for inviting me to be a part of your world. Amen*

Dropping Anchor: *The edges of our perceptions border on the eternal.*

____
____
____
____

Lemon Yellow

"If the Son therefore shall make you free, ye shall be free indeed."
John 8:36

My very first car was a lemon yellow VW Beetle. Perhaps I should stop right there at the word "lemon." Although I loved driving it, dependability was not its principal appeal. It was an adventure—that much you could depend upon. I loved that old clunker the way everyone loves their first taste of driving freedom. You have your own set of wheels. You can come and go as you please. The world is your oyster... until you put the key in the ignition and it won't start.

The Volkswagen Beetle was very basic transportation. Back in that day, the car came with no cabin comforts such as ventilated, forced air. In other words, there was no fan to blow warm air on your windshield (or your freezing fingers for that matter) in winter, and no cooling flow of air through the cabin when the weather was warm. Thus, in winter diving, the trick was to get up enough speed to send some outside air through the narrow vents in hopes that a peep-hole would open on the icy windshield before you hit something ahead of you that you could not see. Meanwhile, the so-called heating vents on the floor (pulling a small lever would open them) would fry your ankles to a crisp at highway speeds while the rest of the car's interior remained chilly. It was difficult to manage the little vehicle. However, the open road never felt as inviting as in those initial days of auto ownership. The highway was home and as long as I was tucked into that little yellow car, I didn't require a destination. It was enough just to be driving.

The "driving" feature however, seemed to have come as an option on my VW. Many mornings I would summon my roommates to come to my aid and push the uncooperative car so that I could jump start it as I headed off to work. From my driveway to the job site, it was always a game of riding the clutch, hoping not to stall in traffic. More than once, upon stalling, some kind stranger offered to push while I popped the clutch to get underway again. I was a traffic jam looking for a place to happen.

Once at a friend's house, I could not get the car to start, no matter what I tried. A kindly uncle who was part mechanic, part mad scientist, rigged something up with an extension cord that ran back to the engine and another that hung down the center of the windshield. I am uncertain to this day how it worked—or why—I can only testify that when the two cords were plugged together, the car started like a charm. Curious passengers would often ask how the system worked as they watched me plug in. "Faith," was always my reply.

Like my Volkswagen, we are sometimes ill prepared for the elements of life. We strain to see what is before us but we can't seem to get a clear view. Often, after finally getting up some speed, we must tend to an annoyance or two, not unlike fried feet on a cold winter's day. In the jumble and traffic of life, we sometimes need a push from a friend, or a friendly stranger. We forge ahead, hoping not to stall out. In the end, it is faith that keeps us going. I can't explain it. I just know it works. And, when all has been said and done, you have to admit… it has been quite a ride.

Father God, You stretch out my life like an open road before me. And then you teach me how to drive. You tell me how to keep things running smoothly. I will trust your manual and follow your will. Amen

Dropping Anchor: *The open road holds no allure if you always need a push.*

____

____

____

____

Hilda

"Watch ye, stand fast in the faith,
quit you like men [act manly], *be strong."*
1 Corinthians 16:13

I grew up in a home where pets were scarce. Like most boys, I would routinely petition my parents for a dog. My grandparents had a black lab named 'Circy' and I considered that old dog to be a grand thing. Circy looked forward to my visits as, once there, I would head straight for the cupboard and begin feeding her from a box of doggie treats. I never got tired of running her through her paces which she would willingly perform in order to qualify for the little bone-shaped biscuits. That dog never seemed to grow weary of the games. She would roll over, play dead, sit, speak… you know the canine basics. After each antic I would merrily toss her a reward which she usually caught mid-air, before hunkering down and crunching away. I reckon these episodes worked favorably on my behalf, for one day my parents announced that I was ready and responsible enough to get a dog of my own. Promising to feed, water and walk this would-be, could-be pup, I waited for the day when my parents would take me to the pet store and there allow me to choose a worthy dog for my own. It didn't quite happen like that.

Hilda came to us in a second hand sort of way. A member of my dad's congregation was moving to Pennsylvania and was told that her new home had a no-dog policy. Well, she had a dog, a feisty little dachshund named Frau Hilda. It was decided by the adults that Hilda would make the move to our house and become mine. The day she arrived was memorable. I was delighted beyond words. Hilda's soon-to-be former owner, a kind, elderly woman, was a torrent of tears. "She's yours now, son" offered my dad, unsure which emotion he was supposed to tap into. "Why not take her outside and show her the yard?" I needed no prodding. Out the door we went a tangle of dog, boy, and leash.

She was the smallest dog in the neighborhood, her tiny legs supporting her sausage body with barely inches of ground clearance. Her diminutive frame, however, made no difference to her self-esteem. She patrolled our property daily, chasing any dog visitors from the yard, no matter what their size advantage. I once saw a German shepherd scamper away, tail between his legs, looking back over his shoulder at the barking brown missile headed straight for him. We soon understood—Hilda was in charge.

She was as smart as she was sassy. She comprehended orders like "Stay out of the garbage!" and "Kitchen!" (My mother insisted that our spacious kitchen was enough indoor area for such a small dog. That one word would stop her dead in her tracks). Hilda was always the first to greet anyone at the door. After a morning of errands, we would return to a royal greeting from our canine friend, that is, unless she had broken the rules while we were gone. What a conscience! In the case of mischief or misbehavior on Hilda's part, she would not come out of hiding to welcome us back home. Her retreat was always made to a spot way under the table, where she would sit, obviously under conviction, thumping her tail as if trying to at least sound like a good dog. Whenever she hid and thumped—we knew we would find the trash barrel overturned or a box of shredded tissues somewhere in forbidden territory. Not unlike our first parents who ate the fruit of the wrong tree in the Garden, my dog would go into hiding, thus exposing her guilt. It was positively Biblical. The book of Genesis had come to life in our kitchen! "Hillllddaaaa!" came the scolding voice from whoever discovered the trespass. Out she would saunter, head low and pace slow. She was in the doghouse and she knew it.

The night Hilda left us came unexpectedly. Many years had passed since she had been delivered to our door. I was in my last year of high school and headed for college. Hilda's face had turned gray, and her pace had slowed a bit. "Hilda didn't touch her supper." My mother's words reached me in the front room where my dad and I were watching the evening news. I looked toward the kitchen and saw her standing in the doorway, earnestly looking my way. "Come here, girl," I called, and to my side she came—breaking the kitchen rule. Somehow on this night it didn't seem so important. Cuddled by my side, she drew deep sighs of contentment, occasionally thumping her tail. The next morning she had gone. She lay motionless in her bed and I could tell that she wasn't with us any longer. Dad found a box which we decorated with bright colors and we laid her to rest in it. We marched single file to the woods where we buried her, singing an old Vacation Bible School song, Boys and Girls for Jesus. "It was her favorite song," offered a friend. We walked back to the house in silence.

I learned a lot from that little dachshund. When I think of her now, decades later, I call up images of her chasing away stray dogs, geese, or newspaper boys; any intruder was sent packing. She guarded the home like it was her job. The application is obvious; we should all guard our homes from intruders in the spiritual realm just as Hilda would do in the natural. A good friend once put it this way; "If a filthy swine came bursting into your house and proceeded to track mud all over your carpet and furniture, you wouldn't stand idly by and hope the animal would eventually find his way out. No! You would grab a broom or its equivalent and try your best to drive it out. There would be no rest until the job was done." So, we must patrol the borders of our lives like a spiritual watchdog. If the opposition seems to be bigger than you—no matter you have God-given authority to drive out all enemy intruders… just like Frau Hilda.

Father God, many of us have animals that are like family to us. Thank you for the creation of these loving companions. May we be as loyal to you as they are to us. Amen

Dropping Anchor: *Properly weilded authority can chase away the big dogs.*

____
____
____
____

Disaster Or Adventure

"And He said to them all, If any man will come after Me,
let him deny himself, and take up his cross daily
and follow Me."
Luke 9:23

Many years ago, it so happened that I was standing on a stark, frozen mountainside far above the tree line—with a group of teenage boys in my care. The icy wind was whipping at our clothes and our only protection against the wild environment was a canvas tent and our sleeping bags. We were miles away from any other human being. Night was falling and we had no choice but to hunker down and ride out the darkness. For most people, the situation would mean disaster. For us, however, it was sheer adventure. We wanted to be there! We had chosen to ascend to the mountain's peak to earn merit badges for our climbing club, and the exciting prospect of reaching the summit would come with the dawn. There is a fine line between disaster and adventure.

My son, Brett, was quite a skateboarder in his teenage years. I can recall watching him doing flips and leaps, planted precariously on four little wheels, and sometimes only two little wheels. Once, while I was at the indoor skate park, waiting for him to wrap up an afternoon of skateboard antics, I witnessed him going airborne over a set of ten steps and landing on the hard floor surface below with his perfect center-of-the-board position and posture well intact. If it had been me going airborne at the top of ten stairs it would have only been disastrous and a really big mistake. If I were somehow unfortunate enough to involve small wheels in the tumble—it would only get worse.

Life offers us many stark realities. They, too, can be viewed as disaster or adventure. Chief among them is the brevity of our time here on earth. Life ends for all of us at some point. Most of us are much closer to the end than we would like to be before we begin to consider this truth. We have ascended the mountain and just the peak awaits. We are leaping off the top step of the staircase and are airborne—no turning back. But, a good mountain climber has prepared for the elements. A skateboarder is well practiced before attempting a leap. We, too, must prepare and practice life. Will the end come as disaster or adventure? I choose adventure and you can too. Here's this pastor's perspective on how.

Begin by laying your life down now. Don't cling to it. Give it away. How? Ten minutes at a time. Just about every ten minutes of life brings a new choice to be either selfish or giving. Make each choice well. Do I slumber and hit the snooze button or get up and face the day? Do I present cheeriness to my family, or complaints and grouchiness? Do I yield in the traffic during my morning commute, or do I honk and curse and push my way through? Do I pray, or turn on the distraction of the radio? Do I perform my job to the best of my abilities, or do I settle for 'good enough?' Do I listen to my children at the dinner table as they describe their day, or do I turn on the game and ignore the family? Every choice has a consequence. Every choice matters.

Laying your life down is a practice that requires patience. Jesus told us that this is the only way we can truly follow Him. He has ascended the peaks before us. He has made all the leaps. He shows us how it is done. If we learn from Him, then, when the final challenge arrives and we must lay life down one last time, we will say, "I know how this is done." The mountain's peak will have been reached. The landing at the bottom of the stairs will be perfect. You have prepared for this moment. You've climbed dozens of hills, following the Guide. You are ready for the last mountain. You have jumped over many obstacles and are ready for this great and final leap. The end does not hold disaster. It is surely a grand adventure as you discover that you can do this! A lifetime of practice has made you ready to enter the gates of the Kingdom. Prepare for the adventure of eternity. Ten minutes at a time. The King will be pleased, and He will say, "Not so scary, was it? I knew you could do it! Well done."

Father God, I ask for adventure to thrill my soul that keeps me trusting you. I dare not brave this life without you as my guide. Amen

Dropping Anchor: *Life's final leap lands in love.*

Philippi

"Around midnight, Paul and Silas were praying and singing hymns to God..."
Acts 16:25

"How does that song go - the one we learned in Lystra?" The Apostle Paul's voice was weary, but clear, despite his bruised and swollen lips. His companion, Silas, lay next to him on the cold, stone floor of the innermost cell of the prison in Philippi. Both men had heavy shackles around their ankles. Their hands were bound with ropes, secured to the rock wall that surrounded them. "It's the one we learned at young Timothy's house. I'm thinking it would be a good time to sing it..." Silas chuckled under his breath. "You are serious, aren't you? You are something else, brother Paul" Silas' laughter quickly became a moan as he tried in vain to sit up. "Owwww. It hurts when I laugh," he remarked. "But, how did the song begin?" Paul asked again. "If you get me started I am sure the words will come back to me."

Silas began to sing. "That's it! Yes..." Paul joined him as together they raised their voices.

Praise our Jehovah God
Praise His beloved Son.
The timeless plan, redemption's song
Is written now upon my heart

It was past midnight and it had been a long day. Indeed it had been many long days in the ancient seaport city, named for Philip, the legendary father of the Great Alexander of Greece. Paul and Silas had been street preaching and with no little opposition. There had been a young witch that had been following them and disrupting their open air meetings outside the temple. Finally, Paul had enough and cast a demon spirit from her, causing her to lose her powers and thereby causing her influential owners lost revenue. When she publicly announced herself to be Christian, her former owners sent a message to the chief of police, demanding the arrest of Paul and Silas. A mob had quickly formed and the whole city, it seemed was in an uproar. The local officials wanted to get control over the mayhem and called on the security guards to drag the two men into custody. Severely beaten by rods, Paul and Silas were thrown into maximum security and ordered held until court could convene in the morning. Official charges would be made at that time.

I am in awe of Jehovah's love
Costing Christ his very life
His horrid death upon the cross
The exchange was made sure for me

The voices of the two men carried through the cavernous prison. "You know... our voices sound pretty good in this place. It has a certain echo effect." Paul smiled as he spoke. "You're missing another tooth," Silas observed. The moonlight was enough for the new gap to show as he sang. "I know." replied the apostle. "That makes four missing now, never mind." Paul cracked a wider smile. "It doesn't seem to hamper my singing voice." As they sang, a low rumble shook the prison. The stone floor beneath them rolled like ocean billows as the men watched in amazement. "My hands are free!" shouted Silas. He quickly began pulling at the ropes that held Paul. Within no time, both men were free of the cords. They rubbed their wrists and flexed their stiff fingers. Then a powerful earthquake hit. Walls crumbled and shackles broke from their places. Doors swung open wide on their iron hinges. The jail was reduced to a pile of rubble within a few terrifying seconds. Paul and Silas stood to their feet, unharmed. Free of their bonds, they picked their way out from the rubble and stood at the place that had once been the main doorway.

Seconds after the shaking stopped, the dismayed jailer appeared at the perimeter of the wreckage. Sword in hand, the prisoners were unsure of his intent - to hurt himself or to control them. "You won't need the weapon," Paul said firmly. "We are all here." The jailer fell to his knees. "I heard you preaching in the marketplace yesterday," said the distraught man. "I wanted to know more. Then,

I heard your singing on this very night. I believe you are from God - can I be saved? What must I do?" "You must believe. Yes and your family too," Silas added. "Bring them out to us."

And so it was that salvation came to a family in Philippi. As the jailer bathed the wounds of Paul and Silas, he too joined in the song of Lystra.

Jehovah the most powerful
Reigns in glorious light
Jesus the very Son of God
Reigns now within my heart

Father God, teach me songs in the night that will break chains in the morning. Amen

Dropping Anchor: *Do not doubt in the dark what you believed in the light.*

____

____

____

____

Major League Reid

"...a brother is born for adversity."
Proverbs 17:17

One night in 1982, I stepped off a curb right in front of a Dodge travelling down Route 9 at forty miles per hour. My parents hadn't neglected the "look both ways" lessons as I was growing up; it was just a simple, yet costly mistake that nearly took my life. I spent the next three months as a hospital patient. Still, in my early twenties, I had plenty of friends from college and the workforce who frequented my room at Framingham Union Hospital, just outside of Boston. Indeed, I had many visitors who dropped in to see me over those long weeks of recuperation. I would like to tell you of one in particular.

The Red Sox were nothing special in 1982. They had yet to break the "curse" and "wait till next year!" was our familiar battle cry. They were our home team however, and that year, hopes were again riding high as some young talent had been added to the roster. One player, Reid Nichols, a speedy infielder who could also play the outfield positions, was a frequent name on the lineup card. Reid was introduced to me at one of the Red Sox baseball chapel services. These baseball chapel programs were held every Sunday morning in the clubhouse a few hours before game time. I had been invited to speak at the informal gathering of players and coaches, and that morning I met Reid.

Reid and I hit it off. I was living with some roommates just outside of Boston and Reid became a "regular" at our condo. I think it was my sister's cooking that he really enjoyed, as she was quite accomplished in the kitchen. Her chocolate chip cookies were demolished by the dozens, and there were always plenty to go home with our Sox friend at the close of the evening. During these visits, we always managed to have a game of catch or whiffle ball before supper. Playing catch is more exciting when a major leaguer is on the receiving end of your tosses. All in all, it was shaping up to be a great summer.

That is when I met the sedan on the highway. The force of the collision, metal hitting flesh and bone, knocked the shoes off of my feet. They were recovered at a distance of about ¾ of a football field away from the accident site. I bounced down the pavement with a broken leg and a cracked cranium. I landed in the emergency room with a kindly doctor tending to my injuries. During my chaotic intake, conversation came around to the Red Sox game that night. The team was in Kansas City at the time, in the middle of a lengthy road trip. During the conversation, one of my friends happened to let the ER staff know that I was friendly with Reid of the Red Sox. That was all the prompting the thoughtful doctor needed. He placed a call to the Red Sox front office and they in turn, sent the news of my injuries to the ball club in their Kansas City hotel. Once word reached the players, the telephone rang in my hospital room and soon I was talking to my friend Reid. He promised to come see me as soon as the team made their way back to Boston. Later that evening, Reid asked the television broadcasters to mention that he was playing the game that night with my stricken condition on his heart—and requested that the viewers keep me in their prayers. This they did.

A week or two later, I heard a buzz in the hallways of the fourth floor, orthopedic wing where I was recovering. Nurses gathered around my bed and with a bit of fanfare, parted an opening in the circle to let Reid stand by my bedside. He handed me a "get well" card which he had personally made for me. All of his fellow Red Sox players had signed the card.

As the summer wore on, I was released from the hospital. Yet, my broken leg was slow to heal. There was little progress to report on the X-Rays and an infection made matters worse. To my dismay, amputation was discussed. My spirits were low and remained that way for an entire year. It so happened in 1982, the Red Sox also were skidding, right out of the playoff picture. The final week of the season found them playing the dreaded New York Yankees. Reid was having a solid season, batting just under .300 and playing both infield and outfield. I was his guest for the last home Saturday game of the season. Hobbled though I was, I made my way to my seat behind home plate. In a wild game featuring soaking rain and thick fog, Reid homered in his last at bat. I stood to my feet and applauded him and as he crossed home plate—he tipped his cap.

I lost touch with Reid over the ensuing years. He was traded by the Red Sox in a deal that sent him north of the border to the Montreal Expos. He played his last big league game on my birthday, five years after the 1982 season. My leg eventually healed. In late summer of 1983 I managed to put on a ball glove and play one half of an inning of a church league softball game at first base. I was drained from just that little exercise, over one year after the accident. But I was getting stronger in spirit at a much quicker rate than my physical healing. Everywhere I went, I would meet people who had been praying for me ever since they heard of my accident on the Red Sox network one summer night from Kansas City. My spirits soared every time I considered the kindness of that team effort—a caring doctor, a helpful ball club, a friend who played in the big leagues, and faithful praying people across the country.

Each new season of summer brings with it the memories of Route 9, Reid and my recuperation, aided by the Red Sox. The "Repair of Loren" and the friendship with Reid all started in Chapel… and I have learned since that most good things do. God is a giver of good gifts and He uses His people to deliver them. You don't have to be a major league ball player in order to bring cheer to someone in need… but you will need to step up to the plate.

Father God, may I be a big league friend to someone today. Amen

Dropping Anchor: *The minor leagues teach us character. The major leagues give us a chance to use it.*

____
____
____
____

Hidden

"And the Lord God called unto Adam,
and said unto him, 'Where art thou?'"
Genesis 3:9

My son True is three years old. We have had three years, now, of watching this boy grow into a remarkable little human. He is full of life and love. The other day we were sitting at the kitchen counter. I was on my laptop, while True was working with some modeling clay. "Hey, Mom?" he called out. "Yes?" replied Amanda. "I love my dad," True said without looking up. He was molding the clay into a heart shape. "He needs to make it about fifty times bigger," I thought… It would have to be a grand scale sculpture in order to hold all the love in the house.

True is all boy. He thinks nothing of leaping off sofas or beds, (or onto an unsuspecting dad in HIS bed,) and then landing with a thud and a "Whoa! That was cool…" He has never seen a puddle he didn't like. Oft times, when it is raining, he will come in from the outside with his legs caked in mud. The clothes and shoes are laundered and so is young True. He climbs in the tub like it was the Fountain of Youth and proceeds to splash and soak. If his brother is sharing the experience, they form a tubby tidal wave and laugh themselves silly. When the fingertips are pruney and they've been sufficiently scrubbed behind the ears, we drag them out and dry them off.

True is also a hide-and-seek expert. Technically, he is not that good at hiding. There are several key secretive places where he will station himself as soon as mom's car pulls in the driveway. When she comes through the door, we all play our part by adopting quizzical voices and faces. "Is True with you?" "Help us find True!" We have barely spoken the words when a cabinet door flies open and out tumbles True. He just could not wait to be found. "Here I am!" Hugging his family one by one, True squeals with joy and says "I found you!" More hugs and happiness follow while we celebrate the lost being found—who thought he found us. As a father, it rarely gets better.

We are all pretty good at hiding. But I, like True, undertake a pretense of hiding, for my secluded safe havens are well known to the One who comes looking. Just like the first humans who hid themselves in the Garden of Eden, we hear the voice of Love calling, "Where are you, dear child?" I have learned not to stay hidden for long. I cannot wait to be found. I tumble out of my secret hiding place and fall into my Father's arms. With a wide smile He gathers me up and says, "Yes child… you found Me. Here I am."

Father God, I never want to hide from you. Make my life so righteous that I need not hide from anyone else, either. Amen

Dropping Anchor: *Better not to hide from correction if you want to be found by love.*

____

____

____

____

One Night In Boston

"Thou shalt not take the name of the Lord thy God in vain; for the Lord will not hold him guiltless that taketh His name in vain."
Exodus 20:7

I was at a convention years ago; an evangelical gathering of ministry leaders from all over New England. During the closing keynote address, I saved myself a seat next to Milton Friesen, one of my spiritual mentors. Milton was the director of a homeless shelter in Boston and we had struck up a meaningful friendship over the years. Together we sat on the risers that spanned the back of the auditorium.

The main speaker was a well-known author and lecturer, recognized by his passionate preaching and persuasive presentations. He was known as a defender of the faith and more than one in disagreement was shamed into silence after taking him on in a debate. You would most likely recognize his name, however he is not the one you're thinking of—He's the other one. He was calling for a compassionate outpouring of God's love for the unbeliever. His challenge was for those of us in attendance to share the message of the gospel with everyone and anyone we would happen to meet. Then the shocker came. As he was fussing and spitting his way to his passionate point, the dynamic speaker announced, "All around us in the streets of Boston, there are thousands of people on the road to hell." He paused and went on, "The problem is that most of you in this room don't give a ___________." (Expletive deleted) He bravely continued as the audience gasped and grew silent. "The bigger problem is that most of you are more upset that I used a curse word in the pulpit than you are about all those people going to hell."

The silence was deafening. No one moved. After a moment, Milton leaned over and said softly in my ear, "I fear our dear brother is correct." I have never forgotten that evening, nor have I forgotten the lesson. I suppose I never will.

Growing up, I always thought that the Commandment (number four of the Ten) "do not take the name of the Lord in vain," meant 'cussing' was forbidden. Well, it surely should be—but that is not what the law means. Not at all... It simply means that we must not say we belong to God and then live like we don't. That is a far greater problem than swearing for most of us. If a woman marries and takes the name of her husband, then proceeds to live like a single woman, she would have taken his name in vain. Many Christians say they belong to Jesus, but no one would ever know it. Their lives and identities are tied closely to earthbound things, despite being heaven's offspring.

So, I reckon the speaker got it right that night in Boston. My friend Milton passed a few years later. He now enjoys a seat in heaven, so I will have to say it in his stead. "I fear our dear brother is correct."

Father God, thank you for preachers who stir us with the truth, even if it hurts a bit. Amen

Dropping Anchor: *If you take the Name, you had better swear allegiance.*

Whale Watch

"And God created great whales..."
Genesis 1:21

It seemed like a great idea... a whale watch. Several of my friends and I got our heads together and decided that since we lived near New Bedford, Massachusetts, the once and former whaling capital of America, we should endeavor to see some of these giant sea creatures ourselves. We booked tickets for a tour which promised whale sightings by the score. That morning, we left dry land behind and embarked upon the waters of the Atlantic coast. It was quite thrilling, standing up near the bow with the salt spray in our faces, the rolling waves breaking before us. We all felt the excitement of the grand ocean rising in us.

That is, all except for my friend, Al. Something else was rising in him. We were not more than twenty minutes from shore when I noticed he was in trouble. He looked pale. He looked sick. He was both... pale and sick. "How long did they tell us this trip would last?" Al looked desperate as he asked me the question. "Four hours," I replied. "I'll never make it," said Al as he headed for the rest room below deck.

"Al is seasick," I warned my friends. "He looks terrible." We felt badly for him, but there was nothing we could do. After about an hour of heading out to the open sea, we saw our first whales. They were huge, graceful dwellers of the deep - seemingly as curious about us as we were about them. We watched in awe and wonder. But not Al. "Tell them to turn the boat around!" he hollered from his position at the rail. It seemed as though Al had eaten a very big breakfast that morning. I wondered how much more he could put into the sea.

About an hour later I saw him again. It was an "Al sighting." Up from below he stumbled, bursting up from the deep, his face an unsettling hue of green and the splash of breakfast all around him. He was way past caring about his clothes. He was clinging to life.

"Awww, buddy," I muttered to him. "Turn the ship around." he hissed. "Make it stop."

Eventually we headed back to port. The long voyage was nearly over. Al stayed below decks in the little restroom he now called home. He had redecorated the floor and walls and the one seat in the room was where he rested his head. As the gangplank lowered for us to disembark, the human sea parted as Al came bursting forth and dove onto dry land. I have never witnessed such relief. He was off the boat. "For good," he managed. "Never again."

Perhaps there is a rocking boat in your life that you have boarded that has taken you for a ride and is now making you ill. Like my seasick friend, you have no solid ground under your feet. It can be most anything causing you to suffer; too much sugar; too much alcohol; too many pills. "Make it stop!" you plead. But there is only one way to a cure. A wise man once told me, "Sin always takes you farther than you wanted to go." Get off the boat... for good.

Father God, Your creation is magnificent and is worth exploring. You care for the creatures of the sea and you care for men who long to see them. We share the same planet, so help us to appreciate the beauty around us in nature. Amen

Dropping Anchor: *Some things you must go through alone.*

G.I. Joe

*"For the trumpet shall sound
and the dead shall be raised incorruptible,
and we shall be changed."*
1 Corinthians 15:52

It is hard to write about the good old days without revealing one's true identity. So, for the purposes and interests of total truth, let me state for the record, that I am officially an old fogey. I'm not certain of all of the necessary qualifications, but I'll bet I've got 'em, all of them. I recall yesteryear with a certain amount of fondness. And, I wonder nowadays just what this world is coming to. Whatever it is that the future holds, we are not trending upward. Not in my mind at least.

I recall, when I was a boy, I desperately wanted a G.I. Joe action figure. He was a great toy back in that day; eleven inches tall with workable joints and even a battle scar on his cheek. He was every boy's dream toy. He came in naval dress or army attire. He had a scuba suit and diving gear. He had weapons. He was ready for serious play. My parents scraped together enough money to purchase a G.I. Joe for me one Christmas and I was completely transfixed. He was better in real life than I had even imagined. I played with my new companion constantly.

But, I broke it. I just snapped a hand right off. Joe could no longer hold his rifle or fire off a flare gun. He was destined for discarding. Yet, instead of a toss to the bottom of the toy bin, my mother went to the local library and found the address of the Hasbro Company. We then carefully packed the wounded warrior in a shoe box and mailed him to the address the municipal library had provided. We waited. Weeks passed. Joe was surely gone for good. And then, one day he wasn't! He appeared back in my mailbox reconditioned and raring to go. The good folks at the parent company even sent along some action accessories. No charge.

Along with "Fogey-dom" my old age has brought me Parkinson's disease. Like my action figure, G.I. Joe, I am broken. I am wounded somewhere at the core of my brain. But, I do not fear discarding. Loving hands that care for me now, will someday pack me in a box and send me off. I will be gone for a time. But then one day, I won't! I will come back restored and raring to go. That is a truth that we had better hold to throughout our years, until the day comes when we find it is holding us.

So, maybe the future is brighter than my old mind can conceive. I will choose to look ahead, not behind. The past was surely sweeter than today, but the plans for tomorrow are truly amazing.

> *Father God, I was broken, but you restored me. How can I thank you enough? I will try to live this day as a thank you for all you have done and in expectancy of what is yet to come. Amen*

Dropping Anchor: *The past offers us no place to live. The future offers a forever place to live.*

____

____

____

____

Goal!

"Let nothing be done through strife or vainglory; but in lowliness of mind let each esteem other better than themselves."
Philippians 2:3

My freshman year of college didn't get off to a good start. Missing my high school friends, I was feeling empty and homesick. I guess you could say I was lonely. From the moment my parents dropped me off and drove away, I began to seriously consider hitching a ride back home. To accentuate my loneliness, my roommate never showed up. I had been given preliminary information about who I was to expect, so I moved into the dorm, and set up my side of things. But, day after day passed with no sign of my fellow dorm dweller. I found his picture in the Student Directory under "incoming freshmen," which seemed to indicate he had, indeed, made plans to come, but there was no sign, no letter and no phone call. My Resident Assistant, Dave seemed understanding. He would frequently look in on me in an attempt to cheer me, but most efforts fell flat. I was alone in my misery.

In addition to being our RA, Dave was also captain of the soccer team. He and I would often kick a soccer ball up and down the dormitory hallways to pass the time. The trick was to keep the ball centered. If you allowed it to hit the wall—you lost a point. We became quite adept at this little game and we played it for hours. Together we cut out my missing roommate's photo from the Directory and hung it on my door. "Will he show??" read the caption. September turned to October and there was still an empty bunk on the far side of my dorm room. "You look like you lost your best friend," Dave would tell me.

There was no doubting it, I was blue. My best friends were hours away. My dorm room was half empty. My classes seemed to hold no interest for me. And, on the fourth day of October—it was my birthday. As I lay on my bed, trying hard to swallow the lump in my throat, a knock came at my door. It was Dave. "We have a home game this afternoon," he said. "Why not come watch? Tell you what... I'll score a goal for your birthday!" Minimally cheered, I thanked him for his invite and closed the door. To my own surprise, at four o'clock that afternoon, I plunked down on the grandstand at the soccer field. Looking around, I saw no one that I knew. I felt the anxiety rising in my throat, but I took a deep breath and began watching the game on the field.

It was a close game. Tied at one goal apiece, the clock was running down in the second half, when, out of nowhere, Dave intercepted a pass at midfield. With a burst of speed, he ran toward the opponent's' goal. With one defender to beat, he feigned to his left and then let the ball fly with his right foot. The ball nestled nicely in the far corner of the net past the dive of the outstretched goalkeeper. It was a beautiful game-winning shot.

Much to my surprise, Dave did not return upfield with his team. Instead, he trotted over to the stands where I stood. With the crowd cheering, he waved his arms for quiet, pointed squarely at me and shouted, "Loren that was for you! Happy birthday!" Suddenly, I was surrounded by friends, not strangers. There were hugs, and slaps on my back. There were introductions. One cute coed removed my hat and put it in her own head; I must admit, I didn't mind. The crowd of soccer fans had become my new friends.

On the way back to my room, I realized the lump in my throat was gone. It never returned. Upon entering my dorm, I removed the photo of my roommate to be, from his place on my door. I put up some posters. I organized my desk. I was going to be ok after all. As I look back on that October day, I realize that Dave's birthday gift of a goal changed the crowd's perception of me, but the real change was taking place inside of me. Dave didn't kick a soccer ball into a net with the lime light bright upon him to accomplish that. No, it was the hours in the hallway of the dormitory when nobody noticed—kicking a ball back and forth with a lonely freshman.

We all have lonely and anxious people around us. They feel abandoned and fearful and we can be their answered prayer. Oh, you don't need to score a game winning goal. Any act of true compassion can transform a life. Stop where you are and encourage someone. Kindly give them some of your attention. Share the limelight. Make them feel important. The Scriptures tell us to treat each other as more important than ourselves. We should make that our goal, because if we truly do forget about ourselves, we will leave behind kindnesses that someone else will always remember.

Father God, help me to "Make someone's day" Amen

Dropping Anchor: *A genuine kindness is remembered in eternity.*

____

____

____

____

Cause And Effect

"For as he thinketh in his heart, so is he"
Proverbs 23:7

We tend to blame ourselves for things which are truly beyond the range of our influence. It's fairly easy to find a supposed cause and effect for nearly every life situation. In our minds, we pick up the blame for our parents broken relationship, a lost job opportunity or an accident which caused us pain. Truth be told, it isn't always our fault. In fact, we usually have no contribution to the mix that is the way of the world. Our inner musings fall far short of any true historical influence or effect.

However, I once had a pastor friend who was fairly certain he caused the Boston Red Sox to lose the 1986 World Series to the New York Mets. In order to appreciate his perspective you need to understand Sox fans. In 1986 it had been many years since the beloved Boston nine had flown a championship banner over Fenway Park. We were accustomed to losing, but never had we managed to lose in such spectacular fashion as we did in '86. It was classic. You may know the story, how a little grounder up the first base line got under Bill Buckner's mitt and the sure-fire easy out became a run scoring, game winning error. The game was lost and the Series soon followed as the Boston faithful watched defeat being snatched from the jaws of victory. The Mets were world champions, while in Boston; we lamented our rotten luck and wondered if we were somehow cursed. That kind of mindset can be catchy and it certainly was embraced by my preacher friend. He blamed himself, and here's why.

He was a devout man. He was earnest about evangelism and discipleship. His lifestyle was blameless except for one downfall. He was a television junkie – a real TV-aholic. He was addicted to the television and he knew it. He would try and limit his time in front of the "idiot box" as he called it, but he would fall back into the bad habit with such ease that he finally decided to rid himself of the source of his problem. He packed up his television and stowed it away in the hall closet. "Out of sight – out of mind," he considered. It seemed to work well. "I promise God, that I will leave that TV in the closet and spend my time in a more productive manner," he vowed. He did just that. Hours that were formerly spent with the Beverly Hillbillies were now invested in sermon preparation and hospital visits.

Then came Game Six. He was lying in bed, listening on his transistor radio, to what was shaping up to be a Red Sox world championship. With one inning to go, and holding on to a narrow lead, the pastor couldn't take the excitement. "I've got to see this!!" he stated. "God will understand if I watch this final inning. It may never happen again in my lifetime." He bounded out of bed and ran to the hall closet where he pulled out his Sylvania portable television. He plugged it in and sat down to witness the glorious moment. Instead, the game immediately began to unravel. And, when the ball rolled into right field after passing under Buckner's mitt, and Ray Knight scampered home with the winning run for New York, he stood up and exclaimed, "This is my fault! I broke a promise to the Lord and look! We turned a win into a tragic defeat." Years later, when he told me this tale, he still registered shock over the amazing turnaround that coincided with his ill-timed television viewing. "Not a coincidence," he would lament. "It's all my fault!"

Now, of course we don't really think that a broken promise made to the Almighty will affect the outcome of a World Series game. It does offer pause for thought however; now that it is decades after the fact. The lesson learned is a simple one, yet it is one we often forget. The outside world is not under the control of our thoughts and feelings. It is under the control of a Sovereign God who loves us and is executing his master plan deliberately and precisely. We are not the center of this universe. The understanding of God that my preacher friend took away from the Game Six disaster was a life lesson we all can share. It is this. Keep your promises. The World Series may not hinge on it—but those around you, in your own world of influence, do. By putting away the television, a man became a better pastor, a better dad and a better friend to those in need.

Father God, help me with self control. It is possible to keep my attitudes pleasing to you. Make me know the difference between vital things and play things. Amen

Dropping Anchor: *God is always building character, not curses, into His children.*

____

____

____

____

The Show

"Pure religion... is this..."
James 1:27

The problem with big "religion" isn't necessarily found in its bigness. It is not a problem of scope or scale. In other words it's not so much the size that matters. The problem with organized religion is in its very nature. "Religion" is the word that should stick in our craw. A little religion or a whole lot of religion lands us in a danger zone.

"Religion" is man's attempt to impress God with rites, ceremonies and ordinances. We do these "religious things" to get his attention. We attempt to please Him with our devotion and dollars. If we are lucky, we think, we will gain His notice. We then hope and pray that it is His favorable attention that we secure. After all, we don't want Him mad at us. The more impressive that our trappings are... the better our chances at the altar. But, God is not religious and therein lays our problem with much of what we call "church."

It is a lesson as old as mankind. There is no chance that our goodness or devotion will be enough to impress God. Didn't He tell us that even our best behavior is like dirty rags in His linen closet? Even our finest efforts fall far short of gaining favor in heaven.

Remember the Bible story of Naaman? It's found in the Old Testament book of 2nd Kings. Naaman was a powerful military man who found he was powerless against the dreaded disease of leprosy. He was slowly dying. On the advice of a servant girl, he journeys a great distance to the home of the Israeli prophet Elisha. He arrived laden with expensive gifts to buy his deliverance from misery, but they were of no use. His cure was a simple one and was absolutely free - no charge! He was told by Elisha to dip in the Jordan River seven times. That's it. Seven dunks in the drink. Naaman was indignant. It couldn't be as simple as that. He wanted incantations and a religious show. So, he turned on his heel and headed for home, still suffering... still a leper.

Some of his close associates chided him and said, “If the prophet had given you a hard task or many religious hoops to jump through, you would’ve done as he asked. Why not accept a simple solution?” Reluctantly, he agrees and is cured. The seventh time was the charm and he came up out of the water as good as new. No religion was required, Just an act of simple obedience.

Naaman still suffered from the religion bug however. He couldn’t make the gold and gifts matter, so he thought, ”Maybe some dirt will work.” He asks for some dirt to bring home to worship on in his homeland. “Good luck with that,” the bemused prophet seems to say.

We want impressive stuff. We think that will matter. But God is after our heart… and the way is so simple. Many folks are suffering from misery and they chase the next religious show, hoping for a magical moment. But their heart needs the cure - not the body. No gold, no dirt… just obedience. It’s just as simple as that.

Father God, I purpose to be a part of a church where I can learn of you. Amen

Dropping Anchor: *Obedience catches God’s attention.*

___

___

___

___

Plain Packaging

"the kingdom of heaven is like unto treasure hid in a field"
Matthew 13:44

We have all seen it occur. An awkward and unlikely contestant in a talent competition surprises the judges' panel and the entire audience by revealing a spectacular singing voice. The great gift within had been hidden by a dismissive exterior. The resultant shock registers on every face and tears flow freely throughout the performance. You would think we would get used to this kind of thing, but we never do. We register surprise each time we encounter an unlikely hero. Yet, it was God's idea to put the pearl inside the oyster.... the pure gold in a lump of valueless ore.

Once, long ago, God put all of His magnificence and glory into human form. He then put that newborn human into an outhouse stable with an unlikely set of nervous parents. The stable was in a one horse town, not in a shining, capitol city. To accentuate the principle, that town, Bethlehem, was in occupied territory on the remote outskirts of the vast Roman Empire. The subtle incarnation was announced to lowly shepherds, not ostentatious kings. It just goes on and on… God methodically reduces the exterior in order to reveal the precious interior. He wraps priceless gifts in plain packaging.

When you stop and consider, that is what He does with each of us who belong to Him. It continues throughout our lifetime. Age, disease and the rigors of staying alive cause us to 'reduce' our expectations that we place on our fleshly packaging. At the same time, we grow inwardly into a spiritual treasure, the value of which is beyond compare. To maintain focus on our own exterior throughout life is not unlike throwing away the pearl and retaining the oyster shell.

I just read through a list of some of the world's richest women. Excavating and mining had made some of these baronesses wealthy; however the one with (by far) the greatest fortune sold makeup. Attempting to look good is producing more wealth than any other industry. Mankind surely does look on the outward appearance, but God looks at the heart. Some of the ladies on the list had obviously spent a lot of time and money trying to patch up their oyster shell - such a misconception of true beauty.

God wraps beauty in ordinary wrappers. He fashions gems under pressure. He obscures the truth in parables. He loves surprises. All the while, He plants clues as to what He is up to. The homeless vagabond who sings like Pavarotti. The blind beggar who writes poetry that moves the masses. The crippled nursing home resident who paints like Monet. Most of them will never have opportunity to stand before us or a panel of judges. But they are not hard to find, tucked away in alleys and institutions. They roam the streets, singing for their audience of One, the Giver of the gift, the One who placed the pearl within the shell. He is always listening with delight. Their song rises from this tired earth to greet His ears. It is an anthem in the making, and someday soon—it will be the Hallelujah we all sing. That will be the day we shed our shells and reveal our own pearl within, to the glory of God. Tears will flow freely as, with the entire audience, we stand and applaud Him, for no one is crippled anymore. No one is blind any longer. We can all see the true gifts and treasures He has wrapped in such ordinary packaging. And, wonder of wonders—we all have found home.

Father God, help me not to overlook beauty in the ordinary. You don't. Amen

Dropping Anchor: *Not every oyster has a pearl inside but they are still worth looking for.*

Chuck

"Good people often die young, before their time..."
Isaiah 57:1 [paraphrased]

Bad things occur in every life and in every family. We don't go looking for trouble, yet trouble finds us—each one. Those of us who are parents try to keep danger and difficulty away from our little ones, but we know that this is a futile process. We cannot always be there, at every car ride, at every street crossing, at every point of danger.

Thus it was that Pastor Charlie and Ruth Graff lost their nine year old son, Chuck. It wasn't supposed to happen. It was an accident, a momentary mistake, but it changed their lives forever. They were good parents in every way, and Chuck was a delightful part of their family. All boy, he was a young standout in the local Little League. It seemed he always had a baseball mitt on one hand and a bat in the other. "Going next door to play ball!" he announced one afternoon, just as he had done countless times before. "Homework done?" asked his dad. "Yessir," came Chuck's ready answer. "Alright then, just be home in time for supper," said Charlie from his favorite chair. Little did they know that supper would never be served.

"Dad, there's something going on out in front of the house," one of Charlie's daughters said a couple of hours later. Night was falling and it was definitely past time for Chuck to be home. "There's a police cruiser and a fire engine right outside!" she announced as Charlie checked his wristwatch. He walked nervously to the big living room window and peered out into the evening light, He was feeling genuine dread from somewhere he couldn't quite explain.

He saw that his daughter had gone outside to better see the emergency and was now running back for the house with a panicked expression on her face. "Dad! It's Chuck. He's been hit by a car," she exclaimed bursting in the front door. With his worst fears realized, Charlie bolted for the street. Imagining a broken arm or a few stitches, he was shocked by the scene he beheld upon his arrival. An EMT was bent over the motionless form of his son, performing emergency CPR. "He's going to be alright, isn't he?" Charlie asked no one... anyone. He noticed a car pulled up on the curb with a crumpled hood. "The impact was severe," he heard a policeman say. "It doesn't look good." "This cannot be happening!" he heard himself cry.

The next minutes seemed like hours as Chuck was airlifted to a major hospital in the city. Ruth climbed into the family car with her husband and together they prayed all the way to the trauma center. They begged God to spare their boy. They pleaded with the Almighty to show mercy and allow Chuck to live. They fell to the floor as the physicians came to meet them upon their arrival, saying the dreaded words, "We have done everything we can. We're so sorry."

The next days were a blur of well-wishers from the community who brought flowers, meals, and condolences to the grieving family. Charlie chose Chuck's little league uniform to bury him in, a task that would crush the strongest parent's heart. Charlie will tell you that Ruth cried every day for two years.

It's been more than twenty years now, but the Graff family hasn't gotten over the loss of Chuck. "He would be in his thirties now," Charlie says wistfully. Ruth dabs at the tears that still come so quickly whenever they speak of their son. They know they will see him again and that is good. But on this side of heaven it remains as a bad thing that happened to a good family. Yet, a parent's love cannot be quenched by the grave. It is stronger than the things we can control and holds us in times beyond our control. There was a Father who once pulled His own Son from the tomb with strong cords of unquenchable love. He then brought Him back home. You know the place… where Chuck Graff lives. There, a supper table waits for all of us to finally sit down together. Bad things never happen there. Not ever. It is just next door in a manner of speaking, so close.

In the Bible, the ancient prophet Isaiah wrote these words, "Good people often die young, before their time. That is because the Lord takes them away from the evil of this world and enters them into rest and peace with Him." Chuck was one of those who was Loved by Heaven and by earth. Forever. Unquenchable. A fortunate son of two fathers.

Father God, for all broken hearts - you alone can hold them together enough so that we have strength to keep going when tragedy comes. Someday you will restore our broken hearts completely. We wait patiently. Amen

Dropping Anchor: *Some pain, like Love, never goes away.*

Peanut Butter And Gerry

"And God shall wipe away all tears from their eyes;
and there shall be no more death,
neither sorrow, nor crying,
neither shall there be any more pain:
for the former things are passed away."
Revelation 21:4

With one look at Pastor Gerry, you could tell that his life had not been easy. The creases and lines in his face were framed by thick, white hair, which was shaved close to his head in a crew cut. He walked with a distinct limp, and his shoulders were bowed in a permanent slump. It was as if he was carrying a heavy load on his back, and in retrospect, I guess he was. He was retired from the pastorate when I met him, and although he still answered to "Pastor," he had not served in a pulpit for more than a decade. "It didn't end well," was all he would offer as to why he no longer served in church ministry.

He had always had a struggle financially. When I met him, he volunteered in the office where I was employed. He wore the same grey pants and pullover sweater vest every day. I never asked, but I knew that those were the only options available in his wardrobe. His footwear was the same everyday as well. He always had the same pair of well worn, white (or, once white) sneakers on his feet. They were second hand shoes, most likely. "Pro-Keds," Gerry would offer with a smile. "The kind the pro's wear."

His family once survived an entire year on peanut butter and jelly sandwiches. These provisions had come from a local food pantry. "You get a lot of protein from peanut butter," Gerry always told me. We usually ate lunch together in the kitchen at my office building. Lunch, more often than not for Pastor Gerry, was still basic fare, white bread with peanut butter and jelly spread thin.

As poor as he was, Gerry was rich in wisdom. "I've been on the mountaintop and I've been in the valley," he would say. "I have learned that the best fruit grows in the valley." He had an unshakeable faith in God. "We don't usually know what He is up to, but we can trust His love." Here's how Gerry learned that lesson.

Gerry had grown up in a home where peace was scarce. His mom and dad both drank too much. His dad passed away when Gerry was in grammar school and after the loss, his mom's drinking became even more severe. Gerry looked to escape the misery of his alcohol-sodden family life and as soon as he turned eighteen, he headed for the local recruiter's office. It was during a stint in the US Navy that Gerry found God. "More likely He found me," he would offer. His life was never the same. "More than anything, I wanted my mother to discover the joy I had experienced in my new faith," he told me.

Gerry moved back home after his military service. There he set about the business of trying to convert his mom. The more he tried to show her the Light, the more resistant she became. Gerry brought books for her to read and audio tapes for her to listen to, but nothing seemed to penetrate her tough shell. "It's great for you, son, but it's not great for me," was her constant response. Gerry's efforts redoubled after his mother received a diagnosis of liver cancer. The doctors gave her six months to live, but after only a month and a half, her decline was obviously going faster than expected. Only the second month after learning of her illness she was hospitalized. "She won't be going home," the doctors told Gerry. "Mom, you've got to turn your life over to Jesus." Gerry pleaded with his failing mother. From under the oxygen mask, he heard her whispered reply, "It's too late, too late son." He left her room that evening with a heavy heart.

In the middle of the night, the hospital called to say she had passed. Gerry was left to believe that his mom had rejected God's love and was now eternally separated from Him. "I had no hope of ever seeing her again. It was a terrible burden that I carried." Gerry's voice was still choked with emotion, despite the passing of years. "I was left to believe that my mother had rejected the love of God, and would spend an eternity separated from Him." It wore on Gerry like a deep wound that just wouldn't seem to heal.

One summer, many years later, a cousin from Buffalo organized a family reunion. Gerry and his wife borrowed $25 from a friend, filled their gas tank and headed for the get-together. It was a four hour drive, but they arrived safely and immediately started shaking hands and hugging relatives, most of whom they had never met. A cousin from North Carolina approached Gerry with a hot dog in his hand, greeted him, and then began the cordial inquiries as to how they were related. The cousin was a few years younger than Gerry, but both men had served in the Navy. Both men had also become Christians during their time of service to their country. "I recall how it happened," said the former sailor. "I was on shore for a few days, and I went to a tent revival meeting and when the evangelist gave the altar call, I couldn't get down the aisle fast enough! It was the same weekend as when I prayed with your mom and she gave her heart to Jesus..." The words shocked Gerry into a state of speechless wonder. "What did you say about my mother?" Gerry started to tremble as his cousin spoke.

"Sure, I thought you knew," continued the cousin. "I always liked your mom... she was like my favorite aunt. When I heard she was ill, I took shore leave, since we were in port near to where she was hospitalized. When I came into her room, she was crying. She said you had just been there and she had sent you away saying it is too late for her to become a Christian. Well, I was pretty fired up from that tent revival, so I told her it was too late for anything but salvation. She stopped crying and started praying and I left her that night, the very night she died, happier than I had ever seen her. Gerry, I thought you knew all of this."

Gerry was fighting back tears as he embraced his cousin. For the first time in more than twenty years, he knew his mother was not lost for eternity. No, she was in heaven with Jesus. Gerry had carried a heavy burden for decades, but with one glad tiding—it was lifted. "You just can't outrun God's love," he would say between bites of his peanut butter and jelly sandwich. "You never know." I do know this much is true. Gerry was reunited with his mom about ten years ago. Together they dwell in a land where hearts are light and the peanut butter and jelly are spread thick and served with generous amounts of milk and honey. "We don't usually know what He is up to, but we can trust His love."

Father God, I believe today that there is goodness and joy ahead for many who do not expect such happiness. You are full of surprises! Amen

Dropping Anchor: *God generally saves the best for last.*

On The Street Where I Live

"...sin lieth at the door...."
Genesis 4:7

The noise woke me from a sound sleep. It was eerie to say the least. "I think it's a cat fight," said my wife who had also been awakened by the disturbing sound. Together Amanda and I waited in the predawn darkness, ears strained, listening for the noise. Our home is in a rural area where there are any number of animals who prowl the night. And, although we have forest and field surrounding us, the city is not far. A ten minute drive will bring a change of environs as you will quickly find yourself amidst tenement houses, businesses and storefronts.

"I don't think it is a cat," I said to my wife as I put on my shoes. The wail had just sent another chill through both our bodies. "It seems almost human. I'm going out to see." "At four in the morning?" she replied with concern. She then told me of the time her parents had heard what they thought was a lost little girl crying for help in the woods behind their home. They searched for many frantic minutes with their lanterns, calling "Little girl! Run to us! We will help you!" In that instance though, they actually did spy a cat high in a fir tree, howling at the night. "I am sure it's just a cat," she said as I headed for the door.

When I got to the edge of the road that passes in front of our home, I could see my neighbor, pacing across the intersection, obviously concerned and talking on his cell phone. By the light of the street lamp, I saw why. "The police are on their way," he said in a hushed tone. There in the middle of the street was a young woman, or what resembled a young woman. She was battered and bleeding; her nearly naked body a pitiful purple and red. "Is she alive?" I asked. "I think so," said my neighbor with a choke in his throat. "At least she was a few minutes ago." Frankly, I couldn't imagine how anyone in her condition could yet be alive. Just then she wailed in a horrible scream that sent another shudder through my bones. "Should we try and move her?" I wondered aloud, noting that a car could come along at any time and run her over. My question was answered instead by blue flashing lights, as a police car pulled up to the scene.

The officers dared not move her either, but covered her with a thick blanket that they had in the trunk of the squad car. Their radios crackled the report that the ambulance was less than five minutes out. "We will wait for the EMT's" said one of the officers. When they arrived, they immediately realized that any attempt to move the young woman, sent shockwaves of pain through her body. The driver backed the rescue truck very close to where she lay so as to ensure the least amount of motion possible. As they loaded her into the back of the ambulance on a stretcher, the police officer standing beside me said under his breath, "And to think, she was somebody's date tonight." I just prayed as I stood there, taking in his words. All I could think was that a very few years before, she had been somebody's little baby girl—and probably still was.

Dawn was breaking as I finally went back inside my home. The police remained on the scene, looking for clues as to who could have done such a horrible thing. But, I already knew. It was pretty clear someone, who had lost all self-control, had made that short, ten minute drive from the city, had beaten her, cut her, and then, pushed her out of a moving car, right outside my home. The "someone" who would be responsible for such a crime, cares nothing for young women. Nor does he care for young men. He is Lucifer the Murderer and it was clear that he was the one with control. His fingerprints were all over the scene. As I shut my door behind me and turned the lock I considered the awful sadness I had just witnessed. It seemed incredible that such mayhem and heartache could start with someone, somewhere, looking to be gratified in a selfish manner. Before long, a formidable, dark spirit takes control and all hell breaks loose. You can't fight that spirit with a safe address or any security measures. It knows nothing of those physical boundaries.

The weapons we fight with are spiritual and what we must shield is our own heart. We are to tear down strongholds of sin. That scene outside my door stems from an industry that exploits both men and women. Viewing sordid, sensual pictures and indulging in pornographic pleasures results in the battering of a young girl who was carelessly left to die in the street. It's the same lewd, degrading spirit—just a different level. It sneaks into many homes and hearts through internet pornography and its prurient promises. It is not outside your locked door. It is on your phone or your laptop, the street where you live... How do you know if it's targeting your home? It is a stronghold. That simply means it has a strong hold on you. Remember, sin always takes you farther than you wanted it to go. It starts with a toehold, becomes a foothold, develops into a strong hold, and before you know realize, it's a stranglehold. Once you open that door, there is no telling where you will end up. Before it gets out of control, you need to end the sordid viewing and the shame it brings. That spirit wants to destroy your family… including your little girl.

Remember, the young woman who was left in a heap right outside my door was somebody's little baby girl. You can probably still find dozens of photos of her on web sites that would best be avoided. I am certain that, in every one of them, you can yet recognize the half smile that frames the face of the shy little girl, whose grade school class portrait is held in its familiar place by a magnet, there on her dear old Grandmother's refrigerator.

Father God, may you lead me today to someone who needs help and may you grant me the strength to offer it. Amen

Dropping Anchor: *Some tragic nights begin many years before.*

___

___

___

___

A Display Of Grace

*"He that is without sin among you,
let him first cast a stone at her."*
John 8:7

My friend, Pastor Steve Brown of Key Life ministries, understands grace. I have probably listened to more sermons from his heart, than any other preacher in the world. When I worked as a producer for a Christian radio network, Steve was a daily contributor to our broadcast by way of audio tape recordings. He would send us his sermons on cassette (remember cassettes?) and my job was to separate his forty minute messages into 5 to 7 minute segments for the radio show. Thus, I would spend many hours, pouring through Steve's sermons.

I can recall hearing him teach on Luke chapter seven. Jesus was having dinner in the home of Simon the Pharisee. It was an unusual place to find Jesus. He and the religious teachers of the law didn't get along very well. Jesus exposed them for the frauds that they were and in turn, the Pharisees wanted Jesus dead.

Word got out that Jesus was having a meal with Simon the Pharisee and according to Luke, a prostitute crashed the party. Remember? She bathed the feet of Jesus with tears and dried them with her hair. As this was going on, Simon thought to himself, "If this guy was for real, he would know what sort of woman this was, touching him." It was considered wrong for a Pharisee to touch a prostitute. Jesus then answered Simon. But wait! Answered? How? Simon did not say anything aloud, he only thought to himself… I have no trouble believing that Jesus knows our thoughts, but how did Luke know what Simon had been thinking as he penned the words years later?

Pastor Steve explains in a beautiful concept. Simon must have become a follower of Christ. He surely told the story a thousand times… "I was sitting there thinking the worst about Jesus and he answered my prideful arrogance with love—the same love he showed to a woman of the street." The early church probably begged for a retelling of the story over and over again. It is likely that Luke interviewed Simon as he wrote his gospel years later, thus, getting the story first hand. But I think you have to turn the pages of your Bible to get the bigger picture.

John chapter 8 gives us the dramatic tale of the woman who was caught in the act of adultery. The self-righteous Pharisees dragged her to the place where Jesus was teaching near the temple and they demanded her death by stoning. Jesus, instead, bowed low and wrote in the sand. We don't know what he wrote but turning to the angry religious crowd, He simply told them that the one who was without sin could go ahead and throw the first rock. Starting with the older men, one by one, they opened their fists and dropped the deadly missiles and left the scene. My guess it was Simon who dropped the first rock. After the last accuser was gone, Jesus turned to the woman and told her she was forgiven. He then sent her on her way. It's a beautiful story of grace.

Not everyone is comfortable with grace. Many believe we need to merit favor from God. Steve Brown says that he has preached on that passage many times—and every time he does, some modern day Pharisee approaches him at the conclusion of the message and states "Jesus forgave the woman, but don't forget, He told her to never do it again." "Yes," is Steve's patient reply. "And if she had—He would say it again." Grace does not carry rocks. But it'll carry just about everything else—including sinners to heaven.

Father God, make me a trophy in your hall of grace. Amen

Dropping Anchor: *Grace is certainly amazing.*

____

____

____

____

Punch

"Wine is a mocker..."
Proverbs 20:1

I come from a family of non-drinkers. We were Baptists after all. Baptists don't touch alcohol. In church, communion was prepared with Welch's grape juice. At weddings, we were allowed to drink a toast to the bride and groom, but we always had to request non-alcoholic sparkling cider. We managed to still feel guilty with the thought that someone may see us with a champagne glass in our hand and assume we had gone liberal on them. My father's beverage of choice was a coffee frappe. My mom stuck to coffee. She enjoyed the instant kind that you brewed in your mug.

Thus it was that on one Christmas day, my cousin pulled off a spectacular "spiking of the punch" prank that I recall as perhaps the merriest Christmas celebration our family ever knew, for awhile anyway. We had all made the drive to my Aunt Meg's lovely home in the suburbs. She and my Uncle Don had purchased a huge turkey for the holiday meal and as it roasted in the oven, we snacked on trail mix and nuts. And, punch. I saw my oldest cousin secretly pouring a clear liquid into the punch bowl. He poured half of the bottle in, tasted a sip of the tainted fruit drink, then, shrugged his shoulders, smiled, and dumped in the rest of the bottle.

Soon the line formed. "Y'know, this punch is fantastic!" said one guest. "I think I will have another glass!" The television seemed to be at maximum volume as the football game became part of the hum and buzz of the living room. Aunt Meg was whistling Christmas carols in the kitchen as she brought the meal out on trays. Uncle Don broke out his finest cigars - before dinner!

Ninety year old Mrs. Enfield (my great aunt) went up the stairs waving to those gathered below as if she were departing port o' call onboard the deck of the Queen Mary. She blew kisses to all of us and went singing off to bed. It was not quite 6pm.

But, by 7pm things below had gone south. They always do with too much alcohol. My uncle began a rant about his job being unfair and argued politics with anyone and everyone for a solid hour. He mercifully fell asleep on the couch. Everyone felt tired and logy. Conversation did not sparkle. It reduced to grunts and snores. I began to think we Baptists had a point.

I'm not a Baptist anymore and I will drink a toast at weddings without feeling guilty (ok, mostly not guilty) but I have also seen alcohol ruin many families. It always begins with a giggle and ends with a "punch," a resounding last laugh... on you. So, take a lesson, then, from old Mrs. Enfield. Leave the party early. You won't miss a thing.

Father God, there is no substitute for life done right. Indulgence is wrong. I know this is true. Amen

Dropping Anchor: *Friends that come in bottles or six packs really don't love you.*

____
____
____
____

Heartache

"...Christ Jesus, who, being in the form of God,
thought it not robbery to be equal with God:
but made Himself of no reputation,
taking the form of a bondservant, and coming in the likeness of men..."

Philippians 2:5-7

The heartache that separation brings is weighty and very difficult to carry. Life goes on at its maddening pace, seemingly oblivious to our desire to push the clock and calendar backward. We ache with each passing moment because something, or rather someone, is missing. The daily routine rattles on, and we are helplessly swept along by the strong current of time. Whenever we lose someone to the tide of time, we know that nothing will ever seem truly normal again... Their absence is particularly cruel because emotion doesn't die. You still hold all the feelings that were yours while the person was present with you. Now, however, there's just no place for those old feelings to go. We know this as the pain of separation. It strikes harder on special days like Christmas or Thanksgiving. That is when the empty chair seems emptier—and your heart breaks, all over again.

Heaven understands... I came to this truth one Christmas. I was praying for a dear friend who had just said a final goodbye to her husband. He had passed from cancer just weeks before. I wondered what joy the season would bring for her and their two young sons... now without a dad.

The Father took me to a vision of heaven on that first Christmas. Jesus, the Son of God, was preparing to leave Glory and spend thirty three years away on a lost planet. He was coming to earth on a daring rescue mission for mankind—alone. How the heart of Heaven must have ached to see Him go. The angels who gazed upon His beautiful face each day would now look at an empty chair.

There is a legend connected to that first Christmas night in Bethlehem. The angels had gotten together in Glory and planned a proper send off for the King of Kings. Gabriel intended to split the sky with an angelic choir stretching from horizon to horizon. Michael, the archangel, had the starry host ready to light up the night sky over Israel. "That isn't what I have in mind," the Father said to His faithful angels. And, He told them of the stable, and the poverty and pain. He told them of the cross. They stood, heads bowed, listening in sadness and awe.

Just then, Jesus stepped to the edge of eternity, preparing to enter time and space. "Oh, Father!" cried the angels, "you can't let Him go alone." "Alright," said Father God, "But, Gabriel, just a few angels and Michael, plus just one star."

If you are carrying the hurt of separation, Heaven knows just how you feel. The heavenly hosts endured an incredible absence, so that we would never be alone again.

Father God, our fallen world must push us in the direction of your world yet to come. I believe it is close. Amen

Dropping Anchor: *There is nothing about you that heaven doesn't already know - and love.*

____

____

____

____

The Time Out Chair

"Now no chastening for the present
seemeth to be joyous, but grievous:
nevertheless afterward it
yieldeth the peaceable fruit of righteousness
unto them which are exercised thereby."
Hebrews 12:11

The "TIME OUT" chair at our house is used routinely. Having raised eight children over three decades, the chair in the corner has seen its fair share of little bottoms, sitting in every imaginable attitudinal position, from repentance to defiance, and everything in between. Once, one of my young children (I won't say which one) came to me early in the morning and announced "I've got shame on me." He sent himself to the time out chair where we discovered he had wet his pants. Apparently in past pant-wetting episodes we had used those words in frustration, "Shame on you," and they stuck. This was not our best parenting moment.

The time-out chair is comfortable, not menacing in any visible way. I always wondered why it created such a sense of dread in little hearts with nothing but its mere mention. I will be honest to say that if I were having a rough day, and someone directed me to sit down for five minutes, I would be most grateful. However, to my children, the concept of sitting down has always been a trauma. I reckon it is the separation that they fear. Being isolated and alone can be most terrifying.

I suppose the time out chair is preferred by most children as the form of parental discipline they fear the least. This is true especially if the alternative is spanking. Although, I did have a friend growing up whose mom was a soft touch when punishment was warranted. She once spanked him with an empty egg carton. He carried off his part in the discipline drama like an actor on stage… holding his bottom and begging for mercy. "Please stop!" he cried. "You're killing me." Meanwhile his dear mother swatted away. Afterward, he always kept a spare egg box handy to ensure his mother wouldn't go out looking for a more suitable switch.

I am old enough to recall my fourth grade teacher taking Randy Brown behind the upright piano in front of our classroom and applying a thirty six inch ruler to his seat of understanding. She was tough, no doubt about it; she had Randy right across her knee. Never do I recall someone more aptly named than Randy. One dictionary defines the term 'randy' as being rude and inappropriate. He was certainly all that and he had the yardstick marks to show for it. There was no time out chair in my elementary school. I'm pretty sure the kids like Randy would have welcomed one. As for me, I was determined to steer clear of the area behind the upright Spinet. And, I did—until seventh grade.

Late for class, I was running down the hallway of the middle school I attended when I heard the school principal shout for me to stop. "You in the plaid shirt," he thundered. "In my office, now!" I came to a dead stop and obediently sat down in his corner office. I was in trouble and I knew it. Running in the halls was a no-no that he enforced with a strict stance at his observation post outside his office door. His choice of discipline was to make me walk the long corridor back and forth for an hour. I was humiliated and repentant; bursting into tears after my ordeal was done. Being isolated and alone can be most terrifying. To be an outcast is a fright to the soul.

Jesus described the place of eternal punishment as being "outer darkness." If it's anything like a lonely corridor or the isolation of a time out chair, you want to avoid it at all costs. The good news is that we indeed can, because Jesus took my (and, yes, Randy's) punishment on Himself. Our shame was on Him. He still has the marks to show for it. His are the only wounds in Heaven.

Father God, I never want to be away from your presence - not now, not ever. Amen

Dropping Anchor: *The timeout chair would be a rough place to spend Eternity.*

___

___

___

___

Boom Booms

"Now therefore fear ye not: I will nourish you, and your little ones..."
Genesis 50:21

Sometimes, my son True, who is three, is afraid at bedtime. Often when he is going "night, night" he points to the bedroom window and says "Boom booms." It all began back in the summer, when some of our neighbors lit off some fireworks, no doubt leftovers from the 4th of July. I think the neighbors were probably a little 'lit' themselves. Anyway, the rocket's red glare flew by our mailbox and exploded with a bang outside True's quiet room. That was all it took. From then until now, he has been constantly on the watch for more boom-booms. He has awakened from sleep on more than one occasion, crying in obvious terror. Upon being gathered into our arms, he describes the boom-boom that invaded his dreams.

I wonder just what these boom-booms are in his three year old imagination. He knows nothing of our nation's Independence Day. He does not understand explosives. He just knows that a loud noise once disturbed his peaceful world and that it made him unsettled. The explosions are gone, but the fear remains. I cannot erase True's memory. I can only assure him that the season of boom-booms is gone for now. We are all quiet until next summer. And, after more summers and winters pass, True's fear of fireworks will be just a memory.

Memory can be horrid, but it can also sweeten things with time. Looking back on a dreadful period in life that robbed your joy (or sleep) can, through the wash of memory, cause us to allow a small smile to come to our countenance while we shake our head in wonder. How we ever made it through is overtaken by the pleasant knowledge that we did indeed make it through and the memory does not hurt us. I was remembering some things myself the other day, and through the filter of years, the guilt of the past experience came rising to the top as the hardship and inconvenience fell away. Ask any old timer, the days of yore shine brighter than whatever may occur today. That walk to school that we reluctantly undertook each weekday now is summoned to recall and worn like a badge of honor. The tedious hours spent in Saturday catechism or Sunday school are logged in memory's perspective as having been good for us. However hard the memory, it is forever framed by passing time, yielding a life picture that says, "I guess it wasn't so bad after all."

The future yet beckons, as it flies quickly toward us. There will be more boom-booms in the night. We cannot escape them, nor do we know exactly what they will be. Whatever they are, we do know this; they will stay for just a while and then become a memory. True won't fear the boom-booms for much longer, and the frightening dread of the night will dissolve into pleasant memories of a little boy in his little room upstairs, in a big house on a quiet street, with neighbors who drink just a bit too much, in a place called Freetown, in a very big world. And, as for me... I will scoop him up from his nightmare and treasure this little blue eyed boy with a head full of curls. I will always remember that I once was able to make the boom-booms seem not so frightening for this precious boy of mine. Dear God, I pray I never forget.

Father God, help me to be a wonderful parent to my precious children. Make me a safe place in a hard world. Amen

Dropping Anchor: *Unfamiliar noises generally seem more frightening at night.*

____

____

____

____

Mr. Undo

"...and the blood of Jesus Christ His Son cleanseth us from all sin."
1 John 1:7

I have been keeping fairly up to date with my Blog. "Blogging" is not something we did back when I was a boy. No one had ever heard of the concept. My limited research tells me that blog (can be a verb, can be a noun) is a common term derived from the word "weblog." Weblog means just that—the act of logging information onto the World Wide Web. Yet, as I type the term "weblog," my auto-correct underscores the word in red in order to tell me that the system does not recognize this particular word. I talk to my computer to let it know that this is, indeed, a proper use of the original word—in fact; it predates the spell-check-approved term, 'blog.' Blog is merely a shortened form of the word "weblog" (red line again.) Now, to "log" means to record, usually chronologically, an entry—to utilize the system. So a blog is simply a log onto the world-wide web, via the internet. A weblog! But my computer has forgotten its roots. I have seen this kind of thing before. My first computer, a Tandy 386, did not know Jesus. Each time I would enter his name in a document the machine would beep. This audio ancestor of the red underline would sound the warning—"word unrecognized." No wonder the 386 didn't have any future. You have got to know Jesus, friends. Today, I am sure that outdated machine lies at the bottom of a landfill, while the industry marches on with faster, smaller, smarter machines. They still don't know weblog though.

Now, I have done it, I have hit the wrong key. Instead of shift—I hit control (or ctrl) and my weblog disappeared. Gone! Fortunately, I recall that my computer has a feature called the undo option. When you make a mistake, you just click your mouse on 'edit' and then 'undo'... and it does! It undoes... Wouldn't it be great if we all came equipped with an undo button? You blow it with a mistake while trying so hard to capitalize—but instead things go out of control... and you end up with nothing, blank-o. Undo is always there; faithfully making our mistakes disappear (or reappear). Meanwhile, adding another computer-style insult to my paragraph, my spell-check has put a red line under the word "control" back in the first line. I have no idea why. I know that I spelled it correctly. There it sits however, a tribute to the editor-computer, which apparently has understanding of things we can only wonder about.

Amanda wanted my help for a minute or two just now, and after a few "In a minute, Dears," I obliged. But, when I returned to my laptop—there sat small True, typing away. "This could mean trouble," I reasoned. True is three years old and has a limited vocabulary. Still, there he sat, absorbed in his work. There was a red line running through all of it.

"CCCCCCCCCCCCCCCHHHHHHHUJIOPLMNV&&&" was how he worded it. "Daddy, look!" said my young son, pointing to the screen. After separating boy from blog, I went straight to Old Faithful—Mr. Undo. He can even correct a mess we inherited. What authority! What incredible power!

Consider... there is a red line running throughout the history of mankind. We make many mistakes. We all fall short. Life should come with an Undo application… taking care of all our wrongdoing. In fact, it does give us that option. It began on a hill called Calvary and it corrects the errors of every man. You've got to know Jesus - weblog out.

Father God, thank you for the cross - it has erased my sin, completely! Amen

Dropping Anchor: *What man tries to do with the undo button - Jesus did with His blood.*

The Homeless, The Healer And The Howler

*"In the last day, that great day of the feast,
Jesus stood and cried, saying,
If any man thirst, let him come unto me, and drink."*
John 7:37

Introduction

There is a chapter in Scripture that I have long considered my favorite. It is in Mark's gospel, the fifth chapter. It tells the stories of three individuals, each caught in a desperate dilemma and, despite odds not in their favor, and they all end up on their knees before Jesus. There they find healing for body and soul. Mark chapter five first introduces us to Jairus, who was a well-known man about the synagogue. Next came a street woman who had been sick for a dozen years, and whose story impacts Jairus. Finally, we meet a man possessed by many demons. He is out of his mind in misery.

I encourage you to read the original, actual Biblical account thoroughly. Mark, who likely wrote this gospel, was not one of Jesus' twelve disciples. It is, however, probable that he knew Jesus personally. Later in life he became an associate of the Apostle Peter. Reliable tradition tells us that much of the information in Mark's gospel was garnered from his partnership with Peter. It is also considered factual that young Mark was present for such Biblical events as the last supper (served at his home) and that he crept out of bed to follow Jesus and the disciples later that night to Gethsemane. The young man, who had been in hiding and flees the scene at the betrayal and arrest of Christ, is no doubt, Mark himself; still in his pajamas!

What follows is my attempt to flesh out the stories and personalities of the characters we meet in Mark chapter five. For story telling reasons we'll first meet the street woman, Jairus and his daughter, and finally a man possessed by many demons. Using "Sanctified imagination," these next pages are "could have been," events and happenings. These pages are not the Scripture. But, I do hope they will bring you inspiration.

Part One

Today, just another day on the street, another day of begging to stay alive while wishing you were dead. She crawled out from beneath the porch where she had hidden herself during the long night. She was cold and hungry. She was lonely. "Oh, God," she said to no one. She was convinced the Almighty had turned a deaf ear to her plight. She had once been a believer in such things. She was a rich man's daughter, but that was long ago now. Her parents had both perished more than a decade ago leaving her alone in the world, alone and sick. An issue of blood kept her in a state of being labeled as "unclean" so that she was not even able to go to the synagogue to pray for healing. She had spent what money her parents had left her on doctors, trying to find a cure for..."For this," she said aloud while wiping the blood that trickled down her leg. For the last twelve years she had been bleeding and this morning was no different. Tossing aside the rag that she had pulled from her 'ragbag' as she called it; she made her way toward the marketplace to beg for her breakfast. Weak and miserable, she shook off the morning chill and entered the crowded main street toward the market...

There was usually one proprietor she could count on. A hard-boiled egg was sometimes saved for her by some kind marketeer. If not, there were usually scraps from the tables that fell at the feet of those in the local eateries. She would often huddle in a corner and watch at a safe distance, ready to lunge for anything that hit the floor. She was way past being concerned about her dignity at this point. Often her collection of crumbs came with a swat or a curse as she retreated back to her hiding place against the wall. Today there had been no boiled egg so she made her way to the nearest restaurant to wait for her chance at a spill. A young, wealthy couple brushed by her on her way inside. They had just left a corner table and there was a bit of unfinished breakfast where they had been seated. Hurriedly, she swallowed what she could gather in her hands. "Go away, vagrant!" hollered a stern voice. She didn't even turn to look, but ran out the door instead. Quickly, she disappeared in the crowd.

It had not always been this way. She thought back to her youth… Her parents were influential citizens of the Decapolis. An only child, she was raised by her beloved nanny who had instructed her in the ways of Jehovah. It was a good upbringing; that is until her parents had perished in the sacred city of Jerusalem. It was years ago now but she could recall the day, and often did remember the horror that came with it... The Roman governor had been at the end of his patience with the Jewish zealots. These ragtag revolutionaries sought the overthrow of Roman rule in their homeland. Their anti-Caesar efforts had begun to grow in intensity, so much so that the Roman authorities had devised a plan to quell the uprising. They desired to put fear in the hearts of the Jews, in an effort to keep the nation in check. The plan was horrific. During one of the Jewish celebrations, the Roman governor had several hundred of his finest soldiers disguise themselves as Jews. Under their cloaks, however, they brandished swords, and on an arranged signal, they took out their weapons and began to hack away at the crowd. "Run, my daughter! Run and hide," her father's voice was nearly drowned out by the screaming of victims. Run she did, hiding finally in a dark corner under the porch of a large home on a nearly empty side street.

She did not emerge from hiding until evening. Retracing her steps, she carefully picked her way through the bodies of those who had perished. She found her parents near the temple, just two blocks away from her hiding place. They were dead, that much could not be mistaken. Hiking up her long robe, she turned and ran as fast as she could into the evening gloaming, away, away—she wanted to put as much distance as possible between herself and the horror. That night was the first time she noticed the bleeding. That was twelve years ago.

Since that time, life had been hard. She and her nanny lived for a time in a rented bungalow. Together they visited every doctor in the region trying to find a cure for the issue of blood that would not abate. She spent what little wealth the banker's said was rightfully hers, although she believed the banker took advantage of her youth and kept most of her father's money for himself. Finally, penniless she had to bid goodbye to her beloved nanny and the following week, she was living on the street—a beggar. Wishing she would die, she sat down by a fire that some of the other homeless had kindled. Greeting the familiar faces (no one has a name on the street) she slowly brought her thoughts back to the present as she listened to the conversation of the men and women of the street.

"Next town over and headed this way," said one who seemed to be the ringleader. "I heard he fed more than five thousand people with one little kid's lunch." "I saw him make a blind man see—with my own eyes I tell you,"" said another. She listened intently as the talk continued. "Traveling fast with a rich man with him…" "Has ol' Zebedee's boys in his posse. Claim they have left their fishing business to follow the Miracle Man." "They've left the old man high and dry." "None too pleased either. He has made some enemies in the power structure."

She hung on every word. He spoke of lame men walking, and blind men seeing. Could this be her chance? Would the Miracle Man help her? Her thoughts were interrupted by two men, peering down the alley where she sat by the fire." Jairus?" they called. "Nobody here with that name," said the ringleader. "No one here has a name…" murmured another. The two men went on their way still calling for Jairus. "Whoever that is…" she mused.

A homeless street dweller that she recognized joined the circle. Reaching under his shabby cloak, he produced a loaf of warm bread. She knew it was stolen but she was too hungry to care. She ripped off a piece and ate with the others. She could not remember the last time she had tasted something so good.

Suddenly a commotion out on the main street caught her attention. Someone in the road was pointing, "It's him, it's Jesus the worker of miracles." Without a second thought she began to run toward the street, pushing her way past the growing crowd of onlookers. At the center of the moving mass of people was one, dressed like a rabbi. "That must be him," she whispered. She became like a crazed woman, elbowing her way through the people. She was so close when someone shoved her from behind and she lost her balance and fell to the cobblestones. Her hope of meeting the Miracle Man fell with her. All she could do was reach and try to touch… Her hand grasped the flowing cloak of the rabbi as he walked past. She hung on for an instant and then let go. At that very moment, the hard cobblestones seemed like a feather bed. What was this feeling? It was as if the taste of the warm bread she had just eaten was taking over her body. She felt whole. She felt strong. She was well again and she knew it. The rabbi came to an abrupt halt a few yards beyond where she lay and turned. "Who touched me?" she heard him say. His eyes met hers. He smiled, and turned again and was gone. Gone too was her miserable condition. He had taken that with him.

Part Two

Jairus was an important man in his seaside village… in fact all of the region knew him. He was a popular figure at the synagogue, where he held a seat in the assembly. He had been somewhat of a wild youth, some even claimed he had a run in or two with the local Roman authorities during his growing up years – but ever since marriage and the birth of his daughter, his devotion was to family and faith. He absolutely adored his precious little girl. She was almost a woman now, for she had just celebrated her twelfth birthday. Her dad couldn't have been more proud, but this night, he was also worried. Her face was drawn and pale as he studied her across the dinner table. Where was her ready smile tonight? "What is wrong, Talitha?" Jairus' voice was full of concern. He could see sickness behind her eyes. His mind raced as he rehearsed the news reports of a contagious fever that had already claimed the lives of three children in the village. "Call for the physician," he said to his wife. She quickly summoned the oldest servant boy. He was her most trusted aide, and she knew he would understand the importance of this mission. The lad ran speedily through the dark streets to the infirmary where he knew he could ask for help. Considering Jairus' reputation – he was certain one of the doctors would volunteer a house visit.

Meanwhile, back at the home, supper was over. The mood, usually light and cheerful in Jairus' house was instead, on this night, tense and fearful. Jairus had gotten up right after dinner to carry young Talitha from the table and straight to her bed upstairs. "You didn't touch a bite of your supper!" said her concerned mother as father and daughter ascended the staircase to the loft. She felt so warm to him… was it the fever? Was it his imagination? Where was the doctor??

"I'm afraid I can't spare any doctors tonight," said the caretaker at the infirmary. "We've got too many sick with the fever! We are short staffed as it is..." Jairus' servant boy turned and ran back toward the house with the somber news.

All through that night Jairus paced the floor while his wife sat by Talitha's bed. Hour by hour the girl's condition worsened. Beads of sweat rolled down her forehead despite the cooling cloths that the kitchen help sent up every quarter hour. There was no sleep for anyone in the household. Talitha was beloved by family and servants alike. As dawn broke Jairus knew what he had to do. His daughter was now struggling to breathe. Each gasp of air was fought for and her frail chest heaved and rattled with congestion. "Where are you going??" asked Jairus' wife, lifting her head from the edge of the small cot where her daughter lay, weak and trembling. "I've got to do something… she's dying! My little girl is going to die!" The words sounded impossible to consider. "Don't leave us here alone," his wife pleaded. "Jairus, I'm frightened" she breathed – but he didn't hear her. He had already gone down the stairs and out into the early morning sun. His own heart was pounding in time with his sandaled feet on the cobblestones as he headed to the outskirts of the village.

His thoughts raced ahead of his feet. Down by the water—with the fishermen and the dockworkers – that is where he reportedly spends his time. Jairus began planning what to say when he found him. "If I find him..." Jairus said out loud. It was a long shot and he knew it. Jesus the Healer kept a low profile. It was no secret that the religious power structure, some of Jairus' best friends, wanted this

Jesus dead and gone. Jairus had even been invited to some of their clandestine meetings, always late at night in a remote location. The Pharisees feared the people would revolt if they took him out. He was popular with the crowds, but he still managed to operate almost completely underground. No one had seen him for several days and the rumor was that he may have gone across the border into Syria.

As Jairus approached the docks he felt strangely out of place. His expensive cloak stood in contrast to the commoner's' garb that everyone else seemed to be wearing. The air was thick with the smell of brine and the sound of shouting between men on the shore and their coworkers on board ship. Coarse language was everywhere. The synagogue seemed like part of another world. In one of the storehouses, where they kept fishing gear and nets, a large number of dockworkers had apparently gathered for a meeting of sorts. Things seemed to be wrapping up as some were coming out the side door right near where Jairus stood. The rest were still inside the building and he could hear them singing an old Jewish folk ballad. Jairus knew the song well from his days as a youth. He recalled that his servants often sang it to this day. A simple song, it told of God's love for Zion. As the last strains of music ended the door swung open and a lone figure emerged, closely followed by a dozen or so men who seemed to be keeping the crowd at bay.

"Are you looking for someone?" asked the man, emerging from the shadows. Jairus was immediately struck by the noble look the man carried. He didn't realize that his own countenance must have given away the fact that he was on a desperate quest. "The Healer… the Nazarene," Jairus heard himself say. One of the men surrounding the two stepped forward and spit on the ground at Jairus' feet. "He's a friend of Caesar..." he scowled. "Judge him not," said the one in charge. "I think we should hear what is on this troubled one's heart." Turning to Jairus he said "Something is troubling you, friend… what is it?"

Jairus paused. Somehow when the man had called him 'friend,' it had stirred something in his heart; something that was unfamiliar, yet known. He shook his head clear and focused on the man before him. "My daughter is dying and I need to find the Nazarene called Jesus!" exclaimed Jairus. "I am a desperate man who will pay..." The man before him put his hand up and said, "Take me to her at once." "Are you the Healer?" Jairus knew the answer before his mouth formed the question. "At once!" said the Healer and Jairus started half walking, half running toward his village. As they moved out, the ten or twelve men that had been around Jesus followed Him. Word traveled fast... the Healer was on the move... walking with a rich man. The crowd quickly formed around them and Jairus found it slow going as he was now pressed in from all sides. Jesus had his hand on Jairus' shoulder, keeping pace behind him. Some of the men with the Rabbi began to call out, "Clear the way! Let the Teacher through!" Suddenly Jesus stopped. Jairus looked back and saw him standing in the middle of the highway – at a dead stop. He seemed to be looking for someone. Before he could get to where he stood – Jairus was bumped and jostled to the rear of the impromptu audience... He couldn't see through the crowd as to what had happened, or why Jesus had stopped, but he knew time was running out. "Let's go." The calm voice of the Nazarene was unmistakable in the hubbub. As they resumed their pace, Jairus could hear the men around Jesus talking about what had just occurred. "Twelve years on the street she was... dogs have it better than she did." "She's a brave soul to grab the Rabbi's cloak like she did." "Pushed her way through – got to hand it to her." "She claims she is better now." "She's better alright... did you see her face light up? And the way she ran out of there?" "I think I would run too after twelve years..."

Twelve years – the number jumped out at Jairus. His little Talitha had turned twelve a short time ago. Now, it was her life that hung in the balance. His thoughts ran ahead to the little loft where his daughter lay. He couldn't bear to even consider her dying. His thoughts were interrupted—someone was calling his name. He thought the voice sounded like his brother but he couldn't be certain above the din. He strained his eyes and ears trying to locate the source of the voice. He was more certain now. Someone was calling him. "Over here!" called Jairus. "I'm here!" Two men burst through the crowd and stood before the worried father. It was his older brother, and with him was a man Jairus recognized as a doctor from the infirmary. They both looked pale and nervous. "Jairus, we have just come from your home. The news is not good," the two men began. "But wait! I have the Healing Teacher with me," countered Jairus with a nod toward Jesus. "He is coming to our home now to heal my Talitha." Then came the crushing reply, "It's too late... don't bother the Teacher anymore... she's gone." His brother delivered the message while the doctor stood by nodding his head in sorrowful agreement. "There was nothing we could do," he managed. "I came in haste at the moment your brother came to my door. I tried…" The doctor's voice sank as he watched Jairus fall on his face in the dirt. A scream escaped from his lips as he lay prostrate in the roadway. There he stayed… defeated, broken, and alone. He never wanted to move again. There would be no future, no tomorrow without his beloved daughter in it. He sobbed deeply, his tears dropping into the dust. Then, a voice said softly in his ear, "Don't be afraid just trust Me." It was the Healer. Slowly Jairus rose to his feet. "That's it. C'mon," urged Jesus. Jairus did not protest. Instead, he put his arm around the shoulder of the Rabbi. Although weak in his knees, he found himself back on the trail, urging his reluctant feet to move quickly to keep pace. The crowd was thinner here away from the docks. The small band of men moved hurriedly and was soon standing at the gate to the village where Jairus made his home. Moving quickly down some side streets, they arrived at the house where Talitha lay.

Jairus' wife ran from the portico and fell into her husband's arms. Together they shared their grief. There were no words, only sobs. No words could be found to express their loss. It was Jesus who spoke. "The child is only sleeping. She will awaken." The doctor and some of the neighbors snorted. Some laughed aloud. Undaunted by their disbelief, Jesus looked at the couple and spoke. "Take me to her."

The stairs to the loft seemed endless as the small band of friends made it up to the top floor. There lay Talitha, so peaceful in appearance that for a moment, Jairus found himself hoping she really was only sleeping. The doctor must have thought the same, for he went to her bedside and leaned over her tiny frame. Holding a mirror under her nose, he shook his head. There was no doubt—she was not breathing. Jairus stared at the floor, his hand holding the hand of his wife. She was softly weeping. From the downstairs, the cries of the mourners reached them in the loft. Jairus barely noticed that the Rabbi had gone to the bedside of his little girl.

"Hmmm, that tickles!" Jairus looked up in astonishment just in time to see Talitha push away the doctor's little mirror from beneath her nose. Was Jairus imagining what he had heard? Jesus held out his arms to young Talitha and spoke softly, the way Jairus did each morning, "Talitha, it is time to awaken." With that, she sat up and rubbed her eyes. "What is everyone doing up here? I'm hungry—is it time for breakfast?" Her words came like music. Suddenly, the room erupted in joyous laughter. Hugs for little Talitha and slaps on the back for the men came with the grins and guffaws. Jairus stood before the Healer and was at a loss for anything to say. "I wouldn't mind some breakfast, myself," said Jesus. "Food for all then!" called Jairus. "It's a breakfast feast."

Later, around the crowded table, Jairus stood with mug in hand. "God has heard our prayers, and He is with us." Looking squarely at Jesus, sitting next to his little Talitha he repeated the words, "God is with us, indeed."

Part Three

His earliest recollections were of the voices. As a child, he would sit by the fire in the hearth and watch his mother perform her incantations. "Spells" she called them, her "magic spells." Hour upon hour she would huddle over her bowls and pipes, oblivious to the world around her. He knew better than to call for her. He had learned this from the voices. "She's with us—go away!" they had scolded him. They seemed to come from deep within his mother… but her lips did not move when they spoke. "Oh, my darling boy, are you alright?" That voice he knew to be hers. She would draw away from the magic slowly, her return always accompanied by apologies and questions. "How long was I with them? Are you hungry, child? Did they frighten you?"

Always at these times she would hold him close. "I'm so sorry little one," she would whisper. She was his whole world in these moments. "Mama" he called her. She was not his true mother. He had no recollection of her. She had died while giving birth to him some six years before. His father had tried to provide for him, but when he perished at sea some months later, Mama was the only one who had cared for him. "A curse is on that one," the villagers had said about the boy. "Both of his parents are dead." And, so it seemed fitting that he be taken in by another outcast, a worker of spells. "Mama" was what he called her. They lived together, just the two of them... and the voices.

"Pay no mind to insults," she had taught him. Often he would come running to their humble bungalow from the market square, chased by children older than he. Sticks and rocks were thrown at him by these neighborhood bullies, and he often ran home to Mama with a gang of taunting children close behind. She would hear the commotion and swing open her door. One look from her dark eyes would send the youths scampering in the other direction. "She's crazy!" He would listen as they retreated…"They're both deranged!" Still frightened, she would bring him close and wipe his tears. "One day we will make them pay," she promised. He could sense the voices rising within her. "Make them pay," she said again, but this time her lips did not move.

Occasionally, men from the village would visit their home. They would stay for the hours while he slept, and be gone before he awoke. They would leave money and provisions for the pair. "Enough to keep body and soul together," she would say. "We do what we can," he had learned to say after. "No shame in that." He had heard her say it dozens of times. Head down, she was quiet on these mornings. He did not inquire about the men, but if he saw one of them in the market, he noticed they pretended not to know his Mama.

The two lived in one of the ten cities by the sea. The Decapolis Region it was called by the Roman authorities. The Sea of Galilee provided life and commerce to the area. As he grew, he loved spending days down by the docks, watching the fishing boats come in with their daily catch. The Zebedee family owned the biggest boats, and a warehouse on the main thoroughfare bore the name as well. Old Zebedee had many sons. The youngest, John, was David's age. The two sometimes sat together after school, lazing in the afternoon sun. John was his only friend. A warm hearted, compassionate boy, he seemed not to mind that his companion was mocked and jeered by the others. John was the only one, beside Mama, who called him by name. "David, the shepherd king, a noble name for such a rascal," John would laugh. "Rascals together!" he would echo. John had learned stories of King David at the synagogue, but David and Mama were not welcome there. So, John would repeat the tales of giants and Philistine armies to David's eager ears. "Tell me more," he would beg. "Tomorrow," John would say. The two friends would often part company with these words. Later, when he would relate the tales of King David to his Mama, she would listen until the voices came. "Nonsense" they said! Her lips were still. "Shut up, boy. We haven't time for foolish stories." And she would leave him then, muttering over her pipes and bowls.

The Romans controlled the region and they ruled with an iron fist. The governor was no diplomat. He had no love for the Jews of the Ten Cities. He couldn't understand their faith in one God and he had no appreciation for their customs and laws. "Is anything legal in the Jewish system of law?" he would often ask. "There are restrictions, restrictions and more restrictions." He taxed them heavily and made sure some of the surplus ended up in his pockets. "I'll get something out of this pitiful assignment" he would tell his wife.

Herod was king, but a puppet king who had little more authority than the Roman governor. Set into power by Caesar himself, Herod was not a true Jew. "He is not King David's descendant," John explained to his friend David, the outcast, one afternoon as they sat together on a wooden wharf, their feet in the water. He went on to explain how Herod, fearing some Babylonian prophets, ordered the massacre of all the boys their age in Bethlehem, of Judea almost ten years prior. The prophets had reportedly announced the coming of the King of Kings, who was to rule from David's throne. He had been born in David's city according to the foreigners. Herod wanted no competition and thus, ordered the slaughter of every male child four years old or younger. It was tough duty, even for the battle hardened Roman soldiers, who carried out the horrific orders. It was a dark time.

David the outcast had little allegiance to Roman law. He knew nothing of politics and his only encounters with Rome was when a soldier or two would visit his Mama for the night. It was on one such night that the boy nearly lost his life. He did lose Mama.

A centurion had come to the home late at night. David was supposed to be sleeping but on this night sleep would not come. It had been a busy day for the voices. They had taken his mother in the morning hours and she had spent all day over her spells. He could hear them in the back part of the house now. The soldier was talking to his mother in a firm tone. "Something about money," he was able to gather. He would have to get closer. He softly exited his room and came out into the kitchen. There on the table where they could be touched and admired were the Roman soldier's weapons. A magnificent sword lay in its sheath there on the table. It was a beautiful tool of the soldier's trade. David could not resist holding it, hefting its balanced weight in his hand. Suddenly, the commotion in his Mama's room drew his attention away. They were arguing and fighting. He was all of fourteen now, and the man of the house. He was not about to let a Roman hurt his Mama. He drew back the heavy curtain just in time to witness the centurion give his mother a mighty shove, sending her across the room and crashing into the wall. He stood in the doorway. "Leave her be," he heard himself say. The Roman turned and faced David. "Put the weapon down, boy!" he whispered. David realized the sword was raised over his head—ready to strike. "Get out of our home," he replied. "Leave us alone." "I'm not leaving without that," said the soldier evenly, pointing at the sword, still raised in David's trembling hands. His Mama was crying. Getting to her feet, she said "Let us all be careful, now." He noticed her lips were still as she spoke. Then the voices seemed to be everywhere. She shrieked and raised her arms high—a hundred voices coming from her. "Take him, kill him," they began to cry out. "Kill the Roman!" they urged. He could hear them clearly; although the soldier was talking to him as well, apparently oblivious to the cracked sound of the voices. His Mama's lips moved now as well but he could not hear her over the din that was coming from within his own head. "Kill him, kill him…" he heard them chant. Powerless to resist, he ran toward the soldier. A scuffle ensued. He was amazed at the power in his own arms as he battled the soldier. But, the Roman was crafty and with a swift move, knocked him hard in the chest, sending all the air out of his body… He dropped the sword. He was dizzy and he could not catch his breath. As he faded into unconsciousness, the last thing he saw was Mama—rushing toward the now armed soldier, rushing to stop him from…

It was morning when he finally awoke. Sitting up with a start he saw her first. Mama was lying next to him in a pool of her own blood. He knew she was dead. "It's your fault," said a voice from within. "You killed your Mama, foolish boy. Now what are we going to do about that?" "I don't know what to do," he said aloud. His question was answered moments later when the door of the small home burst open, and a faction of Roman Military men came crashing in. "There he is!" cried a soldier and pointing directly at David, he came into the kitchen. David gasped, recognizing the soldier as the one he had struggled with the night before. Now, he had returned with some militia. "He's crazy! He killed his own mother and tried to kill me!" The room was spinning. "Not so! Not so!" protested young David. But, then, came a familiar voice from somewhere inside of him. "I will kill you now!!" the voice was menacing and loud. Some of the Roman guard looked around for the source of the cracked voice that now threatened them. With cat-like agility he had never known, David leaped from the floor and attacked the man closest to him. Wailing away with his fists, the soldier appeared terrified, recoiling in fear from the cacophony of shrieking voices that now filled the house. They were everywhere it seemed—but mostly inside of him. He seemed to know the strength of twenty men as he ripped his fingers deep into the skin of the horrified soldier.

Another garrison of Roman soldiers rushed to the scene,

summoned by a trumpet blast from the overwhelmed guard at the house. Chains were brought and when David saw them, he howled in an eerie voice louder than the trumpet blast itself. It took many trained soldiers to chain the exhausted youth, but eventually they managed to subdue him. Bruised and battered, they dragged him to a waiting cell and locked the iron door behind him. There he sat in the darkness.

"It's just you and us now," the voice came from within. "Your Mama is gone and we are all you've got in the world." David sighed and said aloud, "Let's get out of here, then." His lips did not move as he spoke the words. Moments later he sauntered down the alley, eyes darting... a twisted tangle of bars and chains the only occupants of the cell he left behind.

He awoke to the sound of the voices. He was cold, and his limbs felt stiff. But, where was he? It was pitch dark, only a sliver of a moon shed light into the gloaming. Sitting up, he realized that he was in a graveyard, one of several on the outskirts of town. "Deep trouble," one of the voices was saying. "They'll be looking for us," he heard. "Hide!" urged another voice within. David stumbled to his feet. His hands, he noted, were raw and bleeding. "Metal prison bars..." he mused. "I broke them," he added, wonder in his own voice. "No, that was us," cracked the voices. "We give you strength and power." At that declaration, he leaned back and let loose a shrieking howl that filled the night. He shuddered. "Mama," he said aloud. "Mama, I am sorry."

He sat up on his haunches and waited for daybreak. As the first light opened the sky above, he saw several men near the entrance to the tombs. They had shovels and a simple wooden box. Obviously, they were burying someone, but without mourners or a priest. "A commoner," he considered. He knew beyond doubt whose body they carried; he just couldn't say the name. His throat was choked. He felt nauseous. "Your mama," the voice said for him. "They are burying your Mama," said another. "And that is your fault." The workers did not know they were being observed. David stayed hidden from sight. As soon as they had finished their task, the men turned and made a hasty retreat, looking back over their shoulders. "This place is unusual this morning," he was close enough to hear one say. "He senses our presence," said the voice from within him. "Get used to it."

The sun was higher in the sky now. At "The Tombs," he surveyed his surroundings. Most of the dead were buried in the small natural cave formations that were there. Stones, piled stones sealed each site. He searched for an empty cavern and found one on the far side of the sloping hill. "It'll serve as shelter from the sun and rain," he considered. It was large enough for David to sit in. Sitting now—he realized how hungry he was. He thought how just days ago, he had been awakened to the smell of his Mama's honey cakes, frying on the hearth. Letting his head hang back, he let loose a wail from deep within. "What will become of me?" he asked himself. "Of us..." came the reply from the voices. He was certain the Roman soldiers would be looking for him. Fortunately, Roman superstitions kept them from venturing into the burial grounds. He reasoned that they would probably be watching the small hut where he had lived with Mama, ready to apprehend him if he returned for his belongings. "Not going back there—ever," he said to no one. He spent the rest of the day making his makeshift dwelling more comfortable. He fashioned a bed out of palm branches and sand and when it was finished, he felt better about his sepulcher home.

Night was falling, and David was getting cold. The wind blew in off the sea, carrying with it the smells and sounds of fishermen, finishing up their day. He knew if he waited a few hours he could sneak down the path to the waterfront and find something he could eat. Often, the castaways from a ship's catch were tossed into briny barrels, fish too small to fetch a price in the morning market. He imagined them now. There would be enough meat on the bones to make a small meal and keep him from starvation. Several hours later, he padded down to the wharfs and found his supper. A guard dog growled and barked a warning as he dipped his hands into the big barrel of fish that were deemed to be throwaways, but if anyone had come to investigate the commotion, he did not know about it for he was running back to the tombs with his stolen meal wrapped in his robe. He built no fire. He was too exhausted and hungry to care that the bony fish were raw. In fact, they tasted pretty good to him as he tore into the meat with his teeth. As he sat back in his cavern hideaway, he reflected on his situation. Anger burned within him as he thought about the soldier who had killed his mother. "And, now the whole village will believe his accusation that I had done such a thing," he lamented. He meant to say "Mama" aloud but what came instead was a long howl of eerie wailing that he knew came from the voices that now resided in him. He shivered at the sound and slipped deeper into the dark recesses of the cave.

Morning found him still thinking of the Roman. He had slept very little; snatches of sleep, only to be awakened by the voices. They seemed determined to keep him awake at all costs. Today, though, they seemed to be at odds with one another, debating over he knew not what. He just sensed their restlessness. Something was upsetting them. That much was certain. He tried to listen and discern the issue from within, but all he could manage to hear was "Gone public…, a wedding feast..., and wine of the finest kind..." He wondered what the voices were referring to. He closed his eyes and tried to tune them out. Their agitation was growing, however. They were definitely speaking of someone, and he couldn't make them stop. He picked up a sharp stone and cut himself, deeply on the arm. It felt good somehow so he did it again, and again. As he watched his own blood flow his head swam and he dropped into unconsciousness. It was a sleep he needed badly.

He awoke to someone calling his name. He recognized the voice at once. It was John the son of Zebedee. He was calling from a distance, but it was clear that John, his only friend was searching for him. "David, where are you?" the fisherman friend called again. Instead of coming out of hiding, shame and fear pushed him deeper into the open grave. After a time, the calling stopped. He crawled toward the mouth of the cave, peering out into the sunshine. "Aha," came the voice of his friend! "I have found you..." Then, seeing his blood streaked arms he managed, "What has happened to you?" "Go away, leave me to die," ordered David. "But I have good news, my friend. I have found the Messiah!" With that, David stood and let loose a howl that sent John tumbling back against a pile of rocks. Such a blood curdling a sound came from within him that his friend continued to back away in terror. He howled again, sending John on a dead run for the main road. He watched him disappear into the village—still running. Sinking down in despair, the voice from within said to him, "Get used to it. No one wants you now. It's just you—and us." He crawled back to the cave and waited for nightfall.

Weeks passed. Then months passed. He was out of his mind, he was certain of that. He regularly heard the screams coming from within himself. It was rarely his own voice that he heard. He knew well his own voice... the begging, the pleading, and the praying voice that called out for mercy. He had come to know the others very well, the snarling, swearing, destructive voices that made him crazy. There were still many of these within him.

Lately, the voices would taunt him to action. At these moments, no one was safe. The voices had power. At their behest, he could rip apart a small animal or break fetters with which he was frequently bound. He would cut himself with stones and at the taste of his own blood, he would howl in satisfaction. "The Howler," in fact, was one of the names by which he was known in the village. He howled now at the full moon. The grave markers were his only companions. "The living dead amongst the truly dead," he said in his own voice. It was late in the night; early morning, perhaps. There was a violent storm over the lake. A fierce wind was blowing and he could feel the faint edges of the rain on his skin. The roll of thunder echoed off the hills behind him. Lightning flashed across the blue black sky, momentarily putting his surroundings in a wash of white light. The voices inside were unsettled. Restless, he stared into the darkness over the water as if there were something coming his way. He knew not what it was, but the voices knew something. Of that he was certain.

He sat in the darkness where he usually did. The cave near his Mama's grave. She had been buried there now these past twelve years. Thinking of her, he recalled how she had been known as a worker of incantations or better yet, a witch during her years in the village. Hated by most, feared by many, she had raised her only child to know the dark ways of her magic. He heard the same voices back then, but they came from his mother's mouth… since her passing, they were alive in him…

The voices ruled the night. They ruled him. And on this night, they were in rare form. Suddenly, his attention was arrested by a strange calm in the air. He looked into the faint light of gathering dawn over the lake. There was no sign of the storm. It was as if it had vanished in a moment. The thunder was silent and the flashes of lightning were gone as well. "I care not for this," said a voice from within. "Behold he comes this way." He wondered what the voices knew. Who was coming? He strained his ears to hear the faint sound of oars creaking in their oarlocks—a ship was surely heading his way. He could see nothing through the mist, but the sound was unmistakable. He watched and waited.

Before long, a solitary fishing vessel pulled up at the dock. On board he counted thirteen men. "Just some fishermen—pay no mind," said a voice from within. But they had no catch. Fishing was not their mission. He wandered closer for a better look. One figure stood in the rear of the craft. He could not pull his gaze away. He let loose a howl, not his own. He bent down for a stone and heaved it in the direction of the dock, causing some of the men to scurry for cover. But, the man in the stern, just stared his way. Even from that distance, his eyes penetrated his soul. "Be gone, Jesus," the voices cackled. "What do you want here?" "Him," said the man. "I want him." Jesus pointed at the Howler. With that, the crazed man began to run toward the boat. All the voices within were giving orders to stop. But the voice calling from the boat was stronger and he ran hard for the shore. As his feet pounded the earth beneath him the man who had been standing in the vessel was quickly climbing out onto the dock. They met on the beach and fell into each other's arms.

"I have many within," he said in his right voice. Tears were falling from his eyes. His throat ached with a choking sadness. "They are going now" said Jesus. He said something low and indiscernible but a few seconds later an entire herd of fat swine dashed over the high cliff and into the sea.

The darkness that had been with him for so long had vanished as quickly as the storm from the night before. The Howler felt as though he had just come home from a long journey.

"It is only My voice within you now." said Jesus. They stood together in the morning sun, the saved and the Savior. From that moment on—he was called by a new name. The Howler became The Herald. That was what Jesus had called him. That was what he now was… the bearer of glad tidings.

After a while, John, the son of Zebedee joined them on the beach. "I see you have found the Messiah as well," said his boyhood friend. "Can I go wherever you go?" David asked the One called Jesus. "I have work for you to do here…" came the reply. "You must tell your village about what has occurred." David looked around him now, taking his eyes away from the gaze of the Messiah for the first time. A small crowd of villagers gathered in a circle. Incredibly, their faces were angry. "Go away!" they said as one. "We don't want you here." David thought it strange that the voices sounded familiar. He knew the sarcastic and menacing tone and for a moment he turned his head in shame. Jesus took him by the hand and stood, addressing the villagers. "This man has been delivered from darkness," he began." He is a living testimony to Abba Father's saving grace. I want you to welcome him back to his home in the village."

The crowd slowly dispersed, and Jesus, John and the others got in the boat to return to Galilee. Urging David again to stay and tell of his deliverance, the men pulled away at the oars. That night, there was no howling, no cutting and no fitful dreams. He slept in a deep sleep in the house of his cousin, who had reluctantly opened his loft for David. At breakfast the next morning he ate as much as ten men could handle. He stepped outside, only to find a line of the sick, lame, and demented village dwellers. "What He did for you—can it be done for me?" The question came in a thousand different ways over the weeks that followed. The Herald had but one word in reply. It was the name above all names, Jesus—the healer of the Howler.

Eyes Wide Open

"I see men as trees, walking."
Mark 8:24

You will eventually open your eyes, but this can be a hard decision if you are just "coming to" on a lazy Saturday morning. You coax one eye into an open position, and then the second slowly peeks out on the world and allows for a tiny crack of light to filter in. You rub the both of them with your balled fists and before too long you consider yourself awake. Well, sort of.

Being awakened occurs quite differently… there is no coaxing of the eyelids required. The children come running down stairs and pounce on you like it was Christmas morning, causing both of your eyes to fly open at once. You are suddenly awake, and you are also alert - ready for the next pouncing toddler.

I love the accounts in the Bible of Jesus opening blind eyes. Sometimes He healed them gradually, Saturday morning style, waiting for the formerly sightless individual to slowly focus. Others gained sight immediately and began to dance and leap (and perhaps pounce) all at once. Both scenarios are meant for us to apply.

I have a friend who just can't see his need for a relationship with God. He is young yet and I believe life experience will take care of that perceived lack of need over time. Personally, I have stood beside too many grave sides and hospital beds to leave the "need" question open to perception. So, I am patient with my young friend. I can wait. There are times even now, in some of our late night discussions, when his eyes are almost open, like the young man Jesus encountered who began to see shapes even though everything remained a bit fuzzy. He needed another touch. So does my young friend. Jesus is patient enough to invest the time it will take to get one's eyes focused. Not all meet Jesus in pounce-like fashion. But there are some who do…

A young man under the influence of drugs and alcohol came to my door a number of months ago. My son, Brett, had brought him to our house, knowing he would be safe there. I had no sooner begun to share God's love with him, when he began to shake and cry. He saw it all - and all at once. He couldn't wait to give his life to Jesus. Immediately he became straight and sober; yes, right before our eyes. Come to think of it, he did a little pouncing and dancing as the weight of his sin came rolling off his shoulders and the scales came away from his eyes.

Whether you gain your spiritual sight in an instant, or over time - the first thing you will see clearly is always the same. The beautiful face of Jesus looking straight into your now opened eyes. Behold, He is smiling… a big "can't contain it goofy kind of smile." His eyebrows lift with a question… "Do you see? Is that better?"

If you are having trouble "waking up" here's a possible solution. Listen for footsteps on the stairs. There is laughter in the hallway. The Father is sending His children to tell you it's time to awaken. Just like the time the blind beggar called out to the Christ on the road near Jericho, "I want to see!" Hearing him, Jesus turned to His disciples and said, "Go get him." They received the merry task of "pouncing" because it was time to for the blind one to see.

Now! Brace yourself. The kids are about to pounce. These are the Jesus people in your life. You know… the church crowd. They want you to come and see. So, don't just lie there. Behold, the beautiful face of Jesus is now looking straight into your eyes. That much is clear.

Father God, keep me alert and on the pathway of life. Thank you for "pouncing toddlers" who should start my day with a smile - not a growl. Amen

Dropping Anchor: *We slow our ship as we enter the safe harbor for we are now almost home.*

Our Story

A truly good wife is the most precious treasure a man can find!
Proverbs 31:10

From Loren:
Summer is over. The calendar says it is still around for a while, but you can feel it in the air. It's over. The long, lazy days of ice cream shoppes and lemonade stands are behind us for another year. We made our annual trek to the lake again this summer. That is where we make our finest memories as a family. We cut two weeks out of our busy calendar and head for our vacation destination. The Ford packed to the gills with Deckers, we journey to the place where we know time will be irrelevant for fourteen long summer days and nights. Monopoly games will extend far into the wee hours of the morning, because 'sleeping in' is the only plan for the next day.

Once, during each vacation, Amanda and I get away for a night out as a couple. We treat ourselves to dinner at an expensive restaurant (we have garnered a list of favorites over the years) leaving the kids at home - the older ones watching the younger. I am sure, on these evenings, that I am out with the loveliest of ladies by the lake. We sit across a small table for two and I am torn as to which view is more beautiful… the one outside the window or the one across from me, my Dark Irish wife. I do know this, I married above my station. I outkicked my coverage. I am so blessed and on these special nights, I count my blessings - stopping at one. Amanda.

Afterward, back at the vacation house, I serenade her to sleep. I am no singer, so I use a soundtrack of lullabies coming from the tiny speaker on my smartphone.... Neil Young, Boz Scaggs and Fleetwood Mac. *"Helpless", "Harbor Lights" and "Songbird"* fill the night to overflow. They are my staples, and I often surround those three melodies with a variety of other dreamy numbers. She smiles, pleased with my playlist, now more asleep than awake.

Last night True was awake most of the night with a severe cough and breathing difficulties. I dozed in short snatches, but Amanda did the yeoman's work of comforting and caring for our little boy. It is times like these when I find that she is most wonderful and beautiful to me. She has no makeup - no fancy dress - she just is who she is, black hair falling on strong white shoulders, a tousle of toddler in her lap. She loves her children, and I am the fortunate man who shares them with her in this loving family atmosphere. It is the year filled with these life moments that causes me to look across a candlelit table with genuine wonder on our evenings by the lake. I want to keep her forever I tell myself, and then I tell her. Yet, we were an unlikely combination at the start. By most accounts, we should not be. I believe I will now yield the laptop and let her tell how we came to be... inseparable.

From Amanda:

I met Loren at a neighborhood outreach in our town. Loren was on the back of a truck which served as an impromptu stage. He was speaking to a crowd of onlookers, storytelling as he loves to do. The message was hitting hearts, my own included. I remember thinking, this guy speaks like a favorite author of mine. (Little did I know he would someday write himself.) I lost touch with him after that until he began attending my church sometime later.

One day a friend from church approached me and mentioned Loren was looking for a nanny. As a single dad of five, he was hoping to have reliable child care especially for his three youngest children. My first reaction was to refuse the offer. I was quite happy working at a local daycare and going to college. I have many siblings and had always taken care of them as well. I didn't really want to take on a job with longer hours, less pay and more diapers. I said no thanks and didn't think of it again until weeks later when Loren approached me and asked me directly if I was interested in his offer. I immediately spat out the words "I'll pray about it" as a way to say "no" and left the conversation as quickly as possible.

Back home, I felt a little guilty because I knew Loren was a pastor and would ask if I prayed about it and I couldn't lie and say I prayed if I really hadn't. Moments later I was praying and telling God if He wanted me to do this job, I would do it. As soon as I said the words, I knew the answer.

The next week I was giving my two week notice and soon after I began a journey that has changed my world forever.

After working for Loren for several years, I knew he was the guy I wanted to marry. I used to tease and say "you could save a lot of money if you just married me." He would laugh and say that would never happen.

I remember telling God I didn't think Loren would ever come around, and even though I was so sad about it, I felt I should give up the dream of marrying him and move on. It was a very tough decision, but one I really felt God was telling me to make.

As fall was approaching, I let Loren know I would be leaving the position. The kids had grown and the youngest would be starting kindergarten. There was no need for a nanny because they would all be in school. He reluctantly agreed. The plan was for Loren to go on sabbatical and I would keep the kids with me for the first week, after that I would bring them to the place he was vacationing, say my goodbyes and they would finish out their vacation with him and I would end the position. I dropped the kids off as planned with a heavy heart that Loren never came around and his chapter of my life had ended.

Feeling sad but like I was doing the right thing, I had even made future plans to go on the mission field full time. A few days after quitting the position and dropping the kids off, I got a phone call. It was Loren. "The kids really miss you" he said. "Can you stop by for one of our last days of vacation to celebrate one of their birthdays?" I agreed and stopped by. After the party had died down, Loren admitted he just didn't want to see me leave. "You'd have to marry me to keep me" I jokingly said. I didn't expect the response "Ok...I will."

To be honest, I didn't believe it. I thought he was joking back, but over the next few weeks I could tell something had changed. Loren used to tell me, "if I ever fall in love, everyone will know". And that was so true. Flowers, cards, texts, random kind things...you name it. I actually asked him to tone it down cause I thought he was just doing all this to prove to me he was serious...and he was...he was serious and the kindness never stopped. Having been married over a decade later, he still is that kind. I count myself blessed every day.

Father God, thank you for making something as beautiful as love be the glue that holds hearts together. Amen

Dropping Anchor: *If you want a successful marriage, find someone whose qualities you admire and then fall in love with them.*

____

____

____

____

We Close

"I am Alpha and Omega, the beginning and the end, the first and the last."
Revelation 22:13

As we come to the end of this book, I have one last story to tell, and it's a true story. It's a story that comes not from my imagination but from my heart. It is my story of the Soul Chaser Himself; the Heaven Dweller, who loved the lowly earth and was so fond of those who dwelled there that He redeemed them at a high price. It is a difficult thing to bear a cross, but perhaps even harder to carry a heart of love. Both were his burden. One caused the other and so, He became our King of Hearts.

It makes no sense really. Perhaps that is the beauty of it. You will never reason your way into His paradise. Man has tried over and again to create a heaven on this earth. It has collapsed every time. No society has ever produced lasting tranquility and peace. They are not societal markers by their very nature. Man is not a noble conqueror. His strategies fail. The state of the planet testifies to the truth that mankind is not good. His efforts at civility have disappeared into every generation's terror, crime and war. No, tranquility and peace are personal matters and they transcend this planet. No archeological mound of earth will yield the discovery of their source. They are heaven held possessions and are only available from Soul Chaser's hand of mercy. He places them within. Utopia is a state of being not a place to live. Not here. Not now.

You see, there is but one noble conqueror and He cares not for nations. He chases after hearts. His love disarms you and you are forever captured by His grace. His Kingdom was always an inside affair. He told us that while He was here. Oh, yes - He came once. He walked among us. He called for us to follow - but few believed Him to be true. They would not trust, instead most walked away. But, to those who believed, He made them to be His own. They became "Children of the Heavenly Father." You can tell which earth dwellers are His because they have been undone by Love and are clothed with humility.

This True Noble Conqueror does nothing that appeals or aligns with man's ambition. He, Himself, left Heaven and stooped low in search of hearts that would trace His humility and thus, build His Kingdom. It is a place within where few enter, for our own human hearts, filled with greed and want, block the entrance. One must accept defeat in order to partake in His victory.

I have been conquered by this King. My soul allegiance is sworn to Him. And, if this book of stories has touched you, then my prayer has been answered. It is His nail scarred hand that knocks at your own heart's door. It is His voice which calls your name. He has been chasing you all along. He never relents. If you are wise - you will surrender to Him. In the end, His love will conquer all.

> *Father God, you are the beginning and the end of every story that I tell. I worship you. Amen*

Dropping Anchor: *The aged look at the young with a certain grace. It is pity - not envy that the old man feels for the boy he once was.*

____

____

____

____

Conclusion

My dream at the close of these chapters is simple… I pray you have discovered that life and love pour forth from the perfect heart of The Soul Chaser. They cascade out of heaven on wings of grace and slip silently into the hidden places on planet earth where upon discovery, we can only smile. Smiles turn to laughter as we grow closer to this Source of Life who loves us deeply and beckons us upward, forward—closer and closer until we finally close our eyes... and awaken, to the beautiful face of Jesus.

A word about the dedication of this book

Tom Howard (1950-2010) was a beautiful musician that I met years ago when Christian contemporary music was in its infancy. The first night I heard him play he was at a youth event in Boston. He was playing keyboards in Larry Norman's band, featuring Randy Stonehill. They tore the roof off of old Tremont Temple. I was thrilled by what I saw and heard.

Over the years that followed, Tom and I became close friends. He wrote and played wonderful music, a well of magnificent melodies springing from the beauty that was within him. He composed the theme song for my nationally syndicated radio broadcast. He played at my wedding. We talked a lot on the telephone. Once, while he was visiting in New England we found a lovely song written by Andy Pratt entitled "Keep Your Mind on Me." We were both crazy about the song and over the years I encouraged Tom to cover it on a recording. The last time we were together, he was giving a concert at my church in New England and he closed the concert by surprising me with Andy's song. I cried as he sung. I knew the song was for me.

Tom was an incredible pianist... he could play anything from pop to classical. He was a true artist. It is my hope that my writing within this book will approach the excellence that Tom Howard achieved with his music. And, I pray that one of these stories will have captured your heart in a fashion much as Tom's song took over mine—and you will know that it was here just for you.

Tom, I think of you every day...

Loren Paul Decker

About the Author

Loren Paul Decker.......

Loren Paul Decker has spent a lifetime in the ministry. He grew up as a preacher's kid and eventually found his way into Christian broadcasting. He produced and co-hosted a nationally syndicated radio program, Songtime USA for nearly twenty years before taking a full time pastorate in Middleboro, Massachusetts. He has served as senior pastor of LifeHouse Church since 2009.

Loren is married to Amanda and together they share their home with the Decker children, Ash, Brett, Evangeline, Lane, Mercedes, Prudence, True and Rory. This is his second book.

I Love You, Church

Modern Parables

Loren Paul Decker

Within the pages of this book, you will meet some people you'll never forget. Their stories teach life lessons that will stretch, challenge, and move you. Author Loren Paul Decker has collected these modern-day parables over years in ministry and while raising a family.

As Jesus once told stories about day-to-day realities like farming and sheep to illustrate the kingdom of God, Pastor Decker now relates tales of grocery stores, car trips, and the darndest things his kids say -- all revealing loving messages from the heart of the Father. Many of the firsthand accounts in this book began as sermon illustrations at LifeHouse Church where Loren pastors. Now he shares them with everyone. You will laugh and cry as you follow these stories that point to the deepest truth of all -- that we are loved by God.

Pick up your copy today at your local bookstore!

ISBN 978-1-942056-28-7 [Paperback]
Library of Congress Control Number: 2016943401
Printed in the United States of America

CPSIA information can be obtained
at www.ICGtesting.com
Printed in the USA
BVHW040754291018
531537BV00011B/153/P